Present Continuous
CONTEMPORARY HUNGARIAN WRITING

Present Continuous

CONTEMPORARY HUNGARIAN WRITING

EDITED BY
ISTVÁN BART

Corvina

Translated from the Hungarian by Richard L. Aczel, László T. András, András Boros-Kazai, Georgia Greist, Judit Házi, Gillian Howarth, Etelka Láczay, Eszter Molnár, Christina Rozsnyai, J. E. Sollosy, Kathleen Szasz, Elizabeth Szász and Peter Szente
Translation revised by Bertha Gaster

Second edition
© István Bart, 1985
ISBN 963 13 2352 8
Printed in Hungary, 1986
CO 2447-h-8688

Contents

Editor's Note 7

TIME PAST

István Örkény:
The Hundred and Thirty-seventh Psalm 11
Ferenc Sánta:
Nazis 24
Iván Boldizsár:
Meeting the General 32
György G. Kardos:
The First Lines 44
György Száraz:
Roast Pheasant with Groats 58
László Gyurkó:
A Family Novel (excerpt) 70
Mihály Sükösd:
All Souls' Day—The Resurrection 96
Endre Fejes:
Ignác Vonó 110
István Csurka:
Four Students 119
György Moldova:
Father Fabricius 142
Endre Illés:
Room 212 156
Ferenc Karinthy:
Requiem 164

TIME PRESENT

Géza Bereményi:
The Turned-up Collar 2 183
Endre Vészi:
Ólmosi-Bleier's Last Work 199
Eszter Anóka:
Illatos Street 5, Budapest 215
Szilveszter Ördögh:
Sea with Gulls 233
Erzsébet Galgóczi:
Mother Is Dressing 248
Sándor Tar:
A Winter's Tale 261
Zsolt Csalog:
Looking for my Brother 278
Bulcsú Bertha:
Babylonia 289
István Gáll:
The Great Adventure 310
Ferenc Temesi:
A Story that K. Did not Like at All 334
Ákos Kertész:
Snapshot 344
Gyula Kurucz:
Showdown 352
Miklós Vámos:
A Very Private Affair 383

On the Authors 393

Editor's Note

The editor of this book has attempted to compile an anthology that will hopefully provide some idea of the Hungarian experience of the past forty years. The volume is therefore as much an anthology of recent Hungarian history and society as it is of the modern Hungarian short story. This is why autobiographical writings as well as what Hungarians traditionally call "sociography" or reportage written with literary means, and mostly by writers of fiction, appear side by side with traditional short stories, more or less in the same ratio one would find in a Hungarian literary magazine. In Hungary, such sociographical writing is generally classed with the *belles-lettres*.

In short, the selection that follows has clearly been influenced by historical considerations, and though the writings follow each other in more or less chronological order—or at least, with an eye towards successive historical landmarks—the barriers remain indistinct.

Since the aim above all was to introduce Hungary through her literature, when faced with a choice between two equally good pieces of writing, we always chose the one that contained more insight into the above-referred-to experience. In other words, without detriment to literary value, we have tried to select pieces that are interesting in the everyday sense of the word—something that will hopefully be pardoned even if this was done to the exclusion of several major writers.

We cannot claim that this volume contains a representative anthology of Hungarian literature, nor would it fit within the confines of this small book. On the other hand, it represents modern-day Hungary, and especially how this country sees its recent past and immediate present. We have accordingly selected more recent writings wherever we could, and with the same aim in mind, we have given the younger generation, too, a chance to speak up.

We hope that this anthology will prove that writers are the best chroniclers of their age, even better than the historians or sociologists, and that the faces, stories and events narrated herein will provide a faithful picture of Hungary in the Eighties.

The Editor

TIME PAST

*"Time present and time past
Are both perhaps present in time future
And time future contained in time past."*
T. S. ELIOT
(Four Quartets. Burnt Norton. 1.)

The Hundred and Thirty-seventh Psalm

BY ISTVÁN ÖRKÉNY

We had no stretcher. Maurer and Ligeti carried the patient in their arms and wanted to put him down on the operating-table with his clothes on. They had to be told not to soil the sterilized sheet. After that they reluctantly undressed the man.

I saw Laci Haas without his clothes on for the first time. He had been working all through the five months without a pause, and until the appendicitis attack the day before he had never reported sick. When I looked at him I felt as though needles were being jabbed in the back of my head. There was something unfinished, something you might say, moving, in the way his body was built. It was slim and white like a girl's, the chest a little hollow, the belly sunk, and the flesh desiccated like dried fruit. Lumbermen need 5,500 calories a day; it was the heaviest work we had ever done. Where did a child's body like his keep its reserves of energy? I had no idea. I had forgotten to wonder about it.

The big brawny ones melted away like ice in the sun. A lorry driver as strong as an ox, for instance, was done and finished before the unloading was over, and of the manual workers (we hadn't too many in our company anyway) only this Maurer had managed to survive, possibly because he was just too stupid to give up the ghost. Only a thin chalk line between his brows and woolly hair seemed to indicate the place where his forehead should have been. Sluggish, indolent, callous. A railway engine could have rolled over him. I had only asked him to come and help with the operation because of his strength.

He lifted the patient like a feather on to the operating-table.

I had so much experience by then that I could tell at a glance how long a man had to go. These Laci Haases, unpromising, made of soft wax, could stand anything. It was all a matter of strength of mind. Death is not outside, it is inside us. It is there we have to keep it in check. Let go of yourself for a second and it starts to grow, to divide like a cell, to swell and even without wanting to, kills you like an embryo bursting its mother to pieces.

When he was laid on the table, he said: "Take good care how you kill me, Silberman, won't you?"

And he smiled.

"I don't care a damn about you, if that was a little dig at me," I said. "Why the hell didn't you tell some whopping lie when the company was lined up at Jablonovka?"

"I told them straight: a poet."

"Big joke. A poet's good at any damn trade. Couldn't you have told them something else?"

"It makes no difference what I'm good at," he said, "I can't lie."

"Everybody told lies at Jablonovka," I said. "By the way, I did spend a term and a half at the Medical University in Prague."

"We heard that," he said wearily.

"I did a bit of dissecting too," I went on.

"Cut it out," he waved his hand.

"Did I ask to operate on you?" I asked.

"Cut it out," he said. "Give me plenty of ether. I don't care about the rest."

And he closed his eyes.

At Jablonovka the company had been lined up, and Harangozó ordered every one in the corn trade to come forward. Four corn-dealers stepped out. Harangozó had them taken behind the ramp and beaten to death. That scared us out of our wits. We thought we had got a regular butcher of a commander, but later it turned out he reserved his hatred exclusively for corn-dealers, and wasn't out to get anybody else. When they asked us our trade or profession, forty-seven of us in sheer fear swore we were doctors, or rather forty-four of us did, because three were real doctors. But they are no longer with us. Harangozó looked us over and said:

"That one with the scar on the throat will be the company's doctor."

At nineteen I had had a thyroidectomy and the scar that had remained proved to be a stroke of luck at Jablonovka. But I had never dreamed that I would ever have to operate on anybody. Corporal Bisztrai of the Medical Corps called me to the tool-shed that morning. The operation was to take place there, and he told me to get a couple of others to help get the place cleaned up.

It was woodland all around. The house was built of wood and a pleasant smell of pine came from walls, which made your hands sticky with resin if you touched them. The only snag was that the room was originally intended for storing things, so it had no windows. The resourceful Ligeti had taken the headlamps and the batteries from the company's defunct Mercedes. He rigged the light up just like a real operating theatre. We had the sheet sterilized in sodium and boiled the catgut, the syringes and all the other instruments we could lay our hands on in a hurry. I also had a wash-basin with disinfectant put in the room.

"Wash your hands," I said to Ligeti.

"I have," he replied.

"But you touched his clothes. And you too, Maurer!"

"Does it make any difference to him?" Ligeti shrugged his shoulders, looking at Laci Haas, who was lying white, eyes shut in the floodlight, shyly covering up his private parts with his left hand.

"Go and wash your hands, I told you."

They obeyed, their faces betraying insolence. I had got used to that. At first everybody hated me. Not because of my not being a real doctor and still being the company's doctor, but because I lived and ate with the army guards. In the evenings I listened to the radio in their company. I was exempted from wearing a yellow armband. That was what made them sore. But as time went on they began to realize that I was on their side all the same. There was the time, for instance, when the order came through that from then on those with chilblains had to turn out for work just the same, because the sick roll must never exceed three per cent. But by then I knew about Harangozó's changes of mood and temper. Most of the time I exceeded the three per cent limit; in late December in fact, when the great frosts set in, I managed to exempt twenty-seven men. They saw that I was playing a risky game for them. From then on they hated me a little less.

"What are you doing?" I snapped at Maurer and Ligeti. "There's a clean towel to dry your hands on."

With the same impassive face they dried their hands. Because that impassive, sulky face was there to stay.

They sat on a crate. We were waiting for Bisztrai. Maurer was holding his ham hands away from his body so as not to touch anything, and in the meanwhile he watched my movements. That stare made me jumpy. There was silence. The good smell of pine oozed from the walls, like at home when my father brought the pine tree home for Christmas and hid it in the pantry, and the smell seeped through, betraying its presence. Father had always bought the tallest tree that would fit into the room. He had started life all over again four times because his business had always gone bankrupt; perhaps that was one reason why he had wanted me to become a doctor...

I took out a Russian cigarette and lit it.

"Are we forbidden to do that too?" Ligeti asked.

"Your hands are already disinfected," I said. "But you can smoke, Laci."

He opened his eyes. He sat up. He lit a cigarette. I was a little relieved because it was painful to see him stretched out pale in the white light, motionless.

"Do you want anything?" I asked.

"What could I want?" he asked without interest.

I thought a moment.

"Food is out of the question. Do you want some tea?"

"I don't want tea."

"I may be able to get some rum for you."

"Don't get me anything, Silberman."

There was silence again. Nobody spoke. No noise came from outside because the huts of the army staff were covered halfway up with dung and on top of that a thick layer of snow had fallen. It made the silence lie on your heart like a weight of lead.

"We could at least talk," I suggested.

"What shall I talk to you about?" he asked.

"Recite me a poem."

"I can't think of a single poem."

"Do the one you recited at the social evening."

"It wasn't by me."

"Who was it by?"

"Who knows?"

But whenever it came to discussing poetry he always livened up. This time too he soon recovered and started to talk and gesticulate, even forgetting to keep his left hand on his genitals. He had been the great surprise of the social. A voice as strong as the roar of the wind came out of this soft-spoken boy. It swung over the long sheep pen so that even those with gangrene, whom we didn't dare bring forward for fear Harangozó might see them, could hear it.

We had got up the social on the Regent's birthday on Harangozó's order. He had these fits of humanity. He was in constant conflict with himself, but the boys were unable to see it. He had been ordered to produce so many cubic metres of timber for saw-logs, sleepers and telegraph poles, and in the course of it to exterminate the company. But he had quite a bit of idealism, too. He wanted to maintain the illusion that here everything was as if we had been free people—free as far as anyone could be free in wartime. As long as everyone did his work he wouldn't let anyone so much as eye us. He insisted on our singing and enjoying ourselves in the evenings; occasionally he himself came and mixed with us in the sheep pen. When Laci Haas began to recite at the social he broke into tears. He turned aside and went out to keep his emotions from betraying him. The next day I learned from his batman that he had been pacing his room the whole night, clearing his throat. I daresay that was why he had insisted on the appendicitis operation; he hadn't forgotten Laci Haas reciting those lines.

It wasn't an ordinary poem. It was the Hundred and Thirty-seventh Psalm in some old seventeenth-century version.

"Recite it, please," I asked him.

"I can hardly remember it."

"As much as you can."

"I don't feel like it."

All my prompting was in vain. Then Ligeti, speaking over his shoulder, turned on him:

"Why are you putting on dog?"

At that he obediently rose on one elbow, looked round, and threw the loose corner of the sheet over his loins. He didn't seem to want to recite a poem naked. He spoke very softly, almost inaudibly.

By the rivers of Babylon, there we sat down, yea,
we wept, when we remembered Zion.
We hanged our harps upon the willows in the midst
thereof.
For there they that carried us away captive
required
of us a song; and they that wasted us required of us
mirth, saying, Sing us one of the songs of Zion.
How shall we sing the Lord's song in a strange land?

If I forget thee, O Jerusalem, let my right hand
forget its cunning.
If I do not remember thee, let my tongue cleave to
the roof of my mouth, if I prefer not Jerusalem
above my chief joy.

He fell silent. He got a cramp, and lay back again, drawing up his leg. I started to sweat. If anything makes me nervous the palm of my hand becomes damp and cold sweat comes out on the small of my back. Ligeti was staring in front of him, biting his nail; Maurer was breathing heavily with his mouth open and his sticky fish-gaze fixed on me. Laci panted slightly for a while yet, then once again the silence was complete and again the smell of pine wood came flooding into the stillness. Through my mouth and nose, through my very pores it penetrated; I felt like crying behind my closed eyelids. I was shaken. I thought of things I had never thought of. What life was like, what it was about and who had conceived it, and if it had come about of itself, why did it have to be so full of conflict and self-contradiction, why was it self-suffocating, inscrutable, insoluble... I brushed the thoughts away, but at that moment my father's sallow face as he lay on his sick-bed flashed before me. To shut out the image I tried to imagine myself dead. I did not succeed. I was living even in my death. Not very much alive but just enough to know that I was not dead. Then in came Bisztrai.

He had got bandages but no ether. Instead of that he thrust into my hands a bottle of novocaine. He inspected the headlamps, switched them on and off, smiling complacently. Before he left he snarled at me:

"If the shed is not empty by noon, I'll kick you in the belly, Mr. Silberman."

He mistered me. He didn't like anybody to come into the tool-shed. He lived next door in the room to which the shed was attached. He would lie on his campbed day and night, but eight or nine times a day he came out to see if the padlock on the door of the shed was still there.

We boiled the instruments on the big utility stove. I had only once given an injection in my life, six weeks before, to a chap suffering from dysentery. But it hadn't made difference anyway.

"We haven't got any ether," I told Laci. "I'll do it locally."

"What's that?"

"A local anaesthetic."

"Will I be awake?"

I said yes. He asked if he might smoke. I shrugged my shoulders and handed him the whole packet.

"All you'll feel will be one sting," I said.

In civilian life Ligeti was a drugstore shop-assistant. I knew him to be a clever man, but at this moment he was not particularly exerting himself. He moved about with a slowness that was an ironic comment on the futility of his activity. I had to round on him three times before he shoved the scalpel across to me.

"Now throw away the cigarette," I told Laci Haas.

"Lovely smoke rings," he said grinning, and blew the smoke up into my face.

"If that was intended as sarcasm don't exert yourself," I said. "I sat in the library every day till closing time. I wanted to be a good doctor."

"You've said that before."

"If Hitler hadn't marched into Prague I'd have become one too."

"Oh, well," he said.

"What's that 'Oh, well'?" I demanded.

"That's how we indicate something unsaid in literature."

"What's it all about?" I asked.

"Do you know where the appendix is?"

"I bloody well know," I said.

I think I made the cut beautifully at the right place. To be frank, I felt damp on the forehead and down the neck, but I had stopped trembling now, and the tension I had been living under since the previous day was relaxed. I didn't know what I was doing but something inside me told me that I was doing it correctly.

"Your peritoneum is like mother-of-pearl," I said.

"Don't flatter me, Silberman," he replied.

Up till then there had been sharp knives in everything he said. That was the first sentence with a milder tone. I knew that this softening was not intended for me; it was merely the onset of nerve paralysis, or what we call operational shock.

There weren't enough artery forceps, so the wound had to be swabbed frequently. Slowly, very cautiously I began pulling out the small intestines.

"Does it hurt?" I asked.

"It doesn't."

"You're lying," I said. "Not even Professor Schleiermacher could do this without pain."

"What we tell you cannot be a lie."

"Do you hate me?" I asked.

"Should I love you?"

I did not answer. One does not expect gratitude. Yet I'd walked my feet off before I could cajole them into letting me have the headlamps and allowing me to borrow the instruments from the veterinary clinic. A drop of sweat sprang out from under my hair and rolled down my temple and face. Haas gave a cry of pain.

I ought to have found the appendix by then. On Laci's belly, above the cut, lay the sterilized sheet. I put the bowels on it in apple-pie order. But now my hand stopped.

"Who do you think I'm siding with?" I spoke with irritation, because I was again seized by that internal trembling. "Who's holding the baby for you? Who's hiding the chaps with gangrene? How many times have I put you on the sick list, Ligeti? And you, Maurer? Go on, answer me!"

Ligeti was grinning. Maurer was breathing heavily down my neck. I could feel the hot steam of his breath. I could have killed him.

"Is what I'm doing betrayal? And what you're doing not?"

"It is not," Laci said.

"Not even your reciting at the social?"

"We can do anything," he said.

"Why can you do anything?"

"Because we're going to die anyway," Laci said.

The room was overheated. Everything on me was

drenched through, my neck, shirt, hand. I mopped my forehead with my arm.

"Don't be glad too soon," I said. "You're not going to die. I'll find your appendix in a moment."

"Congratulations!"

"I'd already read all the fourth-year textbooks in my first year."

"It's a pity, all that cramming wasted," he said.

"I didn't think about how much I'd earn," I said. "I wanted to be a country doctor."

"Cut out the talk," he said. "Operate."

Now and again he gave cries of pain, although I took care, because I knew that if I didn't, they would be right. The minutes dragged on, very slowly. Maurer still gaped at me with those paralytic eyes of his.

The bowels were already lying in a big heap placed on top of each other.

"You haven't found it?" Laci asked.

"Don't be afraid," I said, "I'll find it."

"Don't make it a question of prestige."

"Do you want to get better or not?"

"Idiot," he said and closed his eyes.

The trembling had completely taken possession of me.

Schleiermacher had lectured to the fourth year; I had never got as far as that. But his famous sayings were known to everybody at the university. This one, for instance: "Gentlemen, the appendix does not float about like the kidney. The appendix is always in its right place, you only have to find it." I didn't. I had to call Ligeti to help hold the bowels together, when Laci's head slid to one side.

"Finished," Ligeti said.

He turned on his heels and was about to leave everything; he only returned to his place when I shouted after him. The pulse was regular but weak, weaker than it should have been. I had no camphor. I had no caffeine. I told Maurer to prop up the patient's head and throw water on his face.

He let the forceps slip. It was torture to see how he picked up the jug from the ground; it seemed as if this was the first time he'd taken anything in his hands. Then he poured a little water into a tin cup, looking at me every now and then in the meantime, which only made his snail's pace still slower.

"Quick!" I shouted at him.

He started to move with the cup in his hand but no faster than before. He crossed the room as though his feet were entangled in seaweed. He bent over Laci. He looked into his face. He looked at him, then at me, at him, at me again. If he'd looked at me once more I'd have gone mad.

"Don't stare like that, you miserable fool!" I shouted. "You'll kill him if you waste time like that!"

He stood there stock-still. A dim-witted wretch like him needs time before the voice reaches his brain. He stared at me, turned, went over to the jug dragging his feet, and poured the water back into it. He placed the cup back in its place on the shelf, in exactly the same place he had taken it from, going through these actions like a trained gorilla. Then he came over to me.

"Put the bowels back," he said.

"What are you saying?"

"Put the bowels back and sew the cut together."

"You beast," I said. "What do you know about it? You dim-witted, stupid bastard, you crack-brained monkey! You idiot!"

His face didn't as much as move a muscle. The insults had not penetrated his ear-drums.

"Sew him up," he repeated with the same impassive voice, and lifted his hairy-backed hand.

I backed away. He came after me. A prehistoric mammal, a beast rearing on its hind legs, a Neanderthal male. He had been standing there behind my back while I had been working and felt his hot breath down my neck.

The stove began to pour out heat. The sweat trickled down my neck. The pine-wood smell from the warm walls was so strong it seemed as if the wood had come into the room. I sewed the cut together. My father had wanted me to be a doctor. He had said: "Not only because a doctor can make a livelihood wherever his fate takes him, but also because the work of a doctor is noble and honourable. He serves the good of mankind."

Translated by László T. András

Nazis

BY FERENC SÁNTA

The shepherd was getting on in years, perhaps he was sixty or sixty-five. He was chopping wood on a broad, high block. Beside him a boy, about eight or nine years old, gathered together the pieces.

Both of them heard the hoof-beats. They heard the horses stop behind their backs and then the scrape of a match as cigarettes were lit. Still they did not turn, but continued to chop wood as though they had heard nothing.

The two armed men had come from the pine-wood, where they had stood for a long time in the concealment of the trees, gazing at the shepherd, the flock of sheep, the small hut, the barking dog running to and fro. Then they had come across the pasture and reined up their horses behind the shepherd and the boy.

There they sat behind them, blowing out the tobacco smoke and saying nothing. There were pistols at their waists, rifles slung across their backs; their legs hung loose out of the stirrups.

Time passed in silence—as though there were no people standing there, close to each other. Yet they had all been born human beings, the armed men, the shepherd and the child too.

When they had smoked their cigarettes to the end, one of the armed man unhooked a large rubber truncheon from the saddle and called to the old man:

"You, old man!" he said.

The shepherd was just raising his axe for a blow, but he did not bring it down; instead he quickly put it in front of him on the ground, whipped his hat off his head, turned round and, with uncovered head, bowed as low as he could. He didn't speak, didn't raise his glance, just stood there in front of the horse, bowing, hat in hand, his light, white hair fluttering in the breeze.

The child, as though he hadn't heard a word, continued to gather the wood and stack it up in a small pile beside the rest.

More time went by; the armed men said nothing, the old man, bowed there before them, did not move either.

Then later, a lot later—the horses were pawing the ground and tossing their heads—the armed man spoke.

"Did you see anyone?" he asked.

The old man replied quickly, as quickly as when he had put the axe down on the ground in front of him.

"I haven't seen anyone!"

The second armed man moved nearer.

"We asked you: have you seen a man around here?"

"I haven't seen a man around here," said the old man.

He rested his gaze on the ground, saw his laced boot, the grass and the horses' hooves.

"Come closer!" said he with the rubber truncheon.

The old man went over quite close to the horse.

"Still closer!"

He stood right by the horse's leg.

"Closer!"

He went right up to the armed man's boot. He saw the toe of the top boot, the stirrup and part of the horse's belly, and the grass.

The armed man leant down and, putting the rubber truncheon under the old man's chin, lifted up his face. The old man was bent forward at the waist, his head back to the nape of the neck, but he did not raise his eyes; he gazed at the horseman's trouser-encased knee, and the stirrup leather. He wanted to swallow, but couldn't because of the truncheon.

The armed man gazed at his face. His wrist rested on his knee, and thus he held the rubber truncheon under the old man's chin, lifting his head ever higher and gazing into his face.

Then he took away the trunchon and hit the shepherd with it across the shoulders.

There was silence.

"You can go!"

The old man turned and quickly went back to the wood block, put his hat on his head and then took up the axe, raised it high and continued to chop wood.

When he had knocked the fourth or fifth bit into pieces, the armed man called out:

"Old man!"

He turned, whipped off his hat, bowed, his eyes on the ground—everything exactly as before.

"How old is the boy?"

"The boy is eight…"

"You bring him up?"

"I bring him up!"

The other called out too:

"How long have you been bringing him up?"

"I've been bringing him up a year."

"How old's the boy?"

"The boy's eight."

"You bring him up?"

"I bring him up."

They moved closer.

"Have you seen a man around?"

"I haven't seen a man around."

26

"You can go!" said the second one.

They were silent.

"You, boy!" the one with the rubber truncheon said.

The child's arms were full of wood and he had started towards the pile to stack it up beside the rest. He stopped, put down the wood at his feet, quickly pulled his cap off his head, bowed and turned round, still bowing from the waist. The wind tousled his hair too. He too saw his feet and the grass on the ground.

"How old are you?"

He replied at once—in the same manner as he had put down in front of him the wood in his arms.

"I'm eight years old."

"And this old man is bringing you up?"

"This old man is bringing me up."

"How long has he been bringing you up?"

"He's been bringing me up for a year."

"That's the old man?" asked the other.

"That's the old man."

"Your grandfather?"

"My grandfather."

"Come here!" said he with the rubber truncheon.

The child went over—just like the old man—in front of the horse.

"Nearer!"

He went exactly up to the top boot, but he was so much shorter that, bowing the waist, his head did not reach the boot; he was there almost under the belly of the horse. He saw nothing beside the grass and his own shoes.

The armed man moved his foot, thrust the toe of his boot below the child's head, sought for his chin and raised his head.

"Higher!" he said.

The child raised his head higher, pressing it right back

to the nape of his neck. He had never seen the faces of armed men and he felt a great desire to raise his eyelids.

Then he closed his eyes.

"Open your eyes!"

He continued to gaze at the creased leather of the boot.

"Seen a man around here?"

"I haven't seen a man around here."

His mouth also filled with saliva.

"You said that old man was bringing you up!"

"I said that old man was bringing me up."

There was silence. The horses' hooves pawed the ground, the old man's axe clinked.

"Turn round!" said the armed man and lowered his boot.

The child turned round.

"Look in front of you!"

The child raised his head.

"What do you see?"

"I see: far away hills, the sky, trees; then I see the hut and in front of it stakes with the cooking pots on them, I see the goat, the stove..."

"Well, forward march!"

They followed him, let him go right up to the hut. Then they stopped him. It was a low shepherd's jit; in front were a few cooking pots set on stakes, to the right a tethered goat, white as snow, and, nearer among the stones, the morning fire, burned to ashes.

He with the rubber truncheon went and stood beside the child and with his foot turned him towards the goat.

"What's that?"

"It's a goat."

"Take a good look!"

"I'm taking a good look."

The other also said:

"What is that?"

"A goat," said the boy.

The armed man leant his boot against the child's side.

"Turn round!"

There further away was the flock, grazing. Not a single sheep bell hung from the neck of any of them.

"Call the dog here!"

The boy called the dog over. It came slinking over slowly, then sidled up and sat down at the boy's feet.

"Pay attention to me!" said the armed man. "The thing that's lying at your feet, what is it?"

"A dog," said the boy.

"No... the thing that's lying at your feet is a goat, a large white goat! Do you understand me?"

The boy was silent.

The armed man put the rubber truncheon on the boy's uncovered head. He laid it across him. He put it right across the middle of the crown of his head, so that the end stretched out far in front of the boy's eyes. The second armed man came closer and stopped with his horse alongside, quite close, so that the leg of his boot strained against the boy's shoulder.

"Well?"

The boy gazed at the dog.

The armed man who had just come over to the side of the boy took out his rubber truncheon and laid it lightly across his shoulder.

"Speak nicely!"

"Well! What's at your feet?"

The boy gazed at the dog.

"A goat," he said.

"A large, white goat."

"A large, white goat."

The armed man swirled away from beside him, the other

took the truncheon off his head and with his foot turned the boy towards the goat.

"And now... there's the dog. Do you understand me?"

He put the truncheon on the boy's head.

"Yes!"

"A medium-sized, dark brown dog, neither little, nor big."

"Yes!" said the child.

"What's it called?"

"Caesar..."

"Go," said the other, "and stroke him nicely, like you usually do and say his name too..."

The other again raised his foot and planted his sole in the boy's back, carefully showing him forward.

"Caesar!" said the child when he reached the goat, and he put his hand on its head, between the horns. "Caesar!"

"And what else do you generally say to him?"

The boy bent down beside the goat's neck, his cap in his hand, his eyes on the ground.

"My little dog!" he said.

There was silence.

"Come here!"

He left the goat and went over to the armed man; this time, however, he no longer stopped in front of the horse but went right up to the boot. The armed man lifted up his chin. Again he wanted to swallow, but couldn't because of the pressure of the boot against his throat; he would have liked to look up, but gazed motionless at the boot under his face.

"You can go!"

When the boy was half way towards the old man, the armed man called after him. He turned and bowed from the waist.

"Have you seen men around here?"

"I haven't seen men around here," he said.

He still stood there for a while. The armed men lit up, took a puff, and lined up their horses side by side.

"You can go!" they then said.

The old man chopped wood the whole time; he didn't turn round, but worked as though no one was at hand.

The two continued to stand there behind their backs—the child gathering and stacking the wood—until they had smoked their cigarettes. They kept silent, blew out the smoke and gazed at the shepherds. Then they threw away their cigarettes, one raised the reins, followed by the other, and, throwing their rifles behind them as they straightened in the saddle, they continued on their way at a walking pace.

Meeting the General
BY IVÁN BOLDIZSÁR

In my young and foolish days I was mixed up in politics, stopped writing short stories and editing newspapers, and was, for a time, an under-secretary in one of the Ministries. In the spring of 1949 we were expecting a delegation from Bulgaria. The minister did not feel like going to the airport so I had to go. I had a huge, black Hudson—they don't make them in America any more. Airport receptions bored me even more than conferences so, just to make it a bit more tolerable for myself, I took along one of my assistants who was even younger than me. He warned me that one of the members of the delegation was a general and a military guard of honour had been sent to receive him. "Do I have to review the troops?" I asked, terrified but laughing at myself. "You certainly do, sir," replied my assistant. As I said, I myself was young, impertinently so for the rank of under-secretary, but this was a time of the changing of generations. We were born into the war, and this may have been given us in recompensation.

The Ferihegy airport manager greeted me and accompanied me to the reception area in front of the airport terminal. The guard of honour was already there, complete with brass band. The airport chief reported that the plane would be landing in ten minutes. A command rang out and the guard of honour snapped to attention; a captain reported to another officer, then turned back to the troops and ordered a right about-face. The other officer approached me with long, even, dignified strides. I noticed red general's stripes on his trousers.

Before I could blink twice, the general stood at attention before me, reporting. "Mr. Under-Secretary, the guard of honour numbers one hundred and four men." As representative of the Government at that moment he reported to me, but I couldn't get used to it. All my life I have always taken whatever I did seriously, but I never learned how to take myself too seriously. The general requested permission to introduce himself. I nodded and, for the first time, looked at his face. He, too, looked at me for the first time. I felt the blood rush to my head. Immediately I recognized the counter-intelligence captain who, fourteen years earlier, at the Miklós Horthy Avenue prison, had... well... who had dealt with me. He, too, recognized me. He gave his name, but I didn't get it. He had also given it to me at the first interrogation, but I didn't get it then either. True, I'd just had my ear-drum split, so I didn't hear very well. There we stood, facing each other. The general finished his sentence with obvious difficulty, then waited, stiff as a ramrod. There was a slight movement of his right hand. I was expected to offer my hand. My elbow twitched. If someone introduces himself you're supposed to shake hands with him, but my arm refused to rise, not even as much as thirty degrees. I just couldn't touch that hand.

I can still see the general's arm jerk back, and at the end of that arm, the white-gloved hand. Back then he had not been wearing gloves. It was only on the second day that I had been taken to the captain. Stand to attention, the guard had ordered when marching me into the room. Leather furniture, carved desk, curtains at the window. A tall, broad-shouldered man in civilian clothes sat behind the desk. I didn't look at his hands then. Open-faced, sun-tanned and sitting as straight in the high-backed chair as a man on horseback. He looked up once, then turned back to his papers again.

"Your name is Medvei?" he asked.

"Yes," I replied.

"I beg your pardon?" the captain was still not looking at me.

"Report properly," the guard whispered in my ear.

I had not done my military service yet. Uncertainly I said that it was Gábor Medvei reporting.

"Don't be impertinent or you'll regret it."

Vaguely I recalled some military language from novels and plays.

"Gábor Medvei begs to report, sir," I said.

"I thought you knew how to do it. You were deliberately provoking me, weren't you? You want to try my patience, don't you?"

"No," I said.

"I beg your pardon," he said again.

A few years later, a new recruit, a loutish corporal played the same game with me. By then, I knew the right answers but withheld them deliberately. However, there, before the captain, I didn't know what I had done wrong. How could the little word "no" be misunderstood? "No," I repeated more loudly.

For the first time, the captain looked at me. "I'm not deaf, but you will be in a moment. Come closer!" I took a step forward. "Closer. All the way, in front of the desk." I obeyed. The captain rose a little in his chair and hit me full force on the side of the face. The blow landed on my left cheek, the cheek-bone and the base of the ear. My skin smarted as if I had been stung by a mammoth wasp, but the pain shooting through my ear was as piercing as a dentist's drill touching and lingering on a nerve. I reeled, raising my hand to my ear. The pain did not subside. I felt a warm wetness on my palm and looked at it. Blood was seeping from my ear. "I've got to sit down or I'll collapse... sit down, sit down," I repeated to myself, but I would have had to back away two steps to reach the chair and I had neither the strength nor the courage to do so. Ever since I was a child I had hated vomiting. Anything but that. The nausea gave me back some self-control. I staggered but did not fall.

The stony face of the captain merged with the carved animal head on the high back of the armchair. Later I thought that the powerful blow might have impaired the focus mechanism of my vision; for while I saw the captain's face through a haze, I saw his hand with great sharpness. Even in my state of vertigo and nausea I noticed that the captain was wearing a heavy signet ring, not on his fourth, but on his middle finger. The ring was set with a dark purple stone. It was still there on the middle finger of the general at the airport. Seeing it, I backed away a little. I was backing away from myself and my impulse to hit the general with every ounce of strength in me, as I had never hit anyone before, right there, in front of the guard of honour. Then I simply turned away. The general stood there for half a minute and then, like a recruit in the barrack yard, executed a smart about-face, and in a low voice gave an order to the captain of the guard of honour, who at last ordered his men to stand at ease.

The young assistant who accompanied me asked what was wrong. "You look pale, sir." I assured him it was nothing. The young man was observant. "Do you know this general, sir? He behaved very strangely." Strangely? I hadn't noticed anything strange. I didn't even know the general's name. "He introduced himself, sir." Did he? I hadn't heard. "Brigadier-General Lajos Kapy, sir."

I had never again come into contact with the captain's ringed hand. During subsequent interrogations the edge of his palm merely rested on the desk, and when he raised it a little, one of the zealous young men behind me would respond with a hit, twist, wrench or kick.

Six weeks later, thanks to the good offices of a former secondary-school teacher of mine—who in turn had been a classmate of one of the ministers—I was released. Even so I was kicked out of my first job, and had to find a miserable job at Szekszárd. But I was very young, not more than twenty-three, and happy, to be alive.

I had been arrested as a spy for the Czechs. In those days in the early 'thirties I wanted to become an architect. I had been simultaneously fascinated by Le Corbusier and by arcaded buildings. As I couldn't go to see the House of the Sun in Marseilles, I wanted at least to go to Lőcse and Telc in Slovakia and Bohemia to have a look at the arcades in their main squares. That was how I met Straka, the cultural attaché of the Czechoslovak Legation. Those in power did not look with favour upon this connection. They decided to scare young writers, artists and architects away from contact with Straka by arresting me as a Czech spy.

I accompanied the Bulgarian delegation to their hotel then went back to the ministry, but I couldn't concentrate on what was said to me. Again and again I saw the large palm of the captain's hand. A small bottle of Parker's ink on the edge of my desk turned into the purple stone of the captain's signet ring. I felt a sharp stabbing pain in my left ear, although for years that ear-drum had only done service as a weather forecaster. More than once I reached for the phone to call up the Defence Minister and tell him what kind of a general he was employing. Or should I call up Lajos Kapy and ask him: "How are you, Captain? When did you last beat up a Czech spy?" Or should I go to his flat, hit him a couple of times in the face and walk away? Once I went as far as dialling the number of the Defence Ministry but after the first ring I hung up the receiver. I had never before experienced a desire for vengeance but now the new sickness was acute, taking possession of my mind, and I felt feverish.

I rang my secretary, told her not to admit anyone and to disconnect the phone. Then I pushed two armchairs together, lay back in one, put my feet up in the other and began to think. I waited until the tide of fever ebbed from my brain and its convolutions reappeared above the waves. If that man was now a general in the new army he must certainly have done something to deserve it. Perhaps he started thinking after Stalingrad. Perhaps he was in touch with the resistance. Perhaps he was captured and as a prisoner of war had been chosen for anti-fascist training by the Russians.

The tide ebbed further and my brain began to function normally. He may even have been a member of a resistance group. I really ought to ask the Minister of Defence about him, I thought, and turned to the phone. No. Impossible. What am I to say if he asks me why I want to know? That I had just met him at the airport and was curious about his past?

For the atmosphere of those days was already stifling; anyone who was alive was suspect. I would have drawn suspicion to myself by the mere fact that I was interested in a general. I was scared.

At that moment I re-lived every second of my arrest. The cold terror when those two black-hatted men rang our doorbell at six in the morning. The hurried dressing. My mother's wordless trembling. The shame when fear moved my bowels and I had to ask permission, in my own home, to go to the bathroom. And the fury when they would not allow me to close the door. The aching emptiness in my stomach in the black automobile as we crossed Margaret Bridge in the early morning. The despair at the thought that I might not see the Danube again, perhaps for years. They might even shoot me, for there was martial law in those days. I recalled the moment that no writer has so far been able to really describe, though many of them have been jailed: the deafening silence and blind darkness that descends on you when the door is locked on you from the outside. The knowledge that my mother was crying at home. The humiliation of being addressed by my first name by the guards. The split ear-drum. The teeth loose in the mouth. The feeling of utter helplessness because there was no way of proving my innocence. The state of exhaustion after the twentieth interrogation and the hundredth... the hundredth... outrage, and the longing to confess if they'd only leave me in peace. I'll tell them that I received a letter from Benes himself, or whatever they want, if they will only stop! Then, after the moments of weakness, stubborn, tenacious anger. No, and no, I won't say anything, even if they kill me! Even if they start drilling my teeth again I'll scream but I won't say a thing! The soundless weeping at night in my cell, and the harsh voice of the guard: get your hands out from under the blanket! All the way! Do you hear! The shaky hope that they'd release me when, at last, I could talk to a lawyer, and being dead alive when they didn't.

It all came back to me in one chaotic rush and I thought to myself that now, at last, I'll make him pay for it. And for the fact that when they finally released me, knowing perfectly well I had done nothing, and with no other purpose in mind than frightening us, they kept a police file on me and I couldn't get a passport. I was forty-six when I finally saw the House of the Sun in Marseilles. I wanted that man Kapy to find out how it felt to be arrested at six in the morning! Let his mother or wife tremble and cry. I wanted him to find out what it meant to face a desk, and behind the desk a man in whose hands you are more defenceless than a newborn child in the hands of the midwife, or a patient on the operating table in the hands of the surgeon, or any man in the hands of the Archangel Gabriel on the Day of Judgement. That's what I wanted!

I went on thinking. This was not simply a private feud between Lajos Kapy and me. My former captain was now a general in the new army. I didn't know what his duties were, but whatever they were he could do a lot of damage if he were still of his old way of thinking. I really ought to call the Defence Ministry's attention to this man. Or, perhaps, I shouldn't, after all. There were two possibilities: either they knew about his past or they didn't. If they did, then my warning, or, to call the child by its proper name, my denunciation, would be looked on as meddling on my part. I might even get some nasty answers: what did I think, did I perhaps think that they, of all people, didn't know the meaning of vigilance? Vigilance, that was the word, that was the open sesame of those days. But it was a reverse sesame: it closed every door.

I continued to think, still working from the premise that they knew about Kapy's counter-intelligence past. They know it, I thought, but accept it because of his good conduct later on. If, however, I now start the whole thing up again, I upset the status quo, they would be forced to take proceedings against him. Oh, yes, quite possibly Lajos Kapy would be sentenced, but I should certainly make a lot of enemies and I'd have to pay for it.

On the other hand, suppose his superiors know nothing about his past, did I have the right to kick a man back into the dirt? A lot of water had passed under the bridge since he interrogated me in 1935. And the world had changed in the meantime, turned upside down. Perhaps he had already changed his views in 1938. Perhaps he had shown courage in the resistance, or perhaps after being taken prisoner. There was really no room for doubt. He must have done something really important because otherwise, as a former Horthy officer, he could never have become a general in this new world.

If I were to unmask Brigadier-General Lajos Kapy, I thought, not only would I antagonize a few ruthless men, but they would suddenly start to practise their wonderful vigilance on me. They would ask me how it happened that the counter-intelligence branch released me? What? They simply let you go? Are we supposed to believe that? Was that the customary practice of the Horthy police and counter-intelligence? They would then begin to drop hints, dig a bit here and there, or even start investigating to find out what services I had offered in exchange for my release. What little favours, or perhaps important services, had enabled me to be left in peace? How could I prove that I hadn't done anything? In those days the air was heavy with the sulphurous smell of suspicion. No, thank you, I wanted none of that. That's what I was afraid of.

At the same time, I wondered what that man was thinking. He had recognized me. Perhaps he had even dug up my name from the geological strata of memories of countless interrogations. He, too, must be sitting in his office at the Ministry of Defence, or in the barracks, head in hands... and when I got to this point I had to take a second deep breath. Perhaps he is looking at his hands remembering what they had done before he set out on his road to Damascus. Perhaps he is wondering whether he should call me up or even come and see me. Or telephone his minister and report the incident. Perhaps, he's wondering whether he shouldn't take out his service revolver and... He's suffering, I thought. And that was enough for me. For days, for weeks, for months he will sit there, trembling, waiting for me to denounce him. Let that be his punishment. My thirst for vengeance, which earlier on would have needed a microscope to be detected, and which only a few minutes before had been spreading like cancer cells, had shrivelled away in a few hours. I had always believed in the human capacity for change. Lajos Kapy has changed. Let him live in peace if he knows how. And that set my mind at ease.

I was really glad I hadn't told anyone about Lajos Kapy only a few months later, when I learned that he, too, had been arrested in the Rajk affair and later, in October 1949, had been executed.

On trumped-up charges, of course, like the others. Imagine how I would have felt if I thought that my denunciation had even partly contributed to his death. I would never have forgiven myself if my story had figured in the indictment. The human soul is so strangely constructed that I was even sorry for him. I'd never wanted him dead, not even in the cell of the counter-intelligence prison in 1935.

But from then on, the death of Lajos Kapy gave me no peace. For a few months after it happened, it gnawed deeply into my consciousness. I should add that before I never thought of the counter-intelligence prison except perhaps when talking to Czechs, and then I never mentioned that I had once been their 'spy'. What for? It was finished and done with. But in those stifling 'fifties I dreamed every other night that I was standing at attention before Lajos Kapy, in his office, who, wearing his general's stars, humbly informed me, that, on orders from above, he was compelled to hit me in the face. Or I dreamed... no, that was no longer a dream but rather my first, hazy thought on awakening, that it was me he had cursed when he was arrested. He knew himself to be innocent as far as the present was concerned, and he was, so what else could he think but that he had been called to account for the past. And since they hadn't done it before, what other reason could they have now except my vile denunciation? Perhaps he stepped on to the scaffold believing I was his murderer.

Only after 1956 did I really begin to breathe freely, for then I learned from one of the defence lawyers what in fact had happened. It never came out at the trial that Kapy had worked for Horthy's counter-intelligence. They were looking for a square to fit into the mosaic of their fictitious structure, and Lajos Kapy happened to be that little stone. He was accused of having been recruited as a Belgian spy and of working through the Belgians for the French Deuxième Bureau. 'Why the Belgians,' I asked, amazed. 'Simple,' explained the lawyer. 'As a small boy, after the First World War, a relief organization sent him to Belgium to regain his health, along with many other thin and underfed Budapest children. He and his Belgian foster parents had come to love one another, and he kept in touch with them and with his Belgian "brothers". One of the boys who had made a career for himself in diplomacy visited Budapest with an UNRRA delegation in '45 and that was, of course, when he recruited Lajos Kapy. Simple and obvious,' said the lawyer. Kapy had been a Belgian spy just as I had been a Czech spy.

I did not, however, retain my peace of mind.

Lately I have begun to think it would have been better to denounce him. Had I denounced him, it would have forced an investigation. Even if they were aware of his past, there would still have been a scandal. He would have been relieved of his rank, thrown out of the army, indicted and taken before the court. He would have been given five years, or six, or at most, ten. He could have left the country in 1956. Or, he could have stayed and started a new life. But he would be alive. Today, he would be a land surveyor, or a forester, a traffic warden in front of the Annabella Hotel at Balatonfüred or even only a night watchman. But he would be alive. Or his sons would be supporting him and he'd be leading a life of leisure. But he would be alive. Had I yielded to my desire for vengeance, he would already have been in prison by the time the Rajk affair started. They would have had to look for someone else to fit into the mosaic. He would be alive. But I—how can I live on the vessels constricting in my brain, with the knowledge that I was an active participant in an age in which whatever I did was wrong?

Translated by Kathleen Szasz

The First Lines
BY GYÖRGY G. KARDOS

The world I came into was a cramped flat overlooking the courtyard at the back of the house in Király Street, opposite the Király Theatre, where I saw the first theatre performance of my life. Our house was full of market-women, and I was welcome in all their homes. I spent most of my time, however, by Frau Markovich's iron stove stuffed full of apple-peel, listening to horrifying stories of the whining and whimpering spirits inhabiting the stove-pipe. Frau Markovich sold lavender in the Hunyadi Square market. Squatting at the foot of the stalls she chanted with a sad monotony: "lav-en-der ... lav-en-der ..." I would do the rounds of the neighbours in the afternoons, since all the other flats were more spacious than ours. We were crowded together in two tiny rooms, my grandparents, my mother, her elder sister and her three brothers. My mother spent little time at home; she worked as a shorthand-typist in an office. On the other hand her three brothers—a printer, a furrier and a waiter—mostly hung around in the kitchen, since two out of the three were generally out of work. My mother's sister was a visiting manicurist; later she went into service in families hardly better off than ourselves. My grandfather had gone bankrupt through war-loans, his grocer's shop had long ago been sold by auction, so he spent the days running after shady bits of business. He was a dumb little old man, a nitwit of a Jew who only muttered in the synagogue instead of praying, as he was somewhat confused by all the different prayers. My grandfather's father, together with all his forebears, had been a tanner, had fought in Forty-Eight for the freedom of the Hungarians and bore a scar from an Austrian sword for the rest of his life. This was often mentioned in our home, which reeked of fried chips, and on Sundays the light cavalry sword gleamed in the flat in Király Street ravaged by bailiffs. The sword-cut must have caused a slight cerebral concussion as my great-grandfather had become a proud man, had taken to wearing braided and frogged Hungarian dress, and was ashamed to pass on his creditable trade to his sons. He had bought a small grocer's shop in Óbuda for my grandfather, a rather weak man, and had had his other two sons—Uncle Henrik and Uncle Poldi—trained as overseers. I can remember Uncle Poldi, who was forever shouting, as if everybody on the Schlossberger estate where he was overseer had been deaf. Of his face only the long, conspicuous, twirled moustache remains engraved upon my memory. As does his funeral, with the parable of the rabbi of Óbuda about the big oak tree which a woodworm began to gnaw and kept on gnawing until "the tall oak tree ... that proud, tall oak tree suddenly fell ... you, who rest here, Lipót Pollák..." I came to discover my great-grandfather's name not so long ago in a booklet entitled "Hungarian Jews in the War of Independence" with a preface by Dr. Móricz Jókai. There he was, József Pollák, tanner—between Armin Pollacsek, peddler, and Jakab Pollner, synagogue warden.

My grandmother was not my grandmother by blood, as my mother's mother had died of tuberculosis before the war. Very soon the children brought lice home, and consequently my grandfather carried on a close but unsuccessful friendship with all the matchmakers in Óbuda. He had had only a few replies to the advertisements he had put in the papers, in which a Jewish tradesman, free of vices, looked for a compassionate and domesticated woman who could be a mother to his six children. Finally my grandfather had to make do with the hand of a lady with a far from impeccable past and alien religion. The lady answered the advertisement on a postcard with *"Gott strafe England!"* above the address. My grandmother had arrived in Dresden from the Baltic Sea. She had previously lived in Russia for a time, but after the outbreak of the war the Russians had bundled off all Austro-Hungarian citizens, not even sparing innocent Hungarian sparrows chirping around the red-upholstered cabaret tables in St. Petersburg. My grandmother was one of those Hungarian women who had danced, with her two sisters, Aunt Franci and Aunt Olga, all three dressed in hussar uniforms, allegedly in the more elegant night clubs of the Russian capital. But the German steamer, the "Kaiser Wilhelm I" had saved only two of the girls for the Central Powers, and Aunt Olga was left in Russia, where she got married to a journalist from Poltava and sank into oblivion. Aunt Franci conquered the heart of a wartime nouveau riche in Dresden. Soon they had a baby girl, who later married a German baron. My grandmother saw her younger sister in Vienna for the last time before the *Anschluss,* and back home related with heartfelt disgust that Aunt Franci had greeted her *"mit nazionalsozialistischem Grusse"*.

My grandmother was born in Pančevo, in the Banat, and made up her mind to live an improvident life in the midst of all the Eastern church ceremony and banners when she accompanied her first husband, Jovan Tabakovich, a cheerful carrier, on his last journey. So before becoming Mrs. Juda Pollák, my grandmother's perfectly respectable name had been the widow Mrs. János Tabak. I could never understand how on earth she could marry my featherbrained grandfather, whose only reaction to her more liberal comments was "a Jesuit way of thinking." Nor could I ever discover what nationality she was: when she spoke

Hungarian, she would mix in some German words, when speaking Serbian in would come words in Rumanian. Perhaps the only thing really to go by was that she would sing in Serbian while cleaning the windows and doing the cooking, and I always used to sing along: *"Kray Milan putuye, kraytzom serkuye..."* But whenever she hung her lorgnette on a long silver chain around her neck, she would promptly mix French words in her otherwise Hungarian, Serbian and German speech; whenever she played cards with my grandfather she would smash her cards down on the table, calling out the dancing master's instructions in teaching the French quadrille, — and she had all the tricks, of course. And that is how I remember it even today: *"Sénanglé, tourdemi, été, pilé ..."* I used to love to sit next to them when they played cards and listen to all their wisecracks. There was a police officer called Schiffler who used to come and play cards with them, and he would smash his cards down on the kitchen table and declaim: "Service cap?!... Baggy pants?! ... A cinema from a church? ... Madam carrying a shopping bag? ..." I soon learnt and kept on repeating it; I don't know who it was who made me understand that it had been to the rhythm of this peculiar gibberish that the men of the posse had beaten the the members of the village councils in 1919.

Police officer Schiffler had a spine-chilling secret, which he shared with our family alone. His younger son, instead of returning from captivity in Russia, had joined the Red Army and had died in the Civil War. Later on somebody brought home a worn photograph of him lying on the bier, wearing a uniform and a beret with a red star on his head. My grandmother hid the photo between two sheets in the closet. Schiffler's elder son was a terrible character; he was a member of all the Establishment clubs, he never worked but was supported by the Baross Federation; his father listened to his every word with stubborn disgust: "The important thing is that we're Hungarians ... There's no greater thing in the world." Whenever the conversation in the kitchen died away, I knew that Schiffler was silently weeping for his other son, the dead one whose picture no one was allowed to see.

The officer was neither Red nor White, he was a Freemason and a monarchist, and even introduced my grandfather to this harmless conspiracy. The monarchists made their moves under the cover of the Hungarian Inventors' Association; they had a three-roomed office, where they employed my grandfather for a modest salary as a storeman, clerk and general dogsbody. I went to see him once or twice in the office, where he sat nodding off on a chair with a deep sense of responsibility; he guarded fifty boxes of powdered spinach for three months. I can't remember seeing any other invention. The shareholders of the Hungarian Inventors' Association finally failed to restore the Habsburg monarchy and confined themselves—before closing down the office—to sending a delegation to Vienna to lay a wreath on Queen Elizabeth's sarcophagus with the words "To our unforgettable queen from Royalist Hungarians." And we inherited twenty boxes of spinach and a somewhat daft retired general called Sipnetzky, who began to frequent the card games, sitting on the kitchen stool with red stripes down his uniform trousers and declaring *"Rote Hosen tragen die Franzosen"* whenever the trump was hearts.

Although my grandmother was forbidden to talk about her adventures in Russia, whenever we were alone at home she would tell me wonderful stories, and I had to swear by all that was sacred that I'd never tell a soul about the time when she had received a hundred tea-roses in the middle of winter from an officer of the Guards for one passionate kiss. I admired the officers of the Guards, and I admired the

Grand Dukes, and I admired my grandmother, too, particularly when she was in a good mood and sang sentimental Russian songs. When her spirits reached their peak, she would push aside the dining-table and show me how they had danced the can-can in St. Petersburg. *"Raz .. dva ..."* she counted as she lifted her skirt and kicked up her legs in their wrinkled stockings. Our walks were happy and purposeful. We spent whole afternoons in the Meteor Café having coffee with milk on what she had saved from her house keeping money, and watching Sergei Smirnoff and his balalaika band. Then we were off to the City Park later in the afternoon. A Russian immigrant worked as porter at the entrance to Gundel's, always dressed in glamorous Cossack costumes, and my grandmother used to have long chats with him.

But on two occasions I had cause to be ashamed of my grandmother. The first was when we met some Rumanian sailors on Lipót Boulevard, and they invited us on to their barge. The brandy made my grandmother tipsy and she began to sing and, roaring with frivolous laughter, let herself be pinched and fingered. However shameful this adventure was, at least it remained between the two of us, while the other one was far more embarrassing.

I went home from school one day with the news that there was going to be an evening performance in the school gym, in which Eleonora Borodina, former member of the Czarist opera, was going to sing, accompanied on the piano by her husband Prince Tserkasky. Parents were invited to the performance, and my grandmother was more than willing to accompany me. She hung her indispensable lorgnette around her neck and dug up a black velvet hat with a green feather from an old hatbox. This didn't worry me too much, as I was pretty well used to my grandmother's eccentricities.

My grandfather waved his hand and said: *"Schausst aus wie eine Hure"*. But by the time my grandmother had finally settled down on one of the seats reserved for the parents, there was already tension in the air. Then Eleonora Borodina sang an aria from Pique Dame and when she bowed at the end of it giggling could be heard amid the applause, and Prince Tserkasky sternly raised an eyebrow. My grandmother's feathered hat was stealing the show from the former permanent member of the Czarist opera. When it came to Tatiana's song there could be no doubt whatsoever that the green feather was the top of the bill. Roars of laughter burst forth from every corner of the gym. Prince Tserkasky turned round to the audience a number of time while playing the piano and hissed *"Ruhe!"* And once even my grandmother raised her lorgnette and cried *"Ruhe!"*. You can just imagine! Fortunately the performance wasn't long. I sat there all the time as if paralysed, without once daring to look at my grandmother, because whenever she managed to catch my eye she would start waving and gesturing to let me know how much we were supposed to be enjoying ourselves. After the performance I couldn't stop her from rushing up to Prince Tserkasky, who was bad-temperedly gathering up his sheets of music. She placed her hands on her full bosom, bowed and said something in Russian to the Prince, whose face went purple red. He threw the bundle of sheets down on the piano and murmured in a rage: *"Lassen Sie mich in Ruhe, Madame!"*

We walked home wearily. In the gym I had been ashamed of my grandmother, now I was feeling kind of sorry for her. She sighed a lot on the way; she was truly shocked that the Prince had not even condescended to answer her in Russian. I would have liked to ease her mind and wondered how I could console her.

"She sang out of tune," I told her after much deliberation, and felt that she was pleased.

"Well, *siehst du,*" she said. "These are not genuine princes. They're humbug."

Although my grandmother wasn't my grandmother by blood, she was my real grandmother. My father was my father by blood, and yet he wasn't my real father at all. He married my mother a few days before I was born out of some sort of bourgeois piety. I have practically no recollections of him; I'm not sure I ever saw him. A book salesman called Galántai used to turn up on his behalf twice a year, at Christmas and on my birthday, with my father's eccentric gifts; for my fifth birthday I got a set of chromium-nickel-plated Waterman fountain pens, for my sixth birthday an encyclopaedia. On less important occasions Uncle Oscar, the famous storyteller, would also pop in on my father's behalf, sit utterly bored beside me, tell me the tale of Puss in Boots, tell my grandfather a couple of Jewish jokes, then he'd be off to do the same on Margaret Island for the benefit of the capital as a whole. For a long time I was convinced my father was a soldier, as all my mother had of him was a photograph taken during the war, with my father resting his hand on the hilt of his sword and his face held high and grinning impudently under his cocked kepi.

My paternal grandfather was a district doctor in Szécsény and I also met him only once in my life. What I know about him is that he had a silver-handled walking-stick, he adored women, and his heart's desire was to be a Hungarian nobleman. One branch of the family had once been granted the noble patronymic "of Zelenka", for which reason the other branches of the family were constantly besieging the county offices. Even so we never got to be called Kardos "of Zelenka", my grandfather nevertheless made it in society to a certain extent; when he died, the obituary described him as Dr. Sándor Kardos, medical counsellor, honorary chief medical officer of Nógrád and Hont counties.

My father was also going to be a doctor, he even did two terms, but then he fell in love with the former star of silent films, Ica Lenkeffy, and wrote short stories for her. At that moment journalism was only one step away. Then the First World War broke out, and my father, rather young, enlisted. He was wounded, a bullet was embedded in his shinbone—he walked with a limp for the rest of his life—and he was discharged with the rank of second-lieutenant with two Signum Laudises and a lot of other medals. At the end of the war he founded a theatrical review called Comedy, which, according to an old encyclopaedia, was banned during the Hungarian Commune for its patriotic content, and, according to a more recent encyclopaedia, banned during the White Terror for its democratic content.

In point of fact my father had nothing to do with politics. He spent his spare time sitting in actors' dressing rooms, gathering material for the daily gossip column called Backstage in the *Evening Courier*. All that politics meant to him—if it was politics at all—was that he was wont to pose as various sorts of Hungarian army officers. Being a disabled ex-serviceman with many medals, and displaying King Charles's autographed picture on his desk, had boosted his ego. His popularity as a journalist was due to his personal charm; he was one of those charming people who never do anything for anybody, but who always greet others first. His spicy jokes were not always in the best of taste, but his Nógrád accent lent them a special piquancy. People always remembered him for his Palots accent, which gave rise to many an anecdote about him. He left more of these anecdotes to posterity than work of real literary merit.

He managed quite well throughout the hard times, enjoying certain privileges because of his record with the army; he was a member of the local chamber and an air-raid warden. In those years we met more frequently, but didn't know what to do with each other, however hard we tried. I did my best to show off my education, and my father tried to gain my confidence by being bawdy. His impeccable elegance embarrassed me, and his eau-de-cologne mixed with the smell of Virginia tobacco made me sick.

We could never manage to break the ice between us.

After the Second World War I happened to come across an article in some Hungarian paper paying a tribute to my father. It said that when he had been taken away, he had donned his white officer's uniform with all his medals. It would have been an extremely admirable thing for my father to do, it would have honoured the patronymic "of Zelenka" and King Charles's picture on his desk. But it wasn't so. I well remember a photograph of interned Jewish journalists, published in an Arrow Cross paper called *Struggle*, who it said were no longer "poisoning" Hungarian journalism. In that photo my father stood in a shabby black overcoat, embarrassed and confused, with the yellow star on his chest and his characteristic round face rather emaciated. So just how authentic can the following quotation about my father's last day in Buchenwald be? "Pista Kardos, who was always a smart, witty and well-groomed man, examined his shameful prison clothes and said: 'I must have these ironed. After all, you can't go to the crematorium like this'."

My mother was prouder of my father than I. She might have been invented by István Szomaházy, author of Tales of a Typewriter; she was the cheap product of the age, no more than the blurred background of an oak-panelled solicitor's office, who led a tormented life there for a hundred and twenty pengős a month, but who—thanks to my father's well-known name—had something in common with all those people spending their holiday in Abbazia, resting in the Park Sanatorium and eating out at Spolarich's. The most, however, that my mother could afford, was a subscription to *Theatrical Life* for three months in advance, in better years, a cheap season ticket to the opera, spending half an hour in a Buchwald chair, where she always managed in some miraculous way to engage the ladies sitting next to her in conversation, in the course of which she never failed to give her opinion that the public was no longer the same in Siófok as it used to be. We never spent a holiday in Siófok, but my mother's futile daydreams knew no limits. Only once did she risk a holiday in Aliga, for six days in the off-season. We had the mustiest room in the world's cheapest boarding-house, from where she wrote her picture postcards with great relish to her acquaintances, as well as to the heads and clerks of the estimable solicitor's office. It was raining all the time, we hardly ever left the room and we ate sausage and bread all day long. In the evenings, however, we would go and have coffee with milk in the café, where my mother could give full vent to her passion for making friends. She told everybody that we were only on a pseudo holiday, a mere trifle, a whim of hers, and that we were soon off on trip down the Danube, as we had been invited by the Bulgarian government in honour of the medal the Bulgarian Czar had given her husband. The story of the medal was true enough, by the way, as we had read about it in the papers. But I never found out just why my father got it.

That is how we lived on the edge of reality and fantasy. I too, ended up supporting my mother's fantasies, nodding with resignation when she told people that the following year she would be sending me to boarding school in Chalons-sur-Marne. In point of fact, I was one of the worst pupils in school and was expelled in the eighth year because I had failed seven of my exams in the previous term, and had been absent for some three hundred periods. And what if I hadn't been expelled? I would have soon been on my way to the copper mines of Bor just the same...

Let it suffice that I was away for almost eight years. By the time I came back my mother, like many Jewish widows, had found peace in social work. For the first time in her life she was happy, on the go day and night, writing lampoons and making speeches at tenant meetings. She dragged me along to her work-place meetings, even though I was nothing to boast about, because being a bricklayer's mate on a construction site was no great career, not even in those militant times.

For most of my life I meant little happiness to my mother, or to anyone else for that matter, including myself. When my first book was published, my mother didn't want to believe it; she had spread so many stories about my non-existent glory that she took it to be one of her own inventions. And when the truth finally dawned on her she had just enough time to live to herald my greatness far and wide. She was now a pensioner, so she could find time to write to and call all her friends and acquaintances in Hungary and abroad, and the people she used to work with, reading them all the reviews of the book and adding that much better reviews would have been written had it not been for the Writers' Association. She eavesdropped on people's conversation on the tram and became convinced that I was the talk of the town. From then onwards she would introduce herself as "György G. Kardos's mother", and soon applied for membership of the Fészek Club, as "my son is an internationally acclaimed author ..." I was at the height of my success when my mother fell ill one night. The next morning I took her to the hospital, where she lay dying for two days. I stayed with her till the end. She knew very well that she was dying and did her best to prevent me realizing it. When it became impossible to avoid knowing, my mother gave in, and whispered in my ear by way of explanation: "This is the quietus," as if meaning that I should pay close attention, as the observation might some day come in handy. She was a pure and honest soul, and approached death objectively and without fear, paying no heed to the silly efforts of the young woman doctor who insisted: "You'll see, Jolika, in two weeks' time you'll be up and about…" She let the woman doctor too know that her son was a famous writer. My mother's last words were: "Don't forget my watch in the drawer," and passed away after spasmodically vomiting blood. I stayed there while her bed was made, the floor around her washed, and spent some moments more with her behind the folding-screen. Then I cautiously undid the seam on the lapel of my coat with a pair of scissors, that is, I rent my garment. Afterwards I started out on the bureaucratic round of hospital and state office desks in order to reach the funeral. My mother, in the meantime, lay in peace in a steel locker, probably in a decent state, as an autopsy assistant had promised me for two hundred forints. "How we replace the skull is not everything, you know, one must be clever, you know, the hair has to be arranged…"

The Jewish burial society tried to pitch the cost of the funeral sky high, as my mother had asked for what was heathen cremation in her last will. I didn't manage to see the face of the person I was sent to, as he was inhaling and the office was full of the fragrance of camomile. The only time he raised the towel covering his face was when I burst out in praise of the clean and well-kept public cemeteries with reasonable prices. "It's all easy right for them," he retorted angrily. "They have three hundred and fifty funerals a week. We're lucky if we get that many in a whole year."

It was all as simple as that. The furniture didn't creak at night, the glasses didn't break by themselves, and I had no omens in my dreams, even though I had heard so much about such wonders from my grandmother. For her death was just as fabulous as her youth with galloping Cossacks, Grand Dukes and tea-roses. The people in my grandmother's fantasy world passed away with vivid colours, without any disfiguring marks of illness, with gracious movements and final words, corresponding her expectations. My grandmother couldn't let the world be as it was, it had to be the way she wanted it to be. And now there is nothing I long for more than to have my head full of her eccentric daydreams as I write the first lines on a clean sheet of paper.

"Nord-Deutscher Lloyd's steamer Lübeck had been lying for three days in the naval port of Kronstadt with engines going. The fog kept the steam down, and the passengers crowding the deck inadvertently smeared the soot on their faces and started gloomily at the Russian cruiser anchored nearby, its guns trained on the Lübeck.

Further towards the stern, from where the cruiser could not be seen, there were two lonely women ..."

Translated by Judit Házi

Roast Pheasant with Groats

BY GYÖRGY SZÁRAZ

The photograph was taken around the end of November, 1981. In the background there is a steep, tree-covered hillside descending to a footpath; in the foreground a tall, rectangular house, with a glassed-in veranda projecting from the façade. There are two windows on the right, one on the left, and below them a set of stairs leading to the enclosed veranda. In front of the house, there is a long, narrow plot of land, with a few fruit trees.

There are family houses on both sides, built on tiny lots, some with gables and some with tent roofs, every one of them the nondescript style of the past twenty years. In the left foreground, a half-finished structure with twin windows; its open garage doors reveal the back of an old Trabant.

Upon this picture I try to project the other one, which exists only in my memory. If it were real, I would write on its reverse side: Christmas, 1945.

The house is the same, and there are the hillside and the footpath. The plot of land is bare and unfenced: the thick forest growth reaches as far as the back wall. There is barren space all around, with only the occasional rattling dry maize stems, and where the house of the Trabant owner now stands, are snow-capped, frozen cabbages marking the vegetable patch. On this picture one can see the continuation of the footpath: above the house it disappears into a narrow valley. I know that there, beyond the turn, wine-cellars and press-sheds are lined up, with discarded barrels and vats in the snow.

I also know that if I were to go up the steps and cross the glassed-in veranda, I would arrive in the kitchen of the house. There is nothing there but a shabby table, an enamelled stove, several crates draped with some material (these are the seats), and under the back window lookig over the hillside, an open convertible, upon which lies an open book, perhaps Jókai's novel, *The New Landlord*. In the left room there is a varnished suite of bedroom furniture: two twin beds, two wardrobes and two commodes. Only there are no mattresses on the beds, and the wardrobes have no drawers or shelves. On the wall hangs a chromotype: a girl with clasped hands gazing upwards to the sky, wearing a blue cloak over a white robe, her head encircled by a saintly halo. There is nothing in the other room: floor and walls are bare.

In front of the house stands a pile of branches, and the trunk of the tree as well, stripped of its bark, bearing the traces of awkward axe-strokes. The young oak tree stood on the hillside behind the house, and one December afternoon I cut it down. Since I had no saw, I took an axe and chopped away all around the trunk, letting fly with an energy that ebbed and surged: Come on down, come on! The tree finally crashed and lay athwart the footpath. Two old men, wearing boots and short sheepskin jackets came out from the direction of the village; one of them said that he was the village elder and that the tree was village property, promising me no end of trouble because I had cut it down. I stood on the other side of the tree trunk; the old man was fat, ruddy-faced and dragged out his vowels in the manner of Danubian Swabians. Finally I told him to get the hell out of there. I was fourteen years old at the time. He stopped abruptly, looked at me: I glared back at him, my tears welling up in hatred. There were no more words between us, and the two left.

I could not have known at the time that half a year later, during the second wave of relocations, when the police would descend upon the village in a surprise raid, the same old man was to make his getaway through the gardens in the back of the houses, only to hide for several months, spending the remainder of his life in a stable, waiting for his son's return from the war. The boy disappeared at the front in 1943, after enlisting in the Hungarian Army, just to get away from the SS recruiters. At the time of our encounter over the fallen tree the old man must have looked me over thoroughly, and was probably able to determine with a feeling of satisfaction and disgust that I was a good-for-nothing. I certainly had the appearance of one: I was wearing my father's old pair of trousers, shortened with string tied below my knees, and a worn-out military jacket, which I had found at the edge of a deserted trench when the front line reached our home-town. My shoes were patched front and back, and were topped by a pair of leggings, jerry-built from an old pair of peasant boots. As for the tree I cut down, it was not only for firewood. I was hoping that my father would somehow take it to Budapest, and trade it for some kind of decent footwear for me, thereby ending my three-months long quarantine. We had been living in that house since October, and I had not yet seen the village.

We had arrived on a sunny, late summer afternoon. The driver of our dray, a Hungarian-Csángó, relayed the seemingly endless story of his migration from the Bukovina in Rumania to the Bácska region in Yugoslavia and then, crisscrossing the front lines, to his destination near Buda. I trudged along beside the wagon, happy, because this time our destination was not as uncertain as the earlier one that summer when we first set out on the road.

On that early summer afternoon I had walked up the hillside above our garden and stood among the thickening potato plants, taking a last look at the city, nestled in the arc of the high mountains, centred around the square watch-tower. That night we left, travelling on a huge dray: Mother, Father and I, along with a woman schoolteacher, who had even fewer belongings than we had, and, coming from this side of the border, the wife of a customs officer, who had been visiting her parents on the other side, and had a special permit to bring goods and firewood across the frontier. The logs were scattered among and under the crates. Around dawn a rainstorm caught up with us. Up front, the thick-legged wife of the customs officer got under a horse-blanket with the gruff driver, while in the back we tried to cover our stuff, to prevent too much water getting inside the crates. In the morning, by the time the shabby-uniformed border guard had raised the barrier for us, the sun was already shining. We travelled through villages full of ruined houses and saw burnt-out mechanical monsters in the ditches along the road. Tattered children ran after our cart, and the teacher quietly slipped them the logs belonging to the customs officer's wife. We stopped to feed the horses beside a roadside inn, and the teacher told an inquisitive old woman that we were part of a circus, and that in the evening there would be a performance in the main hall of the inn. I was grateful that she said this, because the bitter truth filled me with shame.

So this journey in October was quite different. I knew that beyond the hills, in the direction the Csángó driver pointed with his whip, there would be a home waiting for us, a roof over our heads. Then we passed the little chapel on the right side of the road bearing the sign *"Maria hilf!"*

and I got my first look at the village: houses crowded together in the narrow valley, the Baroque church spire, and the white stations of Calvary on the hillside. And there indeed was the house at the edge of the forest waiting for us, with a stove, the picture of the holy maiden on the wall, and the disemboweled bedroom furniture. We lived in the kitchen, which was the only heatable room. Father and Mother crowded together on the convertible at night, and I slept on the floor, in a nest made of clothes. I was told to stay away from everyone, but the forest was mine, at least until the autumn rains came. After that, I was imprisoned inside the house, and, curled up on the convertible, read through my remaining books.

From time to time, there were visitors.

During the first days a woman showed up. She said the house was theirs, her husband had been expelled by mistake, and the matter was going to be cleared up soon. My mother was contrite, almost humble, promising that we would take care of everything. The woman looked around, went down to the larder, and when she saw the great beech-tree block from which I had been splitting pieces for the fire, broke down sobbing. It turned out that her husband's work was with tripe and sausage-casing (earning enough to have the house built), and the block was one of his tools. ... "My God, where will all this end?" she kept repeating as she was leaving. We never saw her again. There were also soldiers from the neighbouring airfield. They beat a path to the wine-cellars, with square loaves of dark brown bread tucked under their arms. They used to knock on our door as well, asking for wine, offering bread and yellowish sugar in exchange. Finally, I put up a sign on the veranda door: "Vino nyet!" Nonetheless two of them begged their way inside once: they had come from the cellars and had got several bottles of wine already; they were asking for mugs to drink it from. They drank and offered me some wine. One of them took out a photograph: "Wife, children," he said, gesturing that they were his, then indicating that they were no longer alive. "Bang-bang..." He added, "Nyemets bang-bang!" and looked at me gravely. I repeated after him, "Bang-bang!" He laughed, but it was not a good laughter; he pointed his forefinger at me and demanded, "Bang-bang?" Obediently, I answered, "Bang-bang!" His friend stood up, patted me on the shoulder, and before leaving filled a jug with wine, gesturing that it was for me.

In November my father brought home a pistol. It was issued to him for self-defence, because there were rumours of escaped SS-soldiers in hiding; we had even heard of killings, and there we were, right next to the forest, far from the village.

The pistol, a Frommer, was already in the house when one evening a tall, lanky Swabian young man showed up: he was looking for my father, and, not finding him home, sat down without waiting to be asked. While rattling away about a certain vineyard, supposedly his inheritance, he kept telling us not to worry, he would not harm anyone. But I saw that my mother's hand was shaking under her apron, and I sat on the couch, outside the circle of light thrown by the petroleum lamp, and held the pistol in a tight grip under the blanket.

There was a morning visitor too: a man with a moustache neatly trimmed, wearing a short furcoat and close-fitting English boots, one of the supervisors of the relocation organization. He too was looking for my father. As he was leaving, he glanced at my footwear made up of a boot upper and an old shoe, and said, laughing, "Fine-looking tap-shoes, kid..." It was just to show him that I soon got a pair of boots. My father brought them; they were used, but I also got a pair of military breeches buttoning up the side with them and those were brand new. My first trip was to the village barber, because during my three-month-long seclusion a real bush jungle had sprouted on my head. This was in contrast to early summer, when I was bald, and had vowed never again to sit in a barber's chair. Not because of the loss of hair; I was used to that, for my father used to have me shorn every spring, out of conviction that it is healthy for a child. But that spring I had been shorn at school, in the bathroom, and there the other boys did not produce any mocking verses, either in Hungarian or in any other tongue. And two days later, our skinny geography teacher, although he wore a peasant shirt with an embroidered collar, linked arms with me during the school's May Fair, and took me over to an upper class girl, telling me to teach her how to dance the csárdás. She was a pretty girl, ready to smile, and her hip burned my palm through the slippery tickle of her silk dress.

In the evenings I used to think of that girl, or the other one, with whom I had been necking a year earlier, in the alley by the mill. Her face reappeared later in a doorway, above the shoulder of a German military uniform. Her body was covered by the wide-flung folds of the coat, and I heard her whimpering grunts... I also thought of the Swabian girls I saw in the village, with their legs in their distinctive tight white stockings; and I imagined how it would be to squeeze them up against the wall and hear their whimpering ... Of course, by that time, in January, I was roaming the village every night, wearing a pistol and an armband. Every potential deportee was already packed up, and they tried to save what they could not carry with them by smuggling it across to their relatives who were remaining. Once, in the darkness, a girl bumped into me: white stockings gleaming on her legs, a bag crammed full on her back, and carrying a shiny, crisp man's leather coat over her arm. She begged and pleaded, and I did not know what I wanted more: her or the coat. In the end, I took her to the police station, where she was given a receipt for everything and was allowed to go home. The next morning there was no trace of a leather coat among the stuff collected the previous night.

But in December there were no boots as yet, only the smell of the petroleum lamp, and hunger. From the deserted garden I brought in some frostbitten cabbage; my mother cooked it in salt and water. It was faintly syrupy and revolting, because we ate it without bread. On Christmas Eve, I dragged a small pine in from the forest and lay down on the couch to read *The New Landlord*. My mother was already cooking the festive dinner. It was the last of the reserves from home: groats that had become lumpy in the canvas bag, having got wet during that night trip in the dray. Suddenly I heard a rattling noise, directly under the kitchen window facing the forest. The sound went on, so I went out to take a look. I found a hen pheasant caught in the thick underbrush. As I reached for it, it struggled wildly, deadly terror in the leathery-wrinkled eyes ... I took the axe, held the struggling animal with hands and knees on the chewed-up stump, and cut off its head. I carried the lightweight bunch of feathers inside, and put it down in front of my mother. She just looked, and suddenly began crying. "The Good Lord sent something for us, after all ..." she kept repeating even while plucking the bird, wiping her wet face with hands coated with feathers.

My father came home and we ate the roast pheasant with the mouldy-smelling groats.

I could never get to like that village, nor feel that I had anything to do with it. Last year, just before Christmas, my father died, and my mother followed him eight months later. They lived for thirty-five years in that village, the second half of their lives. I buried them in the sandy soil of Rákoskeresztúr, next to each other. The blue-robed, skyward-gazing maiden wound up in the attic long ago, but the matching beds and the crippled wardrobes lasted the whole time. The new owner asked me what he should do with them. I told him to chop them up for firewood. And yet I can understand my son, who visits the village, his birthplace, from time to time. This photo, too, was a gift from him, an early Christmas present.

By Way of Explanation

The editor had every reason to ask me to attach some notes to the above piece. I have to add, however, that the bare facts are not very useful here. To compress into a brief paragraph the whole tragedy that befell peoples and nationalities who lived side by side, relying on each other and tormenting each other for centuries, is a nearly impossible task. I will try anyway.

At the end of the First World War, two-thirds of the territory of the Hungarian state, a single entity for a thousand years, was distributed among the Kingdoms of the Rumanians and the Yugoslavs, Austria, and the newly born Czechoslovakia. Many of these border districts were inhabited by various ethnic minorities, but the victorious Great Powers drew up the new borders not on the basis of ethnic realities, but according to political interests. As a result large concentrations of Hungarians, who had lived together in the same place for centuries, and who in all made up roughly one-third of the total number of Hungarians, were torn away from their mother country in the territories to other nations. One of the reasons why the Hungarian regimes of the inter-war years sought the alliance of Fascist Italy, and later of Nazi Germany, was the hope that these nations, also opposed to the peace treaties drawn up at Versailles, would help to modify its terms. With the support of these two major European powers, Hungary was successful in regaining two of these lost areas with a mainly Hungarian population between 1938 and 1941, but the price for this was involvement in the war on the side of Hitler. Thousands of people perished, Hungary itself became a theatre of war in 1944, and in the end the regained areas disappeared once more like the gifts of Lucifer.

The "Danubian Swabians", who were the descendants of German peasants settled in Hungarian areas after the end of the Ottoman occupation of the country some 250 years ago, were regarded by the Nazis as the advance parties of German expansionism. As part of the price exacted in exchange for the regained territories the Hungarian state was compelled to give them special privileges. The pro-Nazi mass organization, the Volksbund, ruled supreme in the Swabian villages, and its leaders convinced the German-speaking inhabitants that after the "final victory" they would become the *de facto* lords of this "Eastern Colony". The young men became soldiers in the SS units of the Reich, first as enthusiastic volunteers, later as conscripts, and indeed ceased to consider themselves citizens of a "foreign" nation, that is, of Hungary.

It was the age of a new *Völkerwanderung* in the Carpathian Basin. In 1939 a wave of Polish refugees from the German invasion of Poland flooded still-neutral Hungary, and the Hungarian families who had originally fled or been expelled after 1918 from the lost territories headed north and towards their former homes in the recovered territory, while those newly resettled, Czechs, Rumanians, were also on the move. In 1941 came the Csángó Hungarians from beyond the Carpathians, the area of Bukovina. The Hungarian Government settled them in the south, in the villages vacated by Serbian peasants who had arrived after 1920 and were then thrown out. And then the most monstrous "mass migration" of all began: the Jewish inhabitants were taken to the German death-camps, first from Fascist Slovakia, then, after 1944, from German-occupied Hungary. But the smoke of the deporting trains was still in the air when the roads again became covered by convoys of wagons, this time heading west: as the front line neared them, Transylvanian Hungarians and Saxons, and Swabians from the old German settlements in the Banat left their homes to escape the fighting. And, after two years of resettled existence, the Csángós, now doubly "stateless", once more were on the move.

Even the first years of peace brought no rest.

In the aftermath of the Potsdam Agreement, the states of East Central Europe prepared, or were forced, to get rid of their German minorities. Hungary also followed suit. As a result the flotsam of the mass migration fetched up in the old Swabian villages, the refugees from North, South and East, who found themselves faced with the closed borders of the re-established 1920 frontiers, were collected in these former Swabian villages in Hungary. The reborn Czechoslovak state decided to free itself of their Hungarian minority, as well as the Germans or Sudeten Deutsch, applying the principle of "collective guilt" to them as well. Hungarian families were expelled one after the other, and preparations were made for a great mass relocation.

These new Hungarian homeless needed homes: several Swabian families in Hungary were forced to move in together, and the emptied houses taken over by embittered new settlers. They sat down at someone else's table, lay down in someone else's bed, and the whole thing was beginning to appear natural: after all, someone else sat down at their table, and lay down in their bed. They did not even feel sorry for those preparing to depart: after all, they had left their own cemeteries, their own orphaned dead. The date was 1945; the guns were silent, but the war was not yet over.

This is the background to what I have written above.

Translated by András Boros-Kazai

A Family Novel

Excerpt

BY LÁSZLÓ GYURKÓ

My family fell apart years before Karl died. The war and history had seen to that long ago. As strong and great as this family had been, so unenduring it was now. It survived only a single generation.

And yet my uncle's death was the conclusion. He had been the last of the siblings, the last head of our unenduring family.

The head nurse called at seven in the morning, telling me that Karl had departed that night. That is how she said it: departed. The young doctor on his ward had said it that way, too, a few days before: "Uncle Karl will be departing soon."

The world changes. We no longer die, we just depart.

I took a green suitcase with me to the hospital, it had been the first one I could find. The nurse put everything in it that Karl had left behind. Pyjamas, towels, a pair of slippers, an electric razor and some cutlery. I felt like leaving everything there, but I couldn't very well ask the nurse to throw it all into the dustbin. I had to take all the stuff with me, knowing that no one will ever have any use for it, take it over to where the rest of the junk was, over to the hacienda. How symbolic, this thought, at eighty Karl's life had been of no use to anyone either.

"Do you want to look at him?" the head nurse asked.
"No, thank you."

I had seen him the day before, he was already unconscious.

He was lying on his back, blueish veins crisscrossing his parchment-white face, his sunken lips moving as if he were chewing on something. I had seen him quite often in the past three years; he had been evading death with an endurance so characteristic of our family. His cerebral sclerosis was incurable, he was hardly able to walk, I dragged him from one hospital to the next, once to a horrible chronic ward that was like a pit in hell, and back home whenever I could. But always he wanted to go home, back to his hacienda. Then he fell and hit his head, in the hospital he had a heart attack and then got pneumonia. He survived it all. Even though he was no longer fighting for his life. Granted, he did not give it up either. Once I sat at his bed for hours, he didn't let go of my hand. He didn't hold it tightly, he didn't clutch it, he just held it. He had a temperature of a hundred and two, he was breathing heavily, unconscious, but if I moved my hand he opened his eyes. That's another thing we know nothing about, that territory between life and death. "I was half way over the hill then," he would say later with a smile. He lived for nearly one more year.

In the last few years quite a few people I knew have departed. Almost all of them at night. I wonder why?

The front door of the house had a rusty padlock on it: the padlock was so simple even the clumsiest robber could have opened it with a single nail. He wouldn't even need that, he could just tear the latch out of the decayed wood with his bare hands. But I had to put the green suitcase down in the mud to undo the padlock.

The door was also locked with key. With a serial key, the kind that you could get at any ironmongery. Karl had insisted on having both a lock and a padlock on the door. He considered it his duty to lock the house; fortune must be protected. The fact that the house was never broken into was not because of the lock or the padlock.

The entrance behind the front door had been built much later than the house itself, when Karl was already an old man. This must have been the last of his many projects, which he always planned, one after the other, reconsidering them endlessly, making sketches and calculations, and finally completing them by literally depriving himself of his daily bread. With each one he hoped that it would change his life. I will get back to them later.

The entrance was intended to serve as a windbreak, but it had turned into a lumber room and a firewood shed. "And we'll no longer carry the mud inside," Karl said contentedly when the rectangular, awkward box was finished — it had of course cost a lot more and taken a lot longer than he had calculated, ruining for good the building's already disfigured exterior.

As I went into the house, the green suitcase in my hand, I found a large heap of coal dust in the corner in which a few briquets were embedded. On the unplaned shelf which Karl had concocted, its cheap curtains torn off long ago, there were cans and cracked jelly glasses full of crooked nails, screws with worn threads, rusty hinges, rancid grease, broken tools, a broom without a stick, and wire; there was a wobbly, filthy kitchen table with leaking pots, pieces of wooden boards, a leash of cracked leather left behind by the dog that had died a year before, bent cramp-irons, and a bucket without a handle. Karl never threw away anything. On the hacienda, there was use for everything. If not today, then tomorrow, but one of these days for sure.

My favourite toy as a child had been a small chest of many drawers that had copper knobs and were filled with the most wonderful things. Because Karl let me play with everything. I could climb up on his couch or his huge armchairs, he didn't even mind my jumping around on them, unlike my other uncles and aunts, as at Aunt Stefy's, where

Uncle Gyula would always be telling me to take care and not scratch the furniture. Indignantly, I told Karl and Sara about it then; they just looked at each other and laughed.

Karl played too. In a cabinet, behind its glass door, he had tin soldiers lined up for battle, galopping cavalry with their swords drawn, artillery-men standing to attention somberly beside their cannons, lancers ready for attack, and giant foot soldiers in busbies marching to battle. On another shelf there was a whole zoo, a lurking hare, a red-bottomed monkey, a slender deer, a giraffe with its broomstick of a neck, a wolf, its teeth bared, a tame elephant, and a lion with a full mane. Most of all I admired the huge grizzly bear standing on its hind legs and snapping its teeth. There was also an electric railway, with freight cars and a passenger train. The two-level station, the signal box, the buildings of the little village, the stables, school and church Karl had made himself, using a fret-saw and bright coloured paint. All these toys he had bought and made when he was already grown up and married. For his unborn children? For the countless brood of the family? As compensation for the things he never had as a child? Or simply because he liked toys? He would often crouch down with us on the floor, his nimble fingers shifting the points and navigating the train.

In the chest the many drawers were subdivided into compartments. One held screwdrivers of various sizes, perfectly ordered, another a set of pliers with flat noses, and cutting nippers, wrenches, pincers, small and larger hammers, handsaws, well-sharpened chisels, screws carefully classified into flat-headed and rounded ones, hectagonal bolts and long nails of all sizes. It was great fun to spread these treasures out on the table and then put them all back again into the drawers.

The chest Karl had designed himself, handing a meticulously drawn sketch to the cabinet-maker. The tools he had bought himself too, and he used them, but he wasn't the one who kept them in order. As long as he had the money he paid someone to do it, and when the money was gone, others who loved him kept his things in order for him as much as they could. When they, too, had departed, leaving Karl to himself on his hacienda with his dog and his cats, the objects he had collected all his life foully conspired against him: they crammed all niches of the house, every crevice, closing in on him without mercy like the vines of the jungle that engulf the ruins of abandoned cities. But Karl stayed on among the ruins, he lived for many years in the house, among his proliferating objects, unperturbed by their tyranny. Time was increasingly losing its meaning. He had more and more time, as if the days came to consist of more than twenty-four hours; his diminishing strength and weak legs allowed him less and less use for it. He adhered to his habits in order to keep his composure, to give some structure to his life. When he departed, he did not take these habits with him; they stayed here on the hacienda, mere in the form of objects, testimony to man's meagre prospects for attaining immortality.

As I said, the entrance was a forgivable transgression of Karl's in his old age, it was not part of the house. Decay really struck me as I opened the door to the porch. For years I had been watching the house fall apart, and everything that was inside it, but now that night that Karl had departed, the ceiling and the walls seemed to have cracked too. The smell was an undefinable mixture of mould, dust, of peeling paint and rags stuffed into window cracks, of the fur of dogs and cats long gone, and of cushions riddled with moths. I knew that smell well. While Karl was alive it didn't bother me, because it was a part of him, something his existence could make me forget. But now that I knew Karl had departed, that smell had become foreign and appalling and sickening and choking. How could Karl have lived in this smell for so many years? He who at one time had freshly washed and ironed underwear set out for him every morning, who shaved twice daily, who changed shirts in the evening too if he had company, who had two toilets in his flat and a huge bathroom with chiselled glass shelves holding lotions, eau de cologne, creams, shampoos and talcum powders, all lined up in due order.

In this house at Pesthidegkút you couldn't even take a bath. Though there was a bathtub in the always cold bathroom the water couldn't be heated up, hot water had to be boiled in the kitchen in huge pots. In the beginning they did this once a week, but as time went by the strength of the residents waned, then Sara departed, and then Aunt Emma departed, too. For twenty years, Karl washed himself in a huge, increasingly rusty white enamel bowl, every day, very thoroughly, surely shivering; but he clung to the hacienda. He clung to his two thousand books, permeated with dust and mould, which never came off the sagging shelves since, as he said, he had already read them. He clung to his ragged Persian rugs which the not always housebroken cats and dogs had thoroughly worn out. He clung to his wall rugs now threadbare, to his many paintings which almost covered the walls, some of them his own creation, he clung to the shabby embroidered and Gobelin tapestry cushions, to the fat cats purring on his stomach, to the blind dog which could no longer find the way to the door. He clung to every inch of ground on the hacienda, the dilapidated sties, sheds, the chairs with their covers turned inside out, the armchairs with their broken springs, the couch which, propped up with bricks, could not be moved, and under which you could never sweep out the dirt. He clung to the motheaten clothes of his dead wife and mother-in-law which were hanging in the attic, where once legs of ham, sausages and pork cheese had hung; they were covered by brittle newspaper under a thick layer of dust. For years before his death Karl was unable to climb the steep stairs to the attic.

He clung to money. He spent it while he had it, whether or not he was asked to. He felt it his obligation to help out all the world, especially the family of course. And since the number of his immediate relatives, including his wife's extensive family which he also made a part of ours, approached one hundred, it isn't hard to imagine what that meant, even if most of them were never in need of financial support. When he no longer had money, or just barely as much as a beggar, I still never heard him utter a word of complaint. Not out of modesty. Nor could it have been the fear that if he complained I might give him some. Because when I did give him money he accepted it as naturally as when he had handed it out earlier. To me, among others.

Lack of money did not give him a sense of want. Not even when he had to forsake his most basic needs, like wine and soda twice a day, or coffee after lunch, cigarettes or meat.

He did like two or three glasses of wine, though, or a sort of schnaps, if someone brought him some, and a smile would then come to his face. He would probe with his tongue the flavour of the coffee he had been given as a present.

But even then it was he who evaluated what to sacrifice for what. He concluded that although life was not unbearable without wine, coffee, cigarettes or perfumed soap, his cats and dogs did need milk and chicken legs. He always offered his guests a drink. What was left of that pauper's pension he got and the scanty income which flowed in by driblets he needed to carry out his plans, which until the end of his life he refused to abandon. A penniless kid from the working class turned well-to-do citizen, he had never learned to respect money, the basic ingredient of the life-style of the bourgeois.

So every junk-souvenir of Karl's life that could not be turned into money survived, and everything that could be sold for money disappeared like a puff of smoke. I have only a rough picture of all his wife's necklaces, rings, earrings, of his cufflinks, tie pins, his gold watch and silver cigarette cases that made their way to pawnshops and loan sharks. Month after month he had tried to save or scrape together the little money—though I know today that to him these sums had been enormous—which was necessary to renew pawn tickets and credit bills. With the utmost secrecy he had asked for a loan from one of his friends, only to pay back what another friend had lent him.

Fortunately, and I mean that literally, it took less than ten years for this nagging, humiliating situation to be resolved. For pennies, for ridiculous sums, he squandered all their valuables, their jewellery, which considering Karl's former life-style could not have been little. Family legend has preserved the story about the diamond necklace worth ten thousand of forints—this in the early fifties!—which failed to be brought home from the pawnshop because Karl was too bashful to borrow two hundred forints to renew the pawn ticket. That necklace, by the way, can still be seen in the portrait of my aunt painted during the war by a fashionable and expensive, but very mediocre portrait painter. With the passing years and life's adversities the picture has become so grimy that after the death of his wife Karl tried to restore it himself. He met with little success.

Whether the story of the necklace be legend or truth no one can say. But even if it isn't true, it is still characteristic of Karl. Legends generally have a kernel of truth to them. And it is true that their jewellery disappeared, to the very last piece. When Karl departed he left only his wife's and his own wedding ring. And the hacienda.

Karl had said of the house, where after the death of its owner the cadaverous smell became stronger and stronger that it had been designed as a caretaker's house. This is legend, too, even if Karl himself believed in it. The small house had been constructed in 1942, at the zenith of my uncle's life, success and wealth. On the outside the high-roofed, rectangular building was shapely and attractive, and it did suit Karl's taste, but the way it was arranged inside was a puzzle. That is, if we want to accept it as a caretaker's house. The long veranda had originally been an open porch with arches and bulging pillars, like those of the manors in the west of the country, with red geraniums in green containers lined up on the white balustrade. The kitchen was the biggest room in the house, the cooking and serving section separated by an arched doorway; on the whitewashed walls were colourful ceramic plates painted with poppies, cocks and tulips. The kitchen led to the pantry, the size of a room. On dark-brown shelves bordered with flowered strips of paper stood an army of glass pots full of home-made jam, tightly covered with celophane wrap: golden apricot jam with white peeled almonds, ebony-blue plum compote with a flavour of rum, red raspberries, pale yellow pears, little berries of red currant, bright green pickles with red and white wedges of carrots and turnips added, red-hot paprikas, Karl's favourite and the horror of the women of the house, deep purple beets and finely rasped relish. From the pantry a steep staircase led up to the huge attic, where heavy chunks of bacon, Indian-red smoked hams, and round pork-cheeses hung from suspended poles.

From the kitchen you came to the small bathroom with a bathtub, a sink, and a flush-toilet—although for years there was no running water in the house. It had to be drawn from the round well, which had a small roof painted green, and where wine, soda and dark-green watermelons could be let down to be cooled twenty metres below. From the kitchen you could also reach the two rooms, one smaller than the next; the large one was four by four metres, the smaller three by three. The little room did not even have a chimney, it could never be heated.

All his life Karl had a craze for projects. He was a born inventor of schemes. The fact that he could not so much as save even the ruins of his former wealth, that the remains of his riches, his gold and jewellery, turned to smoke so quickly that in his old age he almost starved, was not in small part due to the fact that after his former way of life came to an end he came up with the most fantastic plans for revitalizing his days. These he adhered to, despite all kind words, friendly advice and expert opinions with a stubbornness which was so characteristic of our family. And if he failed in his project of the moment, in dyeing kerchiefs, growing chrysanthemums or selling fruit, he already had a new objective in mind. No failure could weaken his positive outlook and his desire to be active. He never accepted the fact that the world had been turned upside down. Unswervingly he followed his own compass, though it seemed always to point in the wrong direction.

His homes, though, he always planned with precision, good taste and convenience. I knew three of them. In these three he lived for fifty years.

The apartment at Bulyovszky Street (today Rippl Rónai Street) was a place full of wonder to me as a child. Even today I would describe it as an almost perfect home. Karl tore down the wall between two of the five rooms, that way he got a room ten metres long and six metres wide. A Venetian chandelier, the terror of the chambermaids, hung from the centre of the ceiling; it had countless lightbulbs hidden between its lustres. But in each of the four corners of the ceiling in the middle of the plaster rosettes, there were also lightbulbs which could be turned on separately, so that the lighting in the huge room could be varied at will. The room was heated by an ever-burning coke stove; through the glass window on its belly a scarlet glow was cast around.

The other three rooms consisted of a study, a dining-room and a guest room. There was no bedroom in the flat. This was in the thirties! Karl and Sara slept in the big room, on a sofa covered by Persian rugs and wide, wider than I have ever seen anywhere else. I knew those austere family double beds with their grim commodes, those swan-necked canopy-beds with sprung mattresses, the plain sofas and folding beds with mattresses on a wire base, but I never knew a bedstead like this. I imagine it corresponded in size to a normal French bed, but such furniture was not fashionable in my family.

A huge oil painting hung above the couch: a nude lay on her stomach on a bear skin, one leg elegantly flexed. The painting did not win the approval of my family. Gossip had it that the painting depicted one of Karl's lovers. Actually it was one of a series of mass-produced pictures by a successful painter of the time. As the fine dame lay on her stomach, thus not disclosing her breasts nor an even more shameful part of her body, it was only just acceptable to middle-class tastes and morality.

In the thirties Karl also built their summer home at Lake Balaton. Exactly there, where it was appropriate for a man of his standing. Because the Lake Balaton settlements had a rather strict hierarchy. From the three capitals of the lake, Siófok was fashionable, Füred mellow and Keszthely already obsolete. The southern shore communities were primarily made up of the bourgeoisie, with the exception of Földvár, which attracted artists, and aristocratic Fenyves with its few dozen very exclusive villas. On the northern shore it was a little less hierarchical. In Badacsony, Tihany and Almádi the villas of the gentry were cheek by jowl with the houses of peasants.

As obliged by his position, Karl chose Balatonszéplak. This vacation spot was somewhat under the influence of Siófok, but was quite separate from neighbouring Zamárdi, which was very petit-bourgeois. Karl's summer house was more modern than the villas built around this time, more reminiscent of the functionalism and puritanism of the Bauhaus. It was cosy, its three rooms well arranged, pleasant from the outside with a large, semi-circular glassed-in veranda; it was practically at the lake's edge and had its own pier with a boat.

Considering all this I cannot imagine the house in Hidegkút to have been built as a home for a caretaker. Even if Karl did build it on the lower part of the long lot with the intention of locating it as far as possible from the future big house. As a result, however, he had to walk some hundred metres from the paved road where the bus stopped for the house, and this for the rest of his life, in mud, rain, and snow, his legs weaker and weaker, faltering more and more. On this road he often fell.

Knowing Karl, this house, the way it was arranged, could have served only one purpose. On the brick-shaped porch, on the large extending table there was room for twenty persons. The huge kitchen, the pantry and attic made it possible to prepare for week-end gatherings. The two small rooms were for Karl, Sara and Aunt Emma to sleep in on Saturday night. There was also a little room for the maid, just barely big enough to fit a bed in, in the little house which led to the cellar. Because there was a cellar that went with the caretaker's house, too, cut into the clay soil, at least five metres long. Here they kept the potatoes, stuck the carrots and turnips into a heap of sand, here they had a few small barrels of wine, and here they kept cool the food, the cold cuts and the cheese.

A caretaker's house?

Karl's greatest, incurable passion was for company. In company this intrinsically kind man was at his best, his voice smooth, his movements seductive, his mind vigorous. The most beautiful days of his life must have been on Christmas Eve when forty to fifty relatives and friends would gather in the flat in Bulyovszky Street. The library, with the huge Christmas tree reaching all the way to the ceiling, which every year Karl decorated himself with glass ornaments, sparklers, candles, candy and gingerbread men, was laden with presents.

If it had been possible for Karl to be in advance of his time, for which he had neither the opportunity nor the inclination, he would probably have gone in for an extended family life-style like the hippies, something like a commune. I must point out that the aristocracy had already achieved such a mode of living, not to mention earlier social groups. Karl must have sensed that true bonds between people are only born out of work and living together. Within the circumstances of his own life he tried to achieve this as far as was possible. And this was the purpose of his supposedly caretaker's house.

In company Karl was in his natural element. And especially if he was the host.

We all know the clichés of this subject. It is good to be a host if someone wants to show off his wealth, his rank or his wit. If he wishes to force his will, opinions or views upon others. If he desires to smooth his path in his professions, his career and his future. If he wants to have the freedom as a host to do anything he wants and force his guests to conform to his wishes.

None of these explanations applied to Karl. He collected his peacock's feathers for himself, without any desire to flaunt them. I do not recall anyone at his table who could have smoothed his career, but much more those whom he could and did help. If there was any adjustment to be made by anyone in his house, it was for him to do so, the guests could do what they pleased. His role was that of a polite, pleasant, helpful host, never weary of mediating, generous, entertaining, a role that did not include rights, only responsibilities.

This role, I suppose, made him happy. Everyone looks for the role in which he can be happy. He was happy to be able to pour a drink into an empty glass, with his eyes to indicate to the maid an empty plate, to give advice to one who asked him for it, to try to cheer those who were depressed and to be the first of the convivial company.

Or was he happy because at least among a small group, with a few dozen people, for just an hour or so, he succeeded in creating that harmony so vital to man? He was a contemplative person, but not the generalizing type. He did not interpret his qualities through formulas, his instincts through laws. If he felt good he did not seek to find any truth behind his gaiety. He was no saint to sacrifice himself for others. He sought his own happiness in that of his fellow men.

In his old age, when he moved with increasing difficulty, he would shave with special care on Saturdays and Sundays, sling a tie around his neck, put his docile sheepdog on its chain, and he would sit down after lunch in his armchair with the broken springs facing the entrance, his cane leaning against the chair, and he would wait, perhaps a visitor would come. One did not come often. Those to whom his house had once been open had departed. Those who were his guests later were brought up in another world, they had their own problems and joys. This, however, did not deprive Karl of his pleasure in expecting company or in people in general. As I mentioned before, he was an indomitable optimist.

But to return to the house in Hidegkút: with the huge flat in Budapest and the comfortable summer house at Lake Balaton Karl could not admit even to himself that he was building a house for receiving guests. There was no moral law that could have permitted him this. And so the ideology was born, that rationalization which the human race produced for actions which contradict what can be rationalized. He was going to build a caretaker's house of the hacienda.

But the caretaker's house was not only a house for entertainment, but also the model for the real one, the one he desired, the big house of the future, where he would be able to receive as much as a hundred guests, where there would be a winter garden, a pool, an arbour with vines, a palm house, a rose garden and a fountain. Flowers everywhere in hundreds of colours, shady nooks, paths with yellow gravel. Somewhere, on the other end of the huge property, pigs would grunt softly, chickens would be pecking in the dirt, ducks quacking, they would be laying eggs and filling the smoke-house and pots, there would be fruit trees, vine stocks, vegetable gardens disgorging produce so that everyone would have plenty of food and drink. Karl would just sit under the willow tree in a white wicker chair, next to him, on a Turkish table with inlaid mother-of-pearl, would be a bowl of ice-cold punch. And Sara would come to play Chopin on a snow-white grand piano, her waist-long, silky black hair flowing freely down her back, floating around her as she were gliding off to make room for other women in their dresses of red and lilac, their lips like ripe strawberries, their bodies exhaling a scent of the tropics, peacock butterflies beating their wings on their naked shoulders, and honey trickling out of their décolletages. Then the family would gather, coming from the rose garden, the palm house or the barnyard. They would sit down around Karl, Uncle Feri would smoke Havana cigars, not a pipe, Anna would do embroidery, not her sewing, the girls would gossip, Poldi would look spick and span, a chauffeur waiting for him on the paved road in a red Daimler-Benz automobile, the girls' husbands dignified and gay, fine gentlemen all of them, no waiters, barbers or unemployed. The Szőcs's would come too, laughing, talking, and the Vojnich's, their carriage drawn by six horses straight from their estate in Bácska, the men holding a riding switch, the women lacy white parasol. Uncle Aladár would come, wearing a bow tie, his silver head held high, and also Count Przsanovszky, also a relative, a real Polish aristocrat, straight from Monte Carlo, with jetons jangling in his pocket. Uncle Sanyi would light an Egyptian cigarette, and from its exuberantly thick smoke would appear Nicholas Horthy of Nagybánya, Regent of Hungary, in uniform, his left hand resting on his gilded seeman's dagger, Karl would bow deeply but not submissively, wearing white smoking now, the family had disappeared, the two of them sitting under the willow tree, talking, man to man, about the harvest, world affairs, a new play, Karl would expound his views calmly, respectfully, His Excellency nodding attentively, taking the arm of his wife, her face covered by a veil, her dress brushing the lawn, they would walk slowly past the family standing in line there, they would have a kind word for everyone, they would walk off, passing the dark green boxwood on the side of the garden path, the adjutant's spurs jangling, his medals clinking on his chest. Out of the vegetable garden e sus Christ would appear, his linen robe snow-white and reaching to his ankles, barefoot. He would gather the children around him, tell them stories, behind him the sky would be blue, not even a small cloud in it, Jesus would open his arms blessing the family, praying, everyone would bow his head, some would kneel down, peace would enter their souls, Lord Jesus would rise up into the sky. The family would resume their chatter, glasses would clink, laughter would bubble through the air, the whole hacienda pervaded with the scent of roses, Karl leaning back in his armchair, taking a sip of the ice-cold punch, watching his family, happy.

We must not laugh at the dreams of little people; they, too, want to save the world.

There were also other reasons for buying the hacienda. Karl made a lot of money at that time, exactly how much he never knew, but even as a child I sensed the great difference between him and the other members of the family who had climbed the lower and weaker rungs of the ladder of lower middle-class existence. If I consider today that the large flat, the summer house of Lake Balaton, the hacienda, the cook, maid, gardeners, the *chambres séparées* and the champagne, the family members in need of support, the bachelor apartment, the permanent and occasional lovers, the concerts where one could only appear in evening dress and diamonds, where Toscanini conducted or Backhaus played the piano, the many trivial but expensive paintings by fashionable painters, the thousands of books, several hundreds of records, the constant guests, Christmas presents, the legions who came for birthdays and other family holidays, the bouquets for the ladies—Karl must have earned at least twenty times as much as what a well-paid official could live on comfortably.

All that money was blown in by the winds of war; Karl had not yet had anything to do with the war, except for the fact that as a reserve officer he had been in the cavalry that was sent out to aid in the re-annexation of Transylvania. Nowadays, as we analyse our past, we seem to forget that even the shadow of war put money, and quite a bit at that, into the pockets of those millions who made up the then so much discussed middle class. Why should the bank officials, teachers or civil servants, the lawyers, physicians, military officers or merchants, the book-keepers or engineers, the estate stewards, notaries, or judges have opposed the war? Especially as long as they did not have to experience its consequences on their own body.

According to family accounts, Karl was even more generous with his money at that time. Obviously, since he had never had so much, and it kept increasing without him having to move as much as a finger for it. How Karl got into that role of Midas, I will explain in due time. But no matter how much money ran through his fingers, he did not forget the golden rule that in war time money has to be invested. He was not that Bohemian; that role in the family was occupied by his younger brother. He was not irresponsible, either, and perhaps not even as light-hearted as he was kindhearted. Although in the First World War he did not have a penny besides his pay, and had his family to support from that, he had seen, heard and read enough about how after the war fortunes a hundred times greater than his had melted down to nothing.

Land would be the safest, most timeless asset, it could not be stolen, bombs could not destroy it, it could not decay, become outdated, be carried off, a property would be the best, most profitable investment; most people thought so at the time. Except for the professional businessmen, who knew that in war you had to invest your money in goods which you then sold for even more money, with which you would again buy goods and sell them for more money and so on, all the way to infinity, or bankruptcy.

Karl was not among them. He never had a feeling for making his money grow, he never had any talent for it and he was not interested in it. He believed in *avrea mediocritas* and bought land. He was to live forty more years in which to realize the value of land.

At first, true to his characteristic extravagance and without any sense of the limits of his resources, he wanted to buy a whole estate; thirty acres of land, somewhere in the Great Hungarian Plain. For some reason, this transaction never came off. Whether that was lucky for him or not we can consider later on. But that was when he bought the hacienda. Granted, it was just one and a half acres, but on the outskirts of Budapest. In a few months the caretaker's house was built and now the guests came, who in spring or autumn, when the summer house at Lake Balaton was not yet, or no longer open, were most suitably received here, in the hacienda with its geranium-framed porch, its garden filled with flowers, the sheepdog in its green kennel guarding the house, rather than in the flat in Budapest.

Though Karl proclaimed all his business dealings as great successes, I think he was right on one point, he had bought the hacienda for a song. At that time the area was largely unpopulated and Pesthidegkút, which had its own administration, was a dusty village. At that time, so far out, four bus stops from the boundaries of the capital, no one was building there. The area was suitable neither for living nor for holidays. Building was actually prohibited. Because of plans to expand the glider airport lying between here and the city, a building stop had been ordered.

Of course, this did not apply to everyone. By a little legwork, by knowing the right people and having the right connections, by making use of "influence", that badly sounding but very lucrative policy, one could procure a temporary building permit. Maybe this is one of the reasons why the house was called a caretaker's house, to signal its temporary status.

Many people have lived here, but a caretaker never.

The history of the hacienda includes the fact that Karl, like most members of his family, had a love for the land. Next to company this is perhaps what he loved most. I could explain this with some kind of atavism, but what for?

Karl also worked in his garden, eight hundred square yards, at Lake Balaton. He planted vegetables, raspberries, beautiful peach trees and a garden with pines, roses and dahlias. He did not dig the earth himself, but every dawn and evening during his vacation he sprinkled, pruned the peach trees and rose bushes, sprayed insecticide, weeded and trimmed and raked. For his own pleasure, because he could well have afforded to pay someone to do it.

There, on the one and a half acres at Hidegkút he could live out his dreams of gardening. The Herman farmer from whom he had bought the lot and who also had supervised the construction of the house, looked after the hacienda in the early years. I think he earned more from this than from the sale of the land, which was full of alfalfa weeds. The farmer always wore blue aprons, and he had two beautiful horses.

The hacienda was given a vegetable garden as well, but not just a few stocks of peppers and tomatoes as in Széplak. In the long, raked beds were turnips and carrots, kohlrabi, dill, cabbage, radishes, onions and squash. Along the road there were early flowering peonies, the flower garden was filled with roses, tulips and hyacinths. Karl also marked out where the fruit trees were to be planted. As with everything, here, too, he strove for perfection. He had cherries and morello cherries, many kinds of pears, apples, plums, greengages, quinces, strawberries, raspberries, walnuts and currants. He even planted grapes, a hundred stocks, if I remember correctly. We harvested a horribly washy wine every year, till luckily the stocks dried out.

Much later he found that this was a soil and climate that only the cherries could fully appreciate. The plums withered, the walnut trees refused to grow, the apples were full of worms, the pears became maggoty, the peach trees grew bare and the apricot trees collapsed. The German farmer had no intention whatsoever of warning the new owner. He was paid according to the holes he dug, the number of seedlings he planted or poles he set up, or how much he hoed. Although even if he had argued he would not have got very far; Karl, as I said, was very stubborn in sticking to his ideas.

In the autumn and winter of 1944 the little house was filled with people. Sometimes dozens would live there, Jews and half-Jews, Aryans in hiding, and deserters. For a few days Karl was also hiding out there with Sara, for two reasons: my uncle had had enough of having to live a soldier's life with all its restrictions; and his wife was Jewish. It was a gruelling, hard winter in forty-four, and the caretaker's house was heated by a single iron stove. Sara could not take that for very long. They preferred to move to Budapest, armed with the best of papers and documents. They could not stay in the flat at Bulyovszky Street either, because there was no room. That, too, was full of refugees, people in hiding, a bunch of relatives and good friends who could not be sent away. Finally they rode out the siege in Karl's office in the city centre, more precisely the basement of the building, because the office had had all its windows blown out by a bomb blast the very day that they finally got there.

The front moved on, the war in Budapest ended, those hiding moved out of the caretaker's house and back to their own homes, spring came, and the German farmer disappeared along with the cart and the horses. Later he surfaced again, but without cart and horse, those had been consumed by the war.

The house was occupied by Uncle Feri, Karl's eldest brother, who was long widowed and retired. He fed the sheepdog, took care of the garden and the house; because a house also has to be taken care of. At that time, Karl had both hands full of work as most of the country did, but from spring to autumn they lived in Hidegkút, and from there Karl rode to the city centre to work. For Uncle Feri they made a home in the Finnish cabin which had originally served as the site office. Karl liked to give a name to everything he owned. The house, as we know was called the caretaker's house, the estate the hacienda, the maid's room the little house, the planned dream palace the big house, the site office which was to be the tool shack was the Finnish cabin. Let me add that nothing became what it had been intended or named for.

The summer house at Lake Balaton had gone with the wind, almost literally. In the summer of forty-four, I rode by bicycle down to Széplak. I have never again seen a house sacked so meticulously as this one, except perhaps at Gyürüfü, Hungary's first ghost town which had been abandoned by the entire population. But Karl's summer house had not been faithlessly abandoned by its owners; instead the war had pillaged it. Not only every chair and plate had been taken, but the windows and doors along with their frames, the fence and the iron gate. Even the pipes had been torn out of the walls. The rose garden had become a crater, probably from a mine, the ceiling of one of the rooms was black with soot and the floor had turned to coal. For four months the front had stood here. Half the roof tiles had been taken off well. For some reason, the other half had been left on.

Karl did not even go down to Széplak, only once, when he authorized an acquaintance to sell the dump. He wrote it off, wiped it out of his mind, he forgot the villa where he had spent so many beautiful summers. He had another one instead, the hacienda, the one he already loved. He never mourned Széplak, he never even mentioned it. There and gone. I do not know what he got for it, but hardly as much as an upright piano cost. Because there had been an upright piano in the summer house. I have never seen such a thing anywhere else.

Karl's fortunes still favoured him after the war was over. He did not earn as much as during the war, but to the other members of the family who were officials, pensioners or teachers on a fixed salary, so that their pay was just barely enough for their daily bread, he was even better-situated than before. The three-course Sunday dinners at Hidegkút were royal feasts, bowls were filled with fruit, in the evening Sara sat down at her upright piano (because at Hidegkút there was an upright too), engraved glasses were filled with red wine, champagne was kept cool in the well, the pantry shelves sank beneath all the food, around the table sat powerful people and persecuted people, gay and gloomy, relieved and fearful ones, most of them members of the family; they included everything from a Parliamentary secretary to a prison escapee, a corporate director and one who had freed himself from detention. Which of them knew that their world was nearing its end just as they were dipping into Aunt Emma's famous, golden bouillon soup full of thin noodles and a side dish of vegetables, as they were sipping the black market red wine and eating the crunchy cherries, I do not know. Karl didn't, that much is certain. He did not believe in the end of the world, or in the end of anything, for that matter. Deep down inside he was convinced that his wealth and peace would last forever. Nor was his optimism curbed by the fact that this belief of his was wrong.

Uncle Feri died in 1949; cancer finished him off in one week. Karl's business was nationalized a few months later. He was not the only one left without a salary but half the family as well, all those who had worked for him. The large flat at Bulyovszky Street went with the wind also, and in an even sillier way than the summer house at Lake Balaton. Pictures, furniture, glass cupboards, books, bric-à-brac, souvenirs, boxes and suitcases were all crowded together on the hacienda at Hidegkút. Whatever there was room for was in the house, the other things packed into the attic, the wood shack, the chicken house, in sheds quickly knocked together, in the garden under tar paper held down by wooden boards. Not a single object ever left that place, only those that could be sold. All the others were buried at the hacienda, there they rotted, decayed, crumbled and broke, they became shabby and disintegrated as they stood in mud and dirt, under leaky roofs and in mouldy corners.

Karl and Sara moved to the big room. In place of the sixty-square-metre room at Bulyovszky Street that designation now referred to the sixteen-square-metre chamber at Hidegkút. There was of course no longer room for the wide double bed. They slept on two narrow, lumpy sofas for the rest of their lives. Aunt Emma, the mother-in-law whom they never left and who never left them, moved to the little room, where next to an iron bed with a spring-mattress there was room for a closet with three doors and a glass cupboard filled with knickknacks and bric-à-brac. Sara lived here for twenty years, Aunt Emma for twenty-five, Karl for thirty.

The day Karl departed and I felt I could no longer stand the smell of decay in the house, I dropped the green suitcase on the grubby sofa; without even opening it, without unpacking Karl's things, I went out into the grounds. By then everyone was calling it an hacienda, not only the family but friends, neighbours, the postman, the butane-gas delivery man with his donkey cart, the neighbourhood shopkeeper, everybody. This was Uncle Karl's hacienda.

If possible, the hacienda looked even more pitiful than the house. The beautiful countryside was charged with the fresh air that came from Hűvös Valley and Hármashatár Hill; but the garden sent out the same smell of decay as the house. Rust had corroded the drainpipe, and everywhere I looked the bricks showed through the plaster on the wall. At the corner of the house a cheap wooden shack rested its back against the wall. There Karl had collected throwaway plywood, for years no one had opened its door, wired shut. It was a slushy morning in February, grey as a mouse, it made me shiver even more than the morgue where I had declined to visit Karl. In front of the Finnish cabin there was a porch made up of parts of wooden boxes, Karl's own creation. Fortunately, the sub-tenant was not at home so I did not have to talk to him. Nor were any of the others at home, the tenants who lived in the chicken pen, the woodshack and the maid's room. I was alone on the mouldy, stale hacienda. The cellar had caved in, next to it stood a shattered greenhouse, one of the latter of Karl's great projects. The peach trees had dried out, but there was no one to cut them down. The big cherry tree had toppled and lay in the mud, its trunk split and rotting. Only the rusty stakes remained of the fence embedded in concrete. For years we had been digging the holes, mixing the concrete until it was all finished. On the stakes here and there hung a few yards of rusty chicken-wire. Who knows how many notices from the city council to repair the fence were lying in Karl's desk drawer? An early summer storm had torn off the dilapidated little latticework house from the top of the well, which had not been in use for years. In the centre of the hacienda lay the crooked, collapsed frames of what once had been plastic-covered greenhouses; this, too, had been one of Karl's bold and unsuccessful projects, as had the two mudbrick chicken pens now lying in ruins, where once he had used electric lighting to stimulate the not so willing Leghorns to lay their eggs a bit more diligently.

I felt like opening wide the doors of this morgue here at Hidegkút, to let anybody enter and take what he would. If I were God, I would command the winds to lift this decaying hacienda by its four corners carefully, so that it would not fall apart, and to take it far, far away, over the ocean, I would command lightning to set it ablaze, to burn it down, and the winds to scatter the ashes into the never-ending waters.

I clicked the lock back on the door, what must be done must be done. There is no wind that can carry away our past.

At any rate, that grey morning the story of my family was finished.

Translated by Christina Rozsnyai

All Souls' Day – The Resurrection

BY MIHÁLY SÜKÖSD

Why do I hate this cemetery here in Budapest, why don't I hate the other cemeteries I know? The cemetery at Márkod, for instance, why don't I hate that one? What makes me like the Márkod cemetery, which is filled with my own past, with the dead of times gone by?

Márkod (at present known by its Rumanian name of Marcului) is a small community some twenty-six kilometres away from Marosvásárhely (Tîrgu Mureş in Rumanian), in Erdély (Transylvania). It is my father's birthplace. If I'm in, say, Japan or America, and I'm asked about the region to where the village belongs, then I describe it in more or less the following way: Transylvania, County of Brassó (Braşov), the land of Fogaras mountains inhabited by the creature of Bram Stoker's imagination, the blood-sucking vampire Count Dracula. That explanation sees the light of recognition dawn in the eyes of my better educated foreign acquaintances. On seeing that light I hasten to continue: Erdély (Transylvania) was part of Hungary for centuries. Under the terms of the peace treaty which followed the First World War it was transferred to Rumania where it remained for twenty years. On the eve of the Second World War the smaller half of Erdély (Transylvania) was temporarily returned to Hungary. As a result of the peace treaty which followed that war the entire geographical region known as Erdély became once more part of Rumania (which is now known as the Socialist Republic of Rumania).

The cemetery of Márkod is approximately six hundred paces from the village. It stands on an irregular-shaped hill. I'm walking thigh-deep in weeds towards it burial mounds. The population of the tiny village has gradually decreased, those who could have moved to a bigger village or to the town, Marosvásárhely (Tîrgu Mureș), in an attempt to keep body and soul together. There is no institution to care for the cemetery, no private individual to care for the private graves.

Then, too, it was Indian summer, there, in Erdély, an "old ladies' summer" as it is called in Hungarian, a gentle old ladies' summer. Sunlight, the scent of flowers, the buzzing of the last bees of summer, the sigh of the mild breeze in the linden trees, the age-old giant willow trees. We are walking along the overgrown road leading to the cemetery, thigh-deep in weeds, my father, my second wife, my son and I. I think this was probably my father's las visit to his birthplace. Yes, I remember that was the last time he ever visited the cemetery where so many of his family are buried. Marble slabs, shattered, broken loose from the earth, lean lopsided; marble slabs, no longer supported by the earth which once held them, lie the length of the grave, or crosswise, as they have fallen. Rotting, crumbling wooden crosses. The skeletons of bunches of flowers, the skulls of wreaths. Worn gold letters, worn metal letters askew, marble slabs lying face down or sidewise. Disintegrating letters on the rotting, crumbling wooden crosses.

I feel very much at home in this neglected cemetery. Wherever I look, before, behind, sideways, all around, on the slabs, on the woods my name is everywhere. My surname mostly, but also my first name. Wherever I turn, my relations, my ancestors look back at me. Men and women; I turn this way and that, learning the Biblical names which are so rare back home in the capital.

I open up the graves and line up my relatives and ancestors before me. Their names are Moses, Samuel, Gideon, Aaron, Zebulon, David, Gregory, Daniel. They are Sarah, Rebecca, Judith, Esther, Lilith, Regina, Naomi. They live nine days, nine weeks, nine months. (They have no doctor, and if they had one he would not have yet heard of penicillin or antibiotics. He would have no cure for pneumonia or diphteria.) They live forty-three years or fifty-one years. It's mostly the women I introduce myself to, my beloved aunts and great-aunts, these shadows resurrected here in the Márkod cemetery for my sake, in my honour. They are clearly worn out by the six or nine or thirteen childbirths, cooking the midday meal each and every day, not to mention preparing the supper, milking the cows, feeding the pigs and mending the holes in the roof of the house; they don't sleep more than five hours a night, and they feel the growing desire for a longer rest. They live seventy-eight and eighty-four and eighty-six years. Mostly the men, the heads of families, my great-grandfathers, great-great-grandfathers, my forefathers. As I run my eyes over the procession of skeletons rising to greet me in the weed garden of the Márkod cemetery, I see that here too, they are all still over six foot tall.

I shake the skeletal hand of my paternal grandfather and think of the first and last time we met. I see him before me in a bright light. I was eight years old, and father was leading me to him. It was the first year of the war, father's native land, Erdély (Transylvania) was temporarily taken from Rumania and returned to Hungary by the Great Powers, at work way above the head of the small boy that I was then. We were on our way from Budapest to visit grandfather. We spent many hours in the train; two horse-drawn carriages were waiting for us at the railway station at

Marosvásárhely (Tîrgu Mureş) and these took us to our destination, Márkod (now Marcului).

My paternal grandfather was sitting on the veranda of his one-storied house, enthroned on a cane chair. A jug of red wine and a glass stood before him on a cane table covered with a red check cloth. If I have counted correctly, my paternal grandfather was eighty-two years old, and would live another nine years. He remained seated as he received my father, who arrived wearing his uniform, that of a surgeon-major in the Royal Hungarian Army. He had not seen him for more than twenty years. Father, then forty-two, knelt before my grandfather in his field officer's uniform, and kissed his hand. My paternal grandfather did not get up, he did not attempt to raise my kneeling father, he embraced him as he sat, kissing him on both cheeks, then on his brow. I have just introduced myself to my paternal grandfather's black tombstone in the Márkod cemetery, but back then, when I was eight, my paternal grandfather was still the head of the family, an active force. He beckoned to my awestruck mother whom he was meeting for the first time. He looked at her silently, at length, while father watched anxiously, but grandfather must have been satisfied, as he kissed her on the face and brow. The ceremony continued. I felt the palm of my father's hand on my back, with his other palm he directed my little brother towards the cane chair.

That skin, exposed to eighty-two years of wind and sunshine, and pickled to a dark brown; those wrinkles like cuts on the back of that neck and brow, that faultless aquiline nose, that black cap pushed back a little, that homespun white tunic, those direct black eyes, that probing look; that dry, weighty palm on the top of my head, "My two grandsons from Budapest". He said it in a matter-of-fact way. No emotion. No trace of the local dialect. It happens more and more frequently these mornings that when I look into the shaving mirror I see some feature of my grandfather's face there before me on my own mortal face.

My paternal grandfather sat in the cane chair and his wife, his four daughters-in-law, and countless grandchildren took orders from a movement of his only slightly greying eyebrow, his fixed regard, the lift of his hand and a few words of command. He had the women kill a turkey, he felt like turkey stew for supper. The female members of his family, my female relations, caught the bird they wanted and took it to the block. Two of them gripped it by the wings, the third held the head in place by grasping its bound beak, the fourth skilfully brought the axe down on the turkey's bald, throbbing neck.

As if she were chopping wood. If I have an anxiety-filled day to face, then even now in my dreams I see the turkey's dance of death in Erdély, thirty-six years ago in my grandfather's courtyard. At the successful stroke of the axe, the turkey's head flew far from its neck, to be henceforth forgotten, something for the sinewy tomcats to chew. After the execution had taken place, however, the turkey's body danced three times around the yard, blood spurting in an arc from the long headless neck, then flowing in a steady stream. My little brother started to scream and covered his face. Mother comforted him, my Transylvanian aunts and cousins looked uncomprehending; a slaughtered turkey had to bleed, it made the stew taste better.

My paternal grandfather sat on the veranda; he smoked something like eight or ten pipes a day and drank, in small sips, two or three litres of red wine, the product of his own labour. When I saw him then, for the first and last time, aged eighty-two, his mind and body were in perfect condition. At harvest time he would be the first to take up the scythe; before his younger brothers, his brothers-in-law, his sons, his sons-in-law. My forty-two-year-old father took a turn too, but after an hour and a half he was tired out and had to rest. "This is no work fit for our doctor brother," said his brothers and brothers-in-law, protecting him lovingly, respectfully, but also with condescension in their voices. Father was ashamed of himself and took up the scythe again; an hour later his palms were blistered. "We need our doctor brother's hands for other things," said, quite rightly, his sisters and sisters-in-law.

When my paternal grandfather died, aged ninety-one, two years after the end of the Second World War, father, a surgeon-colonel in the Hungarian People's Army, could not get a visa from Bucharest to enable him to travel to Erdély (Transylvania, again) to be present at his father's funeral. My father was always down to earth, trusting in his fate, resigned to it, a staunch believer in Calvin's teachings on predestination. That was the only time I ever remember having seen him suffer. He locked himself away in his room, and I watched him through the keyhole; he was dressed in his uniform, lying on his stomach, his face buried in an embroidered cushion, his epaulettes shaking. Very likely he was crying; probably for the first and last time in his adult life.

My dead grandfather and my dead relations line up and file past me in a slow procession, so that I might mask their death-ravaged faces, their names. I see, I commit to memory the unknown faces I have never seen before, which belong to the familiar names. I accept and return the kiss of greeting on each cheek, and, in accordance with Transylvanian custom, the kiss on the brow. They too are my creators, it is partly with their help that I preserve my own self; without them I would not be here to visit these graves or to exchange the kiss of family greeting with them as they pass before me. There is a gentle breeze blowing, the chestnut trees which grow there in the graveyard let fall their cobs on to the earth below, there is no pathway leading from tomb to tomb, we, the four of us, are walking through thigh-high weeds. Father, who from then on was a living corpse, my second wife, who has since left me, my son, who grew up to become an intellectual, his father's friend and his father's judge.

The Márkod cemetery, the Aleppo cemetery.

I'm looking for General Bem's grave. General Bem, Józef Bem in the original Polish, then Bem *apó* (Father Bem) in Hungarian, and after that Murad Tewfik Pasha in Arabic, died here, in the vicinity of today's Aleppo. This is where he was buried. I am alone, looking for General Bem's gravestone. I'm sure he must have a tombstone, my memory tells me that General Bem played a not insignificant part in the history of Syria. I didn't plan this, my solitary search for his tomb; circumstances have decided matters for me. I arrived in Aleppo at the time of a three-day Moslem festival, due to last over the weekend; all the offices were closed. As for my escort, the guide to whom I was entrusted during my stay in Syria, he installed himself in my hotel room this afternoon. It turned out that he was only able to speak a few words of English, and now, this same Friday evening, he's gone off to his relations in Aleppo. He's going to celebrate the holiday with them, not spend it with me: he's seen to my lodging and to other needs, and will come back for me on Sunday evening. Until then I'm free to do as I please.

I'm sure his intentions were good, but having time on one's hands in Syria is a completely different proposition to having time on one's hands in Hungary. He left me alone this afternoon in my tiny little room on the top floor of the hotel, and as soon as he'd gone I was stunned by my situation. I am alone, I shall be alone for two and a half days. They only speak French and Arabic in this hotel, I shall be a prisoner the whole weekend, out of touch with the whole world. Over supper I begin to wonder what I would do if I had a heart attack at midnight or dawn in Aleppo, on the top floor of the hotel, in my tiny room. Then I am attacked by a bout of anxiety, drink too much whisky and Turkish coffee, and lie on the bed, a detective story in my hand. I fall asleep straight away without even turning off the reading lamp. Before midnight I awake in the lamplight to realize my heart is beating very fast and I have a pain in my left shoulder and in the left-hand side of my chest. I am conscious of the fact that I might die, there is a possibility that I might die, now, any minute, soon, a guest traveller on a fortuitous journey, here in Aleppo, far from home, far from my responsibilities. I am thirty-eight years old, it's not the alarming symptoms in the left-hand side of my chest that I'm afraid of, but being alone, and the fact that I have no telephone in my tiny room, and even if there were, whom would I alert and in which language? I'm apprehensive that when my Syrian escort returns on Sunday evening, all that will remain of his assignment will be a motionless corpse lying on the bed, the stench of death exuding from it. Not that we get on well any way, my Syrian escort and I. I sent a telegram days ago, before leaving Cairo for Damascus, saying that I can speak English, but hardly any French. I arrived at the airport in Damascus in pouring rain, and as I reached the end of the corridor in the terminal an oily-haired, effeminate young man, faintly homosexual in appearance, smiled smarmily and swung his prayer beads towards me. "Vous êtes l'écrivain hongrois?" This was the escort I had asked for; my so-called interpreter, this chap, who claimed to be a writer, standing there swaying his narrow hips, supposedly a government official. He couldn't speak a word of English. I politely asked for another escort who could speak English (as an official guest of the government I felt entitled to do so), but my request was politely brushed aside. Well, during my ten-day stay we managed some sort of communication in sign language, the supposed Syrian writer and I. We made signs to each other on the five-hour car journey from Damascus to Aleppo, as the weekend-long Moslem festival drew nearer. We made endless stops on the way there; every time he saw a decent looking market in a village he would snap his prayer-beads-entwined fingers and the official chauffeur would park the official car and go off to buy tomatoes, cucumbers and honeydew melons while I cowered on the back seat, watching as the car boot was loaded up with fresh fruit and vegetables for his relations in Aleppo.

I am totally alone in night-time Aleppo, my left shoulder and the left side of my chest hurt unbearably, and so I gulp down two tranquillizers, drink water, throw water over my face and wrists and do breathing exercises. My chest still hurts on the left side. In the dark I stumble down from the topmost floor of the hotel to the ground floor, and look for the map which is stuck on the wall in reception. I find the cemetery and set off to seek Bem's grave.

It is a starlit Arabian night, cold winds are stirring. I have the map in my hand, and lighting the way before me with my cigarette lighter I search for the cemetery. Whenever I ask anyone the way he either shakes his head or replies in Arabic, nevertheless I manage to find it. The pounding of my heart lessens, the Arabian night grows colder and colder, and I am alone in my wanderings in the Aleppo cemetery in the glimmer cast by my cigarette lighter, in my clumsy stumbling mortal shell, while

the marble crypts with copper half-moons

the onion-domed tombstones

etched with golden letters signify and praise the Arab dead: the extremely long sentences, the letters and numbers run contrary to my European idea of the way letters and words should run

well-manicured crossroads in the Aleppo cemetery, unknown trees sway in the night wind, flowers I do not know grow around the onion-domed graves, I lift my feet carefully lest I crush one

it is after midnight, the Aleppo cemetery is deserted, I am alone in the Aleppo cemetery, the uninvited guest, the invited visitor

is doing what?

in the light of the sickle-thin moon

holding a map and a cigarette lighter

he's doing ... what?

staring at the sickle-slender moon, at the sky above his head, observing the stars close to him, in an objective fashion, soon he will take his place amongst them, will be their dust and ashes, but until then

he has a task DOWN BELOW, among temporal, worldly things

right now

he is searching for the tomb of General Bem, in Syria, in the Aleppo cemetery, for

József Bem was the Polish-born leader of the Hungarian army fighting for freedom in the last century, who

went into exile after the inevitable defeat of the Hungarians fighting for freedom in the last century, who became a Moslem, a Turkish citizen, who from the age of fifty-five was known as Murad Tewfik Pasha, who fought as a colonel of the Sultan in the Turkish province of Syria to put down an Arab revolt, who wanted to reorganize the obsolete Turkish army and planned to continue the fight against despotism as its general, to resurrect the butchered Polish uprising, the Viennese revolution, the Hungarian war of independence, the seemingly dead world revolution in Europe,

this is the way his thoughts ran, this is how he made his plans, Józef Bem, József Bem, Murad Tewfik Pasha in Aleppo in the mid-nineteenth century right until

the fifty-sixth year of his life, when, in the middle of all his plans he perished in the Syrian sands, perhaps he died of cancer, perhaps it was leukemia, who can give us a correct diagnosis

I am on his track now, after all

we are fellow countrymen; he who on November 19th 1848 arrived in Budapest from Vienna and offered his services to Kossuth, with this deed my fate too was decided, moreover

as far as I can be sure, on this night, at this moment I am the only Hungarian in Aleppo, therefore

I have to find my fellow countryman's grave in the Aleppo cemetery.

A tomb with a cupola: fashioned roughly from black granite. Further back in time, like the birth of my father, my grandfather. I do not know who had it built, who cared for it, who cares for it now. There cannot be many to care for it now because General Bem's black granite tombstone stands askew, it has been dirtied by mud and rain and cracked by the sun's rays.

There are three sentences on General Bem's tombstone. I do not know who incised them, who had them incised, or when, there is no date.

The first sentence is in Arabic. It is much longer than the two which follow.

The second is in French. "Ci-gît Murad Tewfik, auparavant Joseph Bem, bon soldat et patriote fidèle." I can more or less understand it, and I agree with it. "Here lies Murad

Tewfik, formerly Joseph Bem, a good soldier and a faithful patriot."

The third is in Polish. I can understand a few words, or I think I can, it seems to mean the same as the French.

A faithful patriot? Of which homeland? Poland? Austria? Hungary? Turkey? Faithful to the country he was leaving, or was it to the country he was going to? Or was he a faithful son of the Free Republic of Adult Nations? Was he faithful to his great love, world revolution? Why was he faithful? For the very reason that he changed his homeland so often, because his homeland was always the place where (according to his own standards) there was work to be done, work that was worth doing?

I am standing in the Aleppo cemetery at a quarter to two on an April morning in 1971, by General Bem's grave. There are no words of Hungarian on his tomb. I would like to rectify this, to add the missing Hungarian sentence, to etch golden letters on the tomb, to burn them in with a blowlamp, to write my confession, on General Bem, my objective annotations, with a searchlight on the Aleppo sky, but I cannot. I am not enough of a Hungarian, I am an emptyhanded Hungarian in the cemetery in Aleppo. All that I can do, all that I am capable of doing, is to pick one of the Syrian wildflowers growing knee-high by the wayside. All that I can do is to place a Syrian wildflower on the grave of my countryman, General Bem.

Why am I doing this? I think it's a banal and sentimental thing to do. I never take flowers to my mother's grave. I've never planted flowers on it, once a year I change the laurel wreath before the urn containing the ashes of my first wife; nothing more. I never do more than this for the very reason that I find such gestures mawkish and trivial.

So what am I doing now? And why?

When he was leading the Polish artillery, organizing the

defence of Vienna, annihilating Puchner's army at Nagyszeben, shelling the Arabs when they made their attack on Aleppo, General Bem was a patriot without a *patria* (this is no contradiction in terms). The Polish uprising was a failure, Vienna could not hold out, the Hungarian war of independence came to an end, and General Bem, Murad Tewfik Pasha, cast a net around despotism, in Aleppo, for the sake of the revolution. What was he thinking of, what went through his mind in the weeks before his death when he dug himself in up to the neck in the boiling Syrian sand? Under the baking hot sun, in the baking hot sand, drying out his skin covering his skeleton and sinews until it was purple-black, drying out everything that STILL remained of his mortal shell, what was he thinking of?

Then they buried him, but in the Aleppo cemetery. A funeral oration was said above the freshly dug grave, in Arabic, French, Polish, and, one hopes, in Hungarian too.

Perhaps I am placing this Syrian wildflower that I do not know the name of on the grave of General Bem because I am taking part in an official ceremony: here in Aleppo, alone, after my heart attack (was it a heart attack? Will this only be made clear some time in the future by my autopsy report?), before my next heart attack (when will this be? Tomorrow? Next week? Next year?), I am the ambassador of my country, I do not see myself as a "faithful son of my homeland", in any case, not in the same sense as General Bem, in many homelands, homeless in his only homeland. But right now I want to add the missing sentence on stone on General Bem's tomb.

Perhaps that's the reason. Perhaps it's not the only reason.

Perhaps it's also because both the dead man down below, and the visitor to his grave up here belong to the same place. To the piece of Earth known as Magyarország (Hungary in English, al-Madzhar in Arabic, Hongrie in French,

Węgry in Polish). He chose it to be his temporary abode, a base for his plans, and he left it (of his own free will, commanded by the events of history) when things happened the way they had to happen. I was born there, it is my inheritance, not chosen of my own free will, that's the way it is, and so I will strive with all my mortal frame to preserve and make flourish this scrap of land.

The Aleppo night has grown cold, and I shiver as I stand by the graveside. It occurs to me that I am General Bem's successor. I am his successor as well, I don't know what that bare skeleton *down here* thinks of our relationship; I, for the time being, *up here* reach forward and touch his tombstone and the Syrian wild rose.

Translated by Gillian Howarth

Ignác Vonó
BY ENDRE FEJES

They had watched the clouds drifting by since the coming of spring. They sang songs, feared death, and dreamed more and more often of a woman's passionate embrace in the dark Italian night.

"Look, sir," Ignác Vonó said one summer evening to the ensign, "the green-eyed lady is calling me again."

The close-cropped infantry soldiers stirred in the trenches.

"It's daft you are, Ignác," the ensign laughed. "Where's this green-eyed woman of yours?"

"There she sits on top of the poplar tree," Ignác Vonó replied. "She's been winking at me this many a day."

And he pointed up at a twinkling star.

That was when he was shot through the wrist.

There was music in the courtyard of the field-hospital, the nuns smiled, and a general pinned a medal on his breast.

They sent him home.

"That bullet was certainly a good shot," he told his acquaintances, showing them his maimed wrist, "God bless the good Eyetalian for it."

He became an attendant in a local office of the National Social Security Board.

He carried files, spent long hours sitting on the tarnished benches; later brought Irén Olajos paper cups of cocoa with a straw, and soft rolls. They talked as she ate. They spoke of Kassa, of Upper Hungary. He liked the girl's soft voice, bright smock, sharp-pointed pencils, the tiny ruby on her slim finger. At twelve sharp he would knock on Antal Del Medico's door. Antal Del Medico would put his feet up on a chair.

"Why don't you get married Ignác?" he would ask. "You have a bad hand, it's true, but you also have a fine post."

"The time will come, Councillor," he always replied.

And polished Antal Del Medico's shoes with a soft velvet cloth.

One October afternoon Irén Olajos bought several pots of cacti. Ignác Vonó carried the blue-gazed pots to her home in a rucksack.

She lived in a humble flat in Buda, on the right side of the river. She invited him to sit, offered him strong brandy, and spoke of Kassa, of the horse-chestnut trees in the old public gardens.

"Do you remember your home at all?" she asked.

He did. The bubbling brook that ran before his father's smithy. The sugar factory of Nagysurány, where his mother sewed sacks. But he did not speak of them. He spoke instead of battles fought, of a field-hospital, of his medal.

"Oh, it's sad to be alone," the girl sighed. "It's so sad to live alone."

Ignác Vonó threw out his broad chest.

" 'Tis to a woman that I owe this wound," he said. "She was beautiful, green-eyed, just like you, Miss."

The girl put the stopper in the brandy bottle. She stood up and smiled.

"My father was a magistrate at Kassa," she said coldly. "Zsigmond Csergő Olajos was well-known all over the Uplands."

Ignác Vonó followed her silently, watching her swaying hips. Irén Olajos walked with a limp.

In the doorway she gave him one pengő for a tip.

A thick fog had settled above the banks of the Danube. It

shrouded the trees along the riverside. Ignác Vonó stopped on the Chain Bridge and watched the river flow. Beads of autumn rain pattered on his rucksack.

On Sunday he bought a wooden spoon in the hollow of which had been painted a glittering blue-gold heart. Pale sunlight filtered down upon Baross Square. He roamed the streets for a long time, awkwardly, timidly shying away from the boisterous laughter of buxom girls. He was home before the sun had set.

Sitting on the brown-tarnished bench one wintry afternoon he found a strange short story in the paper he was leafing through. Riding her horse by a railway embankment Tekla Zichy caught sight of a railway worker, stripped to the waist as he worked. She fell in love with him, for he was as beautiful as an antique bronze. But when she saw him wearing his best suit she gave him ten pengős and sadly sent him home.

"What can that suit have been like?" wondered Ignác Vonó.

He dared not ask Antal Del Medico about it. But as he wiped the fine dust off his shoes with the velvet cloth he would often say:

"Women are strange creatures, Sir."

And give an embarrassed titter.

Hard times came. Budapest, the gay, the gossipy city turned gloomy-dark. The deserted streets learned to keep silence. With a frightening noise the bombers flew high above the city, invisible to the eye.

"Smolensk is ours," Antal Del Medico said.

Ignác Vonó was glad. Here and there he ran, carrying files in his maimed hand. And when the siren sounded he went to sit peacefully in the air-raid shelter.

"Kassa has fallen," said Irén Olajos one day.

Ignác Vonó stared despairingly at the tears that brimmed up in her green eyes.

At Christmas white-faced people prayed by candlelight. The silent city trembled, torn asunder by bombs and mines.

The circle was complete.

The May breeze found a red flag upon the Reichstag tower in Berlin.

The National Social Security Board became the Trade Union Insurance Centre, the councillor became a labourer. Ignác Vonó remained what he had been: an attendant. Lonely. A bachelor.

Every Sunday morning after mass Antal Del Medico stood him a glass of wine. They drank it in the Bástya beerhouse.

"Europe is asleep," Del Medico said. "Hungary is forgotten."

"We must not lose heart, Sir," Ignác Vonó replied. "We must not lose faith. Salvation will come."

He bought shoes from Del Medico, silk shirts, a pocket watch. This last he paid in three instalments. Finally he bought an antique cigarette case for a hundred and ten forints. A finely chiselled, emblazoned cigarette case. Four days later the councillor died. Irén Olajos did not attend the funeral. There was a Party meeting that day.

"Europe is asleep," said Ignác Vonó compassionately. "Hungary is forgotten."

On his fiftieth birthday he treated himself to a suit made of tropical cloth. It was a beautiful suit, light-coloured. He set off to show it to the town. On Lenin Boulevard a sudden shower overtook him. He scuttled for the shelter of the nearest teashop.

In the crowded room he looked confusedly around him. There was a frail lady sitting by the window. He walked up to her, and having asked her leave, sat down. He ordered a brandy.

Lightning struck nearby. People were hushed, then recommenced their chatter. The frail lady made the sign of the cross over her pale blue blouse. Ignác Vonó revealed that he too was a believer. He crossed himself, exchanging a significant glance with the lady, then drew a cigarette from his silver cigarette case and lighted it.

They began to talk. They spoke of the rain, of his drenched clothes.

"Does Madam live far?" he asked sociably. He shifted politely in his seat. "I would not wish to intrude upon you. Ignác Vonó is the name."

"Not the Pécs branch of the Vonó family?" marvelled the lady. She had an endearing, heart-shaped face.

"No, Madam. Nagysurány is where we're from."

The lady glanced at the antique cigarette case. At the coat of arms emblazoned upon it.

"My name is Tekla Virág," she smiled amicably. "A landowing family, perhaps?"

A spark flashed in Ignác Vonó's eyes. A tiny spark, not bigger than a pinhead.

"One thousand five hundred acres," he said slowly, and removed a shred of tobacco from his lips. "Rich, black earth."

"And now?"

"I am an attendant."

Tekla Virág touched his hand.

"So is Pityu Csáty. Buby Szórády makes sweaters. That's the way it is…"

Ignác Vonó stared up at the ornamented ceiling.

"God will help us," he said at last. "We must pray. Not give up hope."

He ordered two brandies.

Tekla Virág protested sweetly but firmly. She never touched alcohol. It must have been so for it went to her head immediately. She recalled touching memories of Sister Angelica, who had been very fond of her, and spoke of a Franciscan friar who had had wicked eyes. She said she lived alone, loyal and true to her order.

Ignác Vonó spoke of the forests of Upper Hungary where his friend, Antal Del Medico, had once shot a bear. And he a wild boar.

Perhaps that was when they fell in love.

They had a church wedding. A quiet, simple wedding attended by a select number of acquaintances.

Their life, too, was quiet and simple. Tekla Virág got up at dawn and glued tiny paper bags all day. Ignác Vonó carried files or sat on the tarnished bench. He looked down upon Irén Olajos and greeted her politely, with the respect due to a Party steward. After work he took a rucksack full of paper bags to the homecraft co-operative. Later he cleaned the flat. He cherished his balconied, beautifully furnished new home.

He loved his wife with a love that was true. Tekla Virág loved him. They retired to bed early at night.

On Sunday Pityu Csáty, Buby Szórády came to visit. An old priest who liked fatty meat. And dear Mother Terezia.

After a shot of plum brandy Mother Terezia began to giggle and related her favourite anecdote. When the Russian troops were drawing near the convent she gave permission for those who were frightened to don civilian clothes.

"All the sisters were soon dressed up to the nines," she said merrily. "Holy Mother, how their silks clung!"

Buby Szórády was anxious over the shortage of yarn. The old priest munched noisily. Pityu Csáty stared at him with loathing and disgust.

Ignác Vonó spoke of the castle of Nagysurány. Of the

clear, bubbling brook that ran beneath the age-old trees of the park. Of the green-eyed, mysterious lady who walked its moonlit banks, for whom he had duelled and had his wrist shot through.

"I once drank a little bottle of beer for a wager," he boasted. "My friend, Antal Del Medico stood the bill."

"Ignác, old chum," Csáty said, "a gentleman does not drink beer."

"Europe is asleep," he said, sadly waving his hand. "Hungary is forgotten."

They thought highly of the brave and jolly Uplands squire. History had not been able to break him, not for a single instant.

Tekla Virág loved him more every day.

Loved him to distraction.

On the twenty-third of October he was on his way home from the co-operative when he met the students singing in Calvin Square. With his rucksack on his back he joined their ranks and sang beneath their flags all the way across the city. He listened to the speech by the statue of Petőfi and when they reached the statue of Bem he was shouting "Down with Gerő!" in hoarse unison with them.

He met Irén Olajos in front of the Parliament. Irén Olajos was reclaiming Kassa.

He returned home rapturously. Tekla Virág removed a rosette the size of a fist from his buttonhole.

"I fear for you, Ignác," she said. "You are so hot-headed. So rash."

Tekla Virág bought a goose, lard, salami, sugar. She spent three thousand forints on food.

Ignác Vonó brought leaflets home by the ton. He read them out loud in a voice heated with passion.

"Don't excite yourself, dearest," Tekla Virág pleaded. "Come and eat now, there's a good boy."

Szórády, too, tried to calm him. Pityu Csáty sat glued to the radio, tense with excitement. The old priest said grace at the table. Mother Terezia disconsolately exhibited the bullet-hole in her hat.

They all listened to Prince Löwenstein's proclamation. Csáty switched off the set. He paced up and down the room for a long time. Tekla Virág knelt by the sideboard. Ignác Vonó watched his wife pray with a smile on his face.

He loved her with a love that was true.

On the third of November Csáty arrived in a dark-grey raglan, solemn-faced. He bent to kiss Tekla Virág's hand.

"I have brought you a present," he said, looking at her, "but it would not fit in my pocket."

He turned to Ignác Vonó. He tried to control his voice.

"I have charged Doctor Balázs Fazekas, my counsellor-at-law, with the re-acquisition of your estates. Go and see him, Ignác old man, and take your papers with you."

And he smiled. Then placed his foot upon the ornamental handle of the glazed tile stove. A fine dust had settled on his shoes.

Ignác Vonó's face paled as he saw it.

Tekla Virág poured tea into Viennese tea-cups. She spoke of how they had beaten a customs official to death by mistake. Csáty showed them three names written in his notebook. He was going to look them straight in the eye, he said. And not only them. Then he spoke of Otto of the House of Habsburg.

At dusk Csáty took his leave. He extended his hand. It was a thin hand.

As cold as ice.

Ignác Vonó sat down by the tiled stove. He watched the shadows swallow up his home. Tekla Virág came in from the bathroom. She spoke sleepily of Erzsébet Zsabka, who had joined the Party.

"The harlot," she said. "The hussy."

Ignác Vonó coughed into his fist.

"She is your niece after all…"

"They'll all pay dearly for their sins!"

She said her prayers in bed.

You could hardly see the carpet in front of the window. Ignác Vonó watched the darkness engulf the last of his estate.

Then he took off his braided housecoat.

Night fell. The smell of winter was in the air. Clouds obscured the stars. Tekla Virág smiled in her sleep. Silent and still, Ignác Vonó watched her heart-shaped face. Listened to the leaden silence.

The crack of a gun shot him out of bed. He jumped to the window, opened it wide.

"They're shooting!" he cried. He turned his head this way and that in the fresh morning breeze. "Jesus! Loving Jesus!"

Tekla Virág ran to him, ran terrified, threw a warm housecoat across his shoulders. She led, she tugged, she carried her laughing husband to the stove.

"Dearest," she pleaded with tears in her eyes. "Dearest husband, calm yourself."

Laughter bubbled in Ignác Vonó's throat. He pounded his knees with his fists.

With gentle hands his wife caressed his hoary head.

Translated by Eszter Molnár

Four Students

BY ISTVÁN CSURKA

In September 1952 five aspiring dramaturgists moved into the students' hostel of the College for Dramatic Art at 97 Voroshilov Street. Four boys and a girl. The boys were put in a garret room on the second floor, the draughtiest part of the building. The awful draught was the result of a slipshod, hurried conversion job. The conversion had to be done in a hurry because that summer, the summer of 1949, when the building work was being done, there was a strange interlude in the life of the villa: for a week it was the home of a head of state and his party, who were visiting Budapest. The head of state left, the world changed rapidly, the results of the rushed reconstruction were never put right, and by the time the five dramaturgists moved in, the name of the head of state, that one-time revered guest, was only allowed to be mentioned in the students' hostel in conjunction with a dog and a chain, if at all.

The former luxury villa was overgrown with ivy. The poor ivy was old, it sensed that no one had any use for it any more. The iron fence, however, was green summer and winter, it maintained itself very well in spite of the fact that of all the parts and appurtenances of the house the fence was probably the most exposed to tribulations. There was no course for acrobats at the college, even so many chose it as an optional activity, getting their practice by means of a nightly display of fence-climbing acrobatics in order to economize on gate money. Between the fence and the house there was a narrow strip of earth in winter and a tiny football pitch in spring, summer and early autumn. At one time there must have been a beautiful green lawn here, but every year the students of dramatic art trampled the grass down the moment it pushed its head out of the ground. On the whole these students did everything instantly, as soon as the opportunity arose. They were like hungry dogs, they snatched up the morsel the moment it was thrown to them.

There was no particular intention behind housing the first-year dramaturgists in the draughtiest room on the second floor. The other rooms were also cleaned only by the draught—the most one could deduce from the system of room allocation was that the hostel administration cared about the health of the future dramaturgists least of all. The four first-year students, however, had no inkling of this as yet. They did not all arrive at once.

First of all the pert little moustached face of Miki Miklya peeped round the door, and seeing that the room was completely empty, that the beds were bare—they didn't even have mattresses—he walked in confidently, looked around, sniffed the dry air, and, after much contemplation and deliberation, settled for the bed by the window on the left. He reckoned this bed had the best position and light, and its springs were in the best condition. Miklya at this stage was a very skinny individual. He had been worrying about the college the whole summer. Should he come or shouldn't he? Was it worth it? He had got into the college with a specialized matriculation exam. Or rather, he was accepted first and only after that had he taken matric. The college ran its own specialized matriculation course during which those who were considered talented but lacked the necessary schooling were taught all sorts of good things for a year and then presented with a matriculation certificate.

What did someone like him with specialized matric know? He knew that the Mongol invasion came before the battle of Mohács and that "of all the arts the most important for them was the film". And that was quite enough. In these days the college did not require its students to have any specific knowledge. For those who were accepted it was sufficient to know where they could pick up their grant. They could get by on that. Miklya himself thought about the whole dramaturgy business in a similar way. That autumn he was in his twentieth year and he'd read about twenty books from beginning to end in his life. He hated nothing more than unnecessary talk, browsing through books, and theoretical debates with no practical outcome — in other words, all the things that constituted about seventy per cent of a dramaturgist's knowledge and activity. He didn't want to be one in the first place, he wanted to be a film director. He had only 'tackled' his matric in the hope of becoming a film director, but the committee did not find his imagination sufficiently 'visual', and they moved him to dramaturgy. From then on Miklya wasn't the slightest bit keen on the business, he only went on with it because it didn't cost anything.

All his possessions were contained in a UNRRA box tied up with string: three shirts, a change of underclothes, one or two pairs of socks, a towel and a few odds and ends.

The whole thing at that moment — Miklya gazing out of the window in the empty, austere room, the open UNRRA box on the bare bed, with the well-worn, multicoloured flannel shirt straggling out of it, and the date itself, September 2, 1952 at two o'clock in the afternoon in the sharp dazzle of late summer — all this could have been dreadfully symbolic. Except that there was no one to appreciate the symbolism. Miklya saw his situation and the objects as natural and inevitable, and, though they did not make him cheerful, they certainly made him determined. He did not for a minute consider what a long journey the UNRRA box had made from Chicago to Szeghalom, where a few years ago his father had sold the milk powder out of it and then put it away in the storeroom at the back, thinking it might come in useful some time. He didn't see the hidden, yet historic connection between the journey of the box and his journey. He had picked out the UNRRA box himself, objecting strongly to his mother's naive and anachronistic idea that he should pack his things in a nice suitcase. Miklya didn't want to turn up at the college with a suitcase. He wanted to appear poor, poorer than he actually was—a suitcase was out of the question. In fact, though, he could have made done with the poverty he had.

Miklya's father had a grocery cum wine-and-spirits shop in a big village in the marshlands. Or rather, he used to have. Now all that remained was a memory, and the small, modest fortune, a house with its furnishings, a nice family home—which the shop had brought him during the boom war years, together with the handicap of having "Shopkeeper, bourgeois" written in the personal files of father and son. The shop was nationalized in 1951: Miklya senior was given a job in a state shop, while Miklya junior did his best to deny his wretched capitalist past.

There was nothing else he could do. There was nothing hypocritical about that denial, it was both necessary and natural. Miki Miklya could see for himself the fallacy of the life plan set from him when he was quite a little boy—he was to complete four years of high school, and then go into the shop with his father—, which history had now not only made impossible, but ridiculous. Being prevented from doing what had been mapped out for him had the sudden effect of heightening his aspiration, raising his morale. Defiant and resolute, he buckled down to the job of securing himself a place in the world with a wider horizon than his father's which would have been his as well except for the historical changes that had taken place. Miki studied hard, though he didn't like studying. He knew that after finishing school he would become the sort of man his father considered a 'gentleman', but he didn't want to be a 'gentleman'; he only had respect for work, work achieved by real tiring effort. There was nothing he hated more than gentlemen and middle-class children.

He stood at the window of the garret room and looked out, down to the far side of the street, to the few empty tables on the pavement outside the café at the far corner, and then, also on the far side, he looked over the high iron fence into the big garden and, still further, to the big empty mansion belonging to the garden. He tried to guess what it had been before, and why it was that he found it more beautiful, more stately, yet at the same time more graceful, than the Cifra Mansion in Kecskemét, which up till then he had considered the most beautiful building of all. He didn't enjoy this new feeling, this realization. He would have liked to preserve, unimpaired and in its former integrity, the great town experience of his childhood. He had never taken his home town, Szeghalom, seriously as a town, but he was devoted to the real town, Kecskemét, the scene of his short and fragmentary high-school years. And now Kecskemét was gradually being forced to sink under strong pressure from Budapest, and this sinking caused him pain—his childhood was going down with it. As for what took its place: Budapest, and the college, they held out no promise for him. Miklya knew what was in store for him: struggle, fight, a life-and-death tussle. In fact he was prepared for worse than what actually happened to him.

Four years of high school, two years beset with failures, at commercial school, problems with spelling and punctuation, problems with self-expression, no knowledge of languages, but some sound common sense, a good provincial—artisan's—brain, all the ingenuity and self-assurance that goes with it, a degree of folksy, Hungarian traditionalism, a respect and love of the people, a desire to belong and the nobility of that desire, a moderate and level-headed loathing for the new regime, the people's democracy, but which also took account of its achievements—that was Miki Miklya, first-year student in dramaturgy, on September 2, 1952, a day before the college year began, when he took his place in the students' hostel. And by and large he was aware of his own limitations. He didn't delude himself, he reckoned on being, with people who were both cleverer than him and better qualified, and he could only get the better of them or hold his own against them if he were aware of his own abilities and situation. He was only afraid of one thing: there would be clever 'middle-class' boys in his class, maybe here in the room as well. He was always a loser against people like that, at home and in Kecskemét as well, because his hatred paralysed him.

He had just started to put his things into the little white tin bedside cupboard—which he had moved from the far corner of the room because it seemed to shut better than the one beside his bed—when there was a knock at the door.

"Come in," he said from his crouching position, in a voice deepened to a somewhat severe, imposing tone, and gradually straightened up. With the slow uncertain opening of the door a boy even shorter and smaller than he was appeared behind, or rather beneath, a pair of big and very strong glasses.

"Is this room six?" he asked timidly, as if he had done something wrong and was expecting a huge slap.

Miklya, as he was nodding and saying "yes", made a

mental note which for the time being had no emotional content. "Jewish," he thought.

The boy entering the room was carrying a cheap string bag slackly packed with some sort of indefinable yellow material which could have been a shirt, a towel, or even a faded American battleshirt, and he had a thick book under his arm. Walking round the table, he went and stood in front of Miklya, looking shy and awkward.

"Hallo, comrade, I'm József Róbert," he said. Miklya noted that he rolled his r's and wouldn't be a serious opponent.

"Miklós Miklya." They shook hands.

Róbert put the book and the string bag down on the table and leant towards Miklya.

"What? Forgive me, comrade, I'm a bit hard of hearing."

"Miklya," said Miklya.

"So I heard right the first time."

"You heard right."

"Why don't you change your name, Comrade Miklya?"

"I like it."

"Isn't it embarrassing?"

"No."

Róbert looked round the room, then stole another glance at Miklya, who was once again crouching down, arranging his bedside cupboard, and now Róbert too noted something. "Not Jewish." So far there was nothing negative about this conclusion either, though Róbert didn't like the look of his future roommate because from the first instant he felt inferior to him. When he came into the room Miklya was already there and he stood at the head of his bed as if he owned the whole room and he were the room commander.

It was equally unnerving that he didn't show the slightest interest in him, immersed as he was in his bedside cupboard, and for that reason Róbert stood for several long moments between the table, the bed and the crouching Miklya, quite at a loss. He would have liked to go to the window and look out, but he didn't dare. This grave and ostentatious disregard fettered him. So he sat down on the iron bar of the bed, the middle bed, the head of which was up against Miklya's bedside cupboard. Miklya gathered from this—because in fact he was watching intently while unpacking—that Róbert had chosen that bed. This did not please him at all. He would have preferred him to be on the other side of the room. Anyway, for as long as absolutely possible he didn't want anyone near him. But how could he suggest Róbert move away? He soon thought of something.

"Why don't you go down and bring your things up?"

"I have. This is all I've got," said Róbert, with a touch of ostentation. Miklya blushed to be on the losing side. This guy was even poorer than he was, he really was poor if that 'quarter of a kilo' of stuff was all he'd got. Miklya thought in terms of 'quarter kilos', basing his guess at Róbert's wealth on his experience in the grocer's shop. And he hadn't succeeded in getting rid of him either, because Róbert remained seated. In fact he reached out for his book, took it off the table, opened it at a certain place, put it on his lap and began to read.

Miklya was stunned. He looked up at him: he was reading. He took an immediate loathing to him. He could not see this purely as an act of ostentation and perversity. Reading, in his eyes, was something you got down to only if you had nothing else to do. This guy comes in here, into the room where he's going to live for years, and instead of arranging his things and getting settled, he simply starts reading. In his eyes this was showing off, a direct provocation. Lenin's "Learn, learn, learn!"

It was only partly that, however. The main reason Róbert started to read was that he couldn't do anything else, or rather, he didn't really dare do anything else. Ideally he would have liked to stand by the window and look at the view, but he had an instinctive fear of doing that, as if Miklya with his very presence would forbid it, as if it would be altogether forbidden. He could hardly go on standing there between the table and the bed doing nothing, and having so few possessions there was nothing for him to tidy away. All he had in his bag was a pyjama jacket and a ragged little towel with shaving things wrapped up in it. There was really no need to find a place for them.

Miklya didn't understand any of this, all he knew was that his instincts rebelled against this kind of behaviour. An honest, able-bodied man couldn't be so independent of life's material aspects and couldn't immerse himself so deeply in the spiritual world in a book because behaviour like this was a false, deceitful and loathsome demonstration. You barbarian, you immerse yourself in your bedside cupboard arranging your belongings, while I gather the fruits of intellect, knowledge. I'll overtake you and outdo you.

Several minutes passed in this way. Róbert read, though he couldn't really concentrate on the words, while Miklya unpacked his things, not just into his bedside cupboard, but also into his section of the drawer in the big hardwood table, keeping an eye on Róbert in the meantime.

Sitting on his bed his feet barely reached the red, cracked, crumbling lino floor; sloppy, childishly small feet and gym shoes. When Miklya caught sight of those once white gym shoes together with the crumpled, dirty socks, he once again sniffed the air cautiously to see whether the gym shoes had brought any noticeable change to the smell situation in the room. They had. Now Miklya not only hated the bespectacled little boy, he felt his hatred to be justified. "You read when you should be washing your feet!"—that was the gist of his justification.

In the end Róbert's nerves proved the weaker. He sensed that he was spoiling something by reading and that he ought to say something. So he put down his book, banging it shut with a sigh as if he really wanted to get down to something now, some sort of work, and with his sigh he exclaimed:

"Oh, how beautiful."

Miklya snapped back at him.

"What?"

"That." Róbert pointed at his book. "*Far from Moscow.* Have you read it?"

Miklya didn't know what to say to that. It was obviously a book one should have read. Finally he said:

"Not yet."

"It's appalling how much the Soviet people suffered for us," Róbert went on.

"Oh, damn you!" thought Miklya, because although he too recognized it as a fact, and he accepted the Liberation as liberation—even though the subsequent change in regime had deprived his family, his father, of their wealth—yet however much he would have liked to, and in fact, did, would alter his own mind to suit the new requirements of life, he never have been able to say that or any similar sentence in such a sincere, almost beseeching voice, nor did he believe anyone could say it really sincerely. As far as he was concerned the Soviet people were first and foremost Russian soldiers—soldiers. The concept of the world he had brought with him from his home town, Szeghalom, all at once became inconceivable, here in this students' hostel, in the company of this boy, but it didn't cease to exist. It remained there at the very bottom of Miklya's consciousness, brushed aside to the back like a desert island to which one could always swim back if the waves of the newly accepted principles and slogans became unbearable. He only realized ten to fifteen seconds later that he still hadn't replied this political pronouncement—either out of surprise or the distracting effect of self-analysis—though reply he must, and quickly, because every moment of silence or hesitation could be interpreted as a counter-opinion, and that could be fatal. But what on earth could he say?

"A heroic people," he said finally.

"Where were you at the time of the Liberation?" asked Róbert with no transition at all, and he still didn't get up from the bare iron bed.

"In the Marshlands," said Miklya. He pulled himself together and asked back: "And you?"

"In a concentration camp," answered Róbert, and looked at Miklya. Straight into his eyes. Miklya was prepared for this, he was expecting it, and withstood the stare. But Róbert went on:

"I've no mother, nor father, nor brothers and sisters. They killed everyone I had." But this Miklya could withstand no longer. He was beaten. All at once it became clear to him that he didn't stand a chance with his father's closed down and disowned grocer's shop, with his two pairs of shabby shoes, his Szeghalom outlook, and the losses of the "better off" in Szeghalom, in the face of this tragedy. In the face of Róbert's dead parents, his string bag, pyjama jacket, stinking gym shoes and his *Far from Moscow*. And it wasn't just that he had no chance against these odds, he did not even have a say, because although Róbert revealed his sad fate without so much as an accusing undertone, or self-pitying emotion, it was an accusation just the same—if nothing else, the inexpressible, giant-sized accusation of an orphan versus a non-orphan. Miklya swiftly bent down and immersed himself in his bedside cupboard again.

"Have you got a mother?" asked Róbert after a short pause.

"Yes."

"A father too?"

"Yes."

"Grandfather?" That had a slightly sentimental ring about it, and Miklya put that sentimentalism to the test as far as he could. He threw off almost rudely.

"A paralytic one."

"Then you don't know what it's like to be alone," said Róbert, ignoring the 'paralytic'.

"No," said Miklya.

Róbert stood up from the bed, went over to Miklya who was just straightening himself, and held out his hand with a smile.

"Let's be friends, comrade."

Miklya hadn't yet learnt to lie to the extent that he could put on an instant good face at this to his mind dreadfully ill-timed offer, and, unhitched and numb with surprise he at first pretended to be deaf, even clapping his hands to his ears. He leant towards Róbert with a horrified look, flashing with stifled indignation.

"What? What did you say?"

Róbert repeated it, blushing.

"Let's be friends."

Seeing the blush Miklya was jerked back into activity.

"Yes, let's," he said, and he grasped, he accepted the soft damp hand held out to him.

At three o'clock in the afternoon, about an hour after Róbert, the third inmate arrived, Purgacsics. As he entered the room Miklya made an immediate assessment of him as he had of Róbert. "Idiot." That was his assessment, and it was about as appropriate and well-founded as the one he had made of Róbert.

Purgacsics, it should be noted, had arrived in a red Pioneer tie. It was anyone's guess what a moustached Pioneer was doing here in the College of Dramatic Art. An oaf in a red tie who came in with two suitcases, without knocking of course. He looked around the room, put his things on one of the empty beds, then, smiling theatrically like a schoolteacher who wants to be nice to his pupils, he said:

"Well, here I am. Forward!"

Miklya just nodded; no words came to him. His voice and what he said made the newcomer seem even more half-witted than before, almost frighteningly so. Miklya shuddered to think that he would have to live in one room with him. Róbert enjoyed the ingenuity in that greeting of the Young Pioneers.

"Forward, comrade," he repeated, together with the 'comrade', because he stuck 'comrade' on to everything.

"Are you young comrades dramaturgists too?" Purgacsics asked brightly and walked over to shake hands with them.

"Not yet, comrade," said Róbert demurely.

"Yeh, don't bet on it," mumbled Miklya.

Purgacsics stood in front of Róbert. He grinned as if he were trying to talk him into some sort of Pioneer-prank. He had picked up the college manner during the entrance exam: he knew how one introduced oneself here.

"Antal Purgacsics, from Zalatárnok." He thrust his hand out before Róbert.

"József Róbert, from Bergen-Belsen," Róbert quickly replied.

"Christ," thought Miklya, "they've got it taped."

Purgacsics stood before him too, wearing the same grin, but Miklya took his hand dourly and said his name without comment. Purgacsics didn't leave it at that.

"Where are you from?"

"I'm just from the Marshlands," said Miklya.

"Well that's fine," conceded Purgacsics, and skirting the table he went back to his bed in a less ebullient mood. He was bothered by that 'Bergen-Belsen'. He couldn't make it out. He felt it must be some sort of wisecrack, some sort of retort to his 'Zalatárnok', but for all he knew Róbert might well have been born there. Quite honestly he didn't even know where Bergen-Belsen was or whether a Hungarian boy could have been born there.

By this time Miklya and Róbert had already made up their beds, because at Miklya's suggestion they had got their mattresses, sheets and blankets from the caretaker. Purgacsics enquired how he could do the same, and he went down to the basement storeroom, signed for his bedclothes, came back, made up his bed, wearing his red Pioneer tie throughout and puzzling all the time as to where Róbert had been born. When his bed was ready he sat down for a moment's rest, and now with a slightly stern, schoolteacher expression on his face he looked at Róbert, who was reading again, but this time in comfort, lying down.

"Tell me, Comrade Róbert, were you really born in Bergen-Belsen?"

"No. In Makó," said Róbert, and put his book down on his lap. "But I managed to survive there, and that's as good as being born there," he added proudly. He was proud of being so witty, and that they just 'swallowed' by his wit. And swallow it they did. Purgacsics seemed to crumble under it, he looked quite crestfallen as he declared:

"Fascism will never return."

Although Miklya sensed the inanity behind that remark, he nonetheless considered it the wittiest so far, and he was annoyed that he hadn't said something similar to Róbert, a moment ago. "It's too late now anyway," he thought, "next time." If nothing else it made him realize that one had to come out with these platitudes boldly and uninhibitedly here, otherwise one would be the loser and seem like 'the enemy'.

Róbert sat up on the bed and fixed the full force of his glasses on Purgacsics.

"Tell me, comrade, could I ask something too?"

"Of course, by all means."

"Are you still a Pioneer, comrade?"

Purgacsics was offended. He said in a slightly peeved tone:

"No, I'm a Pioneer leader. Or rather I was. Camp commander."

This was a bit too much for Róbert, he tried to cut it down to size:

"A teacher?"

"Supervisor," said Purgacsics.

Miklya couldn't let this pomposity go without comment.

"I thought you were decked out for the freshman's ball," he said glumly to Purgacsics.

"It's usually the enemy who mock at the red tie," retorted Purgacsics.

Miklya wasn't intimidated.

"Time will tell who is the enemy here."

Róbert laughed. He was enjoying this dispute.

"I also think this dispute is a bit premature, comrades. Let's get to know each other first."

And he turned straight to Purgacsics.

"How old are you?"

"Twenty-one," said Purgacsics.

"I'm only nineteen."

Then he suddenly turned round to face Miklya.

"And you?"

"Twenty," said Miklya.

Something heavy hit the door from the other side. Voices: "Not that one, son! This is room six." And another voice, more than likely that of the recently addressed 'son'. "Don't let's take in the stuff." To which came an irritated reply: "How else are we going to unpack?" Then, as the door was opening: "You banged it against the wall, you oaf." "I'm afraid a lot of the eggs are broken." And now the door was open, and an unbelievable, almost fairy-tale sight met the eyes of the three boys inside—not at all what they had expected from the dialogue they had overheard. A dove-grey head appeared, a stooped figure, cramming two practically trunk-sized suitcases through the doorway, which was then completely filled by a body, the huge body of the boy. Who the hell are they? What are they carrying? Father and son? Isn't there some mistake? Ghastly creatures. The two intruders united the three boys inside, they were thinking the same thing at roughly the same time. At any rate things started happening fast. Like a scene from a film: the father carries the load into the middle of the room, puts it down, looks around, shows annoyance that the room isn't empty, but eventually beams a smile at the boys. The young man, however, is empty-handed, because the other two smaller suitcases which he swings about with the ease of a yoyo don't tax his strength in the slightest. He isn't carrying anything, he may well be beyond the force of gravity, he is so huge. All he has is a jam-packed sports bag on his shoulder; with this he does have some sort of relationship, it's his. He stands there, not saying hello, just staring at them. "This lot?" is written on his face.

"Greetings, colleagues!" The grey-haired one, the father, pulls himself together and, with the advantage of knowing how to behave, his age, and his dove-grey hair, goes from one boy to the other repeating his name clearly and significantly at each handshake. The boy follows him round 'like a gentleman' repeating the same name and extending such a vast palm to the three gaping, stunned boys that they hardly dared touch it.

"Ferenc Lovas," repeats the father, almost as a cue that the boys should follow; they are educated people after all, colleagues, dramaturgists.

"Dénes Lovas," says the boy, ashamed, yet accepting his father's name, the consequences of being his father's son, the connection.

"You must have seen one or two of my pictures or heard of me. After all a would-be dramaturgist has to have a wide range of information."

They hadn't heard. They hadn't seen either. Only Miklya had a vague glimmer. An illustration under which this name was written.

"You are dramaturgists, aren't you?"

"Yes," said Róbert.

"So is my son."

The scene hit Miki Miklya the hardest. The thing he most dreaded had happened: the middle-class boy had arrived. There was no doubt about that. "Daddy had brought him up to college." He felt sick. At the whole sight, before him, the father carrying the cases and the boy marching in like an emperor, that sports bag on his shoulder and his childish, rosy, girlish baby-face, his innocent expression, his massive palm, his movements which told of great muscles, and his sizeable stomach. "What could this be?"

The father tried to take the situation in hand.

"Well, son, I think that must be your bed," he said pointing to the bed next to the window opposite Miklya's, "but before you get organized let's have a look at the eggs."

"Here?" protested the boy.

"Where else?"

Then, as an example to the boy of diplomatic finesse and style and of how to win people over, he said:

"I'm sure the colleagues won't take it amiss if we offer them a little home-produced sausages and scrambled egg."

No one said thank-you. There was silence.

After that the boy put the larger of the brown suitcases on the bed, while the father turned to the boys with further explanation.

"I'm a market-gardener. We've brought a little sustenance to starving Budapest," and he laughed, tittering so that the boys would join in his mirth, but they didn't laugh. Purgacsics actually became serious, because he found the thing suspicious, he sniffed 'the enemy'. Miklya on the other hand was furious that he hadn't thought of this deal himself. He could so easily have brought along 150 eggs, and what couldn't he have done with the hundred forints he would have made on them. It was Róbert who smiled, because he only really understood the business when they opened the suitcase and the contents was revealed: an uncountable number of eggs, each wrapped in a separate paper, with the head or staring eyes of an occasional plucked goose, duck or hen in between. Róbert drew closer, watching with interest. He'd never seen so much food at one time in his life. "They can certainly afford to give us something out of this lot," he thought. He had no feeling as yet that they wanted to bribe him.

Miklya too stopped arranging his bedside cupboard and sat down for a moment on his bed to watch the Lovases' activities. 'Artist and smallholder'—these two labels, which incidentally Lovas senior himself had displayed like this, side by side, should have coagulated into a judgement in him too. Had he been ready in his mind to categorize every phenomenon which was not to his liking under the heading 'enemy', he too would have described them as enemies. That not being the case, however, he simply summed them up as 'middle class'.

The father examined every one of the mound of eggs. Only two or three were broken. He told the boy to get a dish out of the other case. The boy was dreadfully ashamed of the whole business, his baby-face blushed as he put the other case on the table and opened it. As the lid was raised the small room was filled with a mild, pleasant, sourish smell of smoke.

Róbert left the case of eggs and stood marvelling over this one, now quite unreservedly. He hovered about between the Lovases' suitcases like a scruffy little urchin 'from the backyard' who's allowed to do anything. Even so Lovas junior took such pains to keep out of his way—even drawing in his stomach when he got close to him—it seemed as if he were frightened Róbert would break if he accidentally brushed against him. In the suitcase on the table there was smoked bacon, in vast quantities. The boy put his hand under one of the pieces of bacon, lifted it and took out from underneath a plate which up till then had been face down and handed it to his father. His father tipped the remains of the cracked and half-split eggs into the plate and asked:

"Has the bacon melted?"

"It's just started to run," said the boy.

"Where can we find a nice cool place for it?"

"Nowhere."

The father lost his temper.

"Nowhere? That's a lot of use. I'll call up your Uncle Jankó and ask him if he can help."

"He'll probably flog the lot right away."

The father became even angrier.

"He won't flog it because I'm going to flog it myself... but not till tomorrow morning in the market. If I've lugged it this far, I'm not going to let it go for nothing."

It was clear from the father's words that he felt very confident under the shelter of the promised scrambled egg and sausages, and he certainly didn't care whether he was consistent: he wasn't ashamed of asking a price for what he'd brought for 'starving Budapest'.

Róbert stood there by the open suitcase. He didn't grasp any of this since he lacked home life experience; all he knew was that his olfactory nerve-endings were being assaulted by the pervading smell. It was so long since he had eaten food like this as a little boy in Makó that he couldn't actually remember the taste, just the lack of it stayed with him, the awareness that he didn't get any of those things. There in the rising smoky smell, the wretchedness of his life, the wretchedness of being an orphan flashed through him again. The sight, and the enticing smell, however, overpowered even this feeling and left him with just one wish: that they should get on with making that scrambled egg. Now for the first time since he had arrived in the room he had a sense of well-being.

"Whew!" he let slip and made a rather poor attempt to click his tongue. Then, to complete his embarrassment, his stomach rumbled so loudly that everyone could hear it. He blushed and winced, wishing he could tear out his stomach, and quickly sat down on his bed again with downcast eyes. Miklya smirked.

In the meantime Lovas senior had finished sorting out the eggs. There was now about half a plateful of whites and yolks, and three cracked but not leaking eggs were ready beside the plate. The old man looked round the room as if he were making a count of those present, those to be fed. Then he broke the cracked eggs into the plate and, with as much show as possible, he took out two whole eggs and broke them too into the plate. After that he said to his son:

"Here, make scrambled eggs for the boys out of this."

Lovas junior didn't take the plate from him.

"Where, may I ask?" he enquired in a provocatively cheeky tone. The father, however, didn't seem to be shocked by this insolence—he must have got used to it—and he answered his son in a sarcastic, preaching, disdainful tone, as if he were talking to an idiot.

"We have here a students' hostel, Mr Lovas. Students are going to live here for months, and it won't be their mothers who'll cook for them, they'll have to look after themselves. There's bound to be a kitchen here somewhere, all you have to do is open your mouth and look for it. If you're so gormless how d'you think you'll ever make a dramaturgist?"

"You think this is the most important thing right now?"

"Yes. You go down and look for Comrade Fóti, the caretaker, you know, and you introduce yourself to him."

"Like this with a plate of eggs in my hand, right?"

"Yes, with the eggs. And the sausage and bacon too."

"You fix that one."

"I'll fix it, you just make the scrambled egg, understand?"

He had raised his voice, it had become incisive and authoritative.

Miklya was the only one of the boys to sense that in actual fact it wasn't what they were talking about that was at stake, but something much more important which they had probably been quarrelling over for a long time and which was most significantly conveyed to him by the sudden mention of the name 'Comrade Fóti'. He was unable to brood on this for long though because Lovas junior, after a slight pause, picked him out as the one he wanted to address.

"Do you know anything about a kitchen here?"

"There is one, but no one uses it. It's got a gas stove but no saucepans."

The father interrupted:

"I told you to go and ask for a pan from Comrade Fóti."

An imaginary, seemingly unattainable scrambled-egg pan, the remains of five or six dashed and flattened eggs, mixed up with printer's ink, and Comrade Fóti popping up out of every egg with threatening significance—what was it all about? What was going to happen? Miklya with his good instincts and excellent foresight guessed that 'these types' wanted to bribe Comrade Fóti as well, and all of a sudden he decided not to accept any of the scrambled egg.

That was still far off though. Right now Miklya just felt that he couldn't stand being in the room any longer with these people. He couldn't go back to his bedside cupboard again because he had tidied everything away; to stand at the window would have been too strong a protest, so, with an almost inaudible 'excuse me' aimed at no one in particular, he went out of the room. Down to the first floor, to the spacious classroom, the salon of the former luxury villa. He sat down and spread out before him a more than two-months-old copy of *Free People* that he found on the table. But he didn't read it, he just looked at it. He saw the objects his roommates had brought with them, Róbert's scanty bag and his *Far from Moscow*, Purgacsics' red Pioneer tie and the Lovases' piles of eggs and bacon. He thought that when the evening had drawn in he would go upstairs, pack his UNRRA box, and leave them without saying goodbye. At home they were building a fishpond up by the Foki Bridge, he could get a job there. It would be much better for him at the fishery.

His meditations were interrupted by the creak of the door. A freckled girl came out of the girls' room behind the classroom. He recognized her: she was the fifth first-year dramaturgist. He had met her this morning. The girl was about to walk through the room, but when she saw him she gave an awkward smile and stopped.

"Are you studying already?" she asked, in a slightly sharper tone than she'd meant to, due to her awkwardness.

The freckled girl's awkwardness produced unexpected strength and superiority in Miklya.

"No. Just my usual afternoon devotions," he said.

"Really?" sang out the girl, even more embarrassed. Then she added:

"Are you religious?"

"Very," said Miklya.

The girl came closer in her confusion, and stopped in front of Miklya.

"What's your room like?" she asked.

"Splendid," said Miklya.

"And your fellow students?"

"More splendid still."

The girl didn't want to start up any new subject of conversation. She stood for a moment in front of Miklya then she said:

"I'm going to buy some soap."

"At least she's clean," thought Miklya and gave an approving nod.

Translated by Elizabeth Szász

Father Fabricius
BY GYÖRGY MOLDOVA

Once, I no longer recall on which holiday, a procession crossed the square. Only a few old men and children walked behind the fancifully embroidered flags as we watched them with curiosity.

"They must have lost their way."

"This is a blue-collar district, people were never religious around here."

Martin, the police captain, who brought his daughter down to the square every afternoon to play, interrupted.

"It's not that simple. Believe it or not, this place produced a priest once."

"Who?"

"Father Fabricius. One of the most interesting men I have known. It's an old story, no longer bound by official secrecy. If you gentlemen have time, I could tell you about it.

Perhaps this priest will sound more familiar if I tell you that his real name was Leipnik. Those of you who have been around a while must remember the Leipnik family. They lived in Szerdahelyi Street.

Old man Leipnik worked at the Ganz Plant. He was a toolmaker. He made decent money, but he was very stingy and eccentric. In the morning he always took the family's bread and sugar bowl with him to work, to prevent them nibbling. He handed out the portions when he got home, a slice of bread for the soup, one cube of sugar for the coffee.

Only the eldest son, Ede, got more once. He had pneumonia, but old man Leipnik would not call the doctor. He gave his son two cubes of sugar saturated with spirits of salt, saying it had quite enough strength to cure the boy. When Ede died anyway, he shrugged his shoulder: even a doctor would have been helpless with a weak physique like that.

As soon as the children were grown, of course they left home. Only two of the eight stayed, Gyuszi and Manci.

Gyuszi turned out just as maniacal as his father, but in reverse. Money ran through his fingers like water. He'd sometimes take ten people out to dinner. He'd spend a week's earnings but figured it was well worth it—everyone said how Gyula Leipnik was no run of the mill sort of chap. And he was particular about his clothes too. When he had a coat made he'd turn up the collar, so that everybody could see what a good lining it had.

Manci went to the bad. At first she was kept by men. One shelf in the closet couldn't hold all her silk stockings. As she got older, she just went from bad to worse. She became a "penny girl" in Fecske Street until the younger hookers forced her out, and then on Sunday she'd cruise on her bicycle in the City Park. At dawn, old man Leipnik waited for her by the gate, searched her handbag, and took away her money down to the last penny.

Daniel Leipnik, later Father Fabricius, was born into this terrible family of selfish maniacs and degraded souls in 1922.

Mrs. Leipnik was taken ill at his birth and had to be operated. As a result of the operation, she could have no more children, perhaps that was why she lavished more attention on Daniel, the last reminder of the motherhood, than on any of her other children. From the time he could walk, the little boy stumbled along by his mother's side. He was the only one allowed to kneel beside her during her quiet prayers at St. Rita's Chapel.

Even later Daniel rarely joined the other children in their

games in the street, and when he did so, he preferred the company of girls. However, as soon as he learned to read from his older brothers and sisters, the girls called him outside in vain.

He sat all day under the only tree in the cobbled yard and read old newspapers stained with mould. His mother picked out the children's colour supplement for him, but he refused to believe in the existence of fairies and witches, he was only interested in articles on technology. He asked his mother for paper and pencil and, considering his age, copied the diagrams of various machines with wonderful dexterity.

School, which laid almost exclusive emphasis on religious studies and nationalist poetry, might have blighted this gift, had not Daniel come under the care of a teacher who cherished no respect for them himself.

This teacher was called Lőrinc Méhész. He had once been a lecturer at the Palatine Joseph College of Technology, but at the time of the 1919 Commune he accepted an official post, and for this he was put in jail, nor did the new regime forgive him after his release. He was not allowed to go back to his teaching in college, on the other hand, to humiliate him, he was given permission to teach at the grammar school at Szerdahelyi Street.

Méhész was happy at this school. He asked for an empty shed and turned it into a workshop with tools he had brought from home. He took the boys who showed most promise—including Daniel—and spent his afternoons here with them.

Daniel was in the fourth class, and in accordance with the regulations of the old school system, he there had to decide whether to opt for the humanities or study something more practical. Old man Leipnik wouldn't hear of more schooling: he had already arranged with one of his colleagues to send the boy to him as an apprentice.

Daniel didn't care. All his energies were absorbed in one great goal: he wanted to build a functioning locomotive from wood. He didn't tell anyone of his plan: he was afraid that his friends would laugh. He lied to Méhész as well about why he needed the diagrams of the locomotive parts.

One night, he sneaked down to the Józsefváros station to steal pinewood for carving out the locomotive. The guard caught him and hit him with the plank until it broke across his back, and then flung the pieces at him. Though his entire body ached from the pain, Daniel had enough presence of mind to grab the wood and run for it.

He measured out the parts on this broken piece of plank. He knew that if he made a mistake he wouldn't be able to get his hands on any more wood. He took care as he carved, too, cutting away only two or three millimetres at a time with his knife. Despite this caution he ruined several parts, and needed more wood. He took his father's old kit box apart. Leipnik found out and beat him bloody, but Daniel didn't care about that either.

He finished the carving the middle of May, rubbed down the pieces with broken bits of glass, took a wide rubber band, assembled them, and installed the engine. He wrapped the finished locomotive in paper; he wanted Lőrinc Méhész to be the first to see it. But his father noticed the package and opened it.

As a result the wheels of the wooden locomotive rolled first along the stone kitchen floor. Leipnik stared at the construction, stupefied; he could not believe that his barely eleven-year-old son had made it. He pushed a pencil into Daniel's hand and made him design it. His doubts were only dispelled after an hour-long cross-examination.

Leipnik rewrapped the train and took it with him to the factory. He went to see the director, Dr. Vilmos Pálvölgyi, and asked for help to educate his talented son. Privately

Leipnik hoped he would be given cash that he could keep for himself. Pálvölgyi let him have his say, then took a good look at the locomotive. But all he said was that Leipnik should send Daniel in to see him the next morning.

The next day Leipnik accompanied his son all the way to the director's door. Pálvölgyi first asked Daniel various questions regarding the locomotive, which Daniel answered with precision. But Pálvölgyi's face showed no satisfaction.

Then he tested Daniel about religion. The boy knew many religious rituals and legends from his mother; the director smiled at last and nodded his approval.

He called Leipnik in from the corridor and informed him that he'd be willing to be responsible for Daniel's education, provided the boy chose to become a priest. Only a few years had passed since the Commune, and if a boy could manage to rise from the ranks of the proletariat, he should pray for the sins of his class rather than open up new opportunities for sin through the study of science. Pálvölgyi was a regular visitor to the Jesuits' retreat in Zugliget, and offered to speak to the fathers about Daniel.

His expectations of gain dashed, Leipnik caught hold of the boy and, fuming mad, took him home. Once home, he pushed Daniel into the middle of the room, and began cursing over the expense of educating him. And now they'd get him for a priest—free! Swearing that Mother Church would get nothing, he tore the crucifix from the wall in his anger, trampled on it, and broke it.

In twenty-five years of marriage Mrs. Leipnik had never opposed her husband with such vehemence until that moment. If Leipnik would not allow Daniel to become a priest, she'd hack him to death with a hatchet that very night. She'd rather spend twenty years in jail than see her youngest child's life ruined too.

Leipnik flung the bedding into the middle of the room

and pressed a match into his wife's hand. Go ahead, set it alight, ruin him as well! But even Daniel could feel that he was putting on an act; in truth, he had given in to his wife's will so suddenly and unexpectedly manifested.

Perhaps it was due to the working wooden train which Pálvölgyi gave to the Jesuit fathers, perhaps to some other circumstance—it is enough to report that Daniel's application was handled with more speed than usual. In the August of 1935 he boarded a train to enrol at the Jesuit school in Kaposvár.

In a certain sense, Daniel was lucky to end up with the Jesuits. The sentimental Franciscan Order would have been foreign to his nature; he would have either rebelled or succumbed, whereas the spirit of the Jesuit Order matched his own inclinations.

The hymns and the legends of St. Stanislas of Kostka made as little impression on him as the colour supplement of the *Friss Újság* had done in his boyhood, but the logical organization of the Order, its structure based on obedience and self-sacrifice, held as much technical appeal for Daniel as the basic laws of dynamics had done in earlier days.

In the restful, quiet church and study hall, where at last there was no danger lurking in the shades, Daniel's soul found peace. His fear of his old surroundings was metamorphosed into contempt, and he developed the aristocratic attitude of men severed from their own class, an aristocratic attitude more profound and definitive than that of born aristocrats.

His keen intelligence and love of knowledge soon attracted his teachers' attention. He was promoted, elevated above his peers, and in 1935 was sent to Württemberg, to the central Jesuit boarding school. Since its establishment this institution had been producing the best soldiers of the Order in their hundreds—men who accepted the duties of priest, missionary or underground organizer with equal zeal.

We know little about the years Daniel spent in Württemberg. He probably received a thorough, complex training, during which Hungary and the changes taking place in Hungarian life could not have been ignored, for Daniel had no difficulty in adjusting to the new conditions there on his return.

It is also probable that Daniel was ordained in the church of that establishment after he had finished his noviciate at which time he was given the name of one of St. Ignatius of Loyola's first followers, Pater Fabricius.

On orders from his superiors, Father Fabricius returned to Hungary in 1945. At the border he did not say that he was an ordained priest; he filled out his papers as a soldier made a prisoner in the war. Though his appearance had changed beyond recognition in the ten years he had been away—the child had become a strong, though thin, prematurely balding man—he avoided his old surroundings, nor did he contact his family. Not that he had any reason for such caution: after all his mother, the only person who would have recognized him despite his altered condition, had died during a raid in a bomb shelter, while his brothers and sisters had gone to the bad, and disappeared.

Fabricius worked as an unskilled labourer for a while, then became a master locksmith at a small factory in Kőbánya. In the meanwhile, he maintained contact with the Jesuit leaders in Hungary, whose addresses he had been given in Württemberg.

In the wake of the 1947 elections the Communists came to power. Fabricius's superiors left Hungary in haste, only avoiding arrest by a couple of hours. Their last communication to Fabricius was to the effect that he would have to fend for himself for the foreseeable future and he was given a free hand in the conduct of his affairs.

Previously, when Fabricius had finished work, he would walk the streets into the night. This he considered the best way of learning about the city and the changes in its life. But now he sat at home for days on end and pondered: how should he set about his task? He gave up his job at the factory, where in any case he had very few personal contacts, and looked for a work that by its very nature would give him an opportunity of meeting people. After several attempts, he settled down as a cabin attendant in the baths of Erzsébet Colony, on the edge of town.

The wooden houses of the Colony were put up during the First World War to serve as a temporary military hospital, but for more than thirty years now they had been home to the lowliest, worst-paid workers of the neighbouring brickworks, brewery and canning factory, as well as to old people and other has-beens. Its sanitary facilities, sewers, piped water and electric cables, meant to serve the former hospital for only a few years, had stopped functioning for the most part, with no repairs in sight. Two wells with pumps supplied all the water, while in a heavy rain the lights would go out all over the settlement.

Their plight went from bad to worse when new apartment blocks sprang up on the other side of the tracks and the people of Erzsébet Colony could not get a single one of these new, all-convenience flats. Just about every month augmented the friction between the newcomers and the old tenants. New shops were opened on the ground floors of the blocks of flats, where there was meat and matches even when the tiny wooden shack in the colony had run out of supplies. But when the people from the colony climbed over the racks, the salesmen in the shops denied having anything left, and refused to serve them. The tram stop too was transferred to the new houses, but the asphalt road was not extended, so that the stop had to be approached by a muddy footpath.

Naturally there were no open flare-ups or outright fights, though the children of the two colonies used to throw stones at each other alongside the tracks. But the indignities lodged themselves in the bosoms of the people of Erzsébet Colony: they'd bring them up night after night as they propped themselves against the zinc counter of the bar. Fabricius could not have found a more suitable place for the realization of his plans.

When he first moved into the attendant's booth at the baths the people of Erzsébet were suspicious of him, as of all strangers. The priest didn't even look as if he wanted to win their confidence. He'd open the bathrooms and take the money with an indifferent air, and only spoke when he could not avoid it. This he knew was the only means of dispelling their suspicion.

He first made friends with the children. Soon about a dozen of the twelve to sixteen-year-old boys were hanging around the bath attendant's booth. Fabricius used to have long talks with them in the evenings. He tried to express himself so that, should the children repeat his words, no one could find a trace of political propaganda in them, but every story he told had this aim in view. He retold the legends he had heard in the seminary; he merely changed the names of the saints, for in the early fifties teaching religion brought imprisonment.

His labours were not in vain. After the humdrum routine of school and workshop practice his stories aroused the boys' innate longing to perform heroic deeds. When after a year had passed Fabricius knew that the time had come to find a circumspect way of realizing their dreams.

Fabricius joined the League of Hungarian Freedom Fighters. He chose an organization where work only progressed sporadically, since its leaders were reluctant to devote their time to it for nothing. With no special effort he soon managed to be appointed head of the excursion section.

Gradually he brought along his students from Erzsébet Colony. By the beginning of 1952 they were all members of the league. Fabricius tried to prevent strangers from joining the group; he only took two or three boys from outside whom he thought would serve his purposes.

Fabricius and his students attended almost every course of the Freedom Fighters' League that could be important from a military point of view. They handled their guns reliably, were familiar with the use of radio and ciphers, had made well over a hundred parachute jumps, and on Sundays went on long treks into the hills. In four years, they became a highly trained combat unit.

Fabricius knew that this sixteen to eighteen-member unit was much too valuable to jeopardize, he mustn't risk it for the sake of a spectacular but insignificant operation—the toppling of a statue or a heroes' memorial. Patiently he waited for a chance for the unit to show its true strength.

On the night of October 23, 1956, the demonstrators brought back the first bullet-ridden flags from the Boulevard, but Fabricius still kept his unit waiting. First he went to the city to look around, and only then did he arm his students with small-bore rifles and machine-guns.

Fabricius's group took part in all the most desperate battles of the uprising. They took up the fight at the tram depot at Bethlen Street against the state security forces and participated in the siege of the main Party Headquarters. They joined the fighting quickly and efficiently and their assistance generally decided the outcome. But after a victory they would not permit the assembled civilians to lionize them like the rebels at Corvin Lane or Bosnyák Square; they did not drink or pick up women, but left the site of a battle promptly. The newspapers did not glorify their deeds; in fact Fabricius would not allow a single picture to be taken of any member of his unit.

On November 5, when a number of scattered groups were still fighting all over the town, Fabricius realized that though the fight could go on a long time yet, its outcome was hopeless; it would be senseless to sacrifice a single member of his unit now. So he sent the boys home with orders that they must try to survive the hard time that were coming as best they could, without attracting attention, and be ready for a new enterprise at any time.

Why Fabricius had kept the unit out of the limelight was clear at last. Their activities were recorded neither by pen nor camera. A few of the boys, who during the fighting were away from home for too long, were called in by the police, but they were set free after a few days' detention.

During the uprising, Fabricius had already found and contacted his former superiors. On their orders he moved down to Eger, taking down with him the arms of his unit in a truck. In Eger he bought a small empty house, moved in, and hid the arms in the cellar.

The next few years brought no change in Fabricius's life. He worked in one of the industrial co-operatives in town as a repair locksmith. During the day he went from door to door with a box on his back, and at home he fitted up a small workshop, bought technical books, and based on the blueprints, made miniature models of serious machines for his own amusement.

Fabricius was barely past thirty-five, but he did not consider breaking the limited pattern of his destiny, even though they urged him at the co-operative to get himself a technician's certificate. With that in his hand he could have immediately had a leading position. Once a month he went down to the small cellar, unwrapped the arms from the papers smelling stale oil, and checked them. Every evening, as he opened the door after work, he looked for the letter bringing orders for a new enterprise.

The letter only came in the spring of 1959, but its contents were the opposite of what Fabricius had expected. It gave immediate orders for the destruction of the arms in his cellar. The letter said nothing more, so there were no instructions on how he should carry out the orders.

Fabricius realized that destroying the arms meant the total abandonment of any future plans. He forced himself to accept his instructions, but could not refrain from seeing the members of his former unit one last time.

According to a plan they had agreed on before they had parted, he notified one of the boys who had acted as his assistant in the unit, and told him to start the chain of messages going. He appointed the small house in Eger as their meeting place, and the time as the night before the first of May. He reckoned that the boys' arrival would draw less attention in the pre-holiday rush.

He waited for the boys from the early afternoon of April 30th, but they came neither by the Pest train, nor by bus. It was already dusk when someone knocked on his window. Fabricius was surprised that, throwing caution to the wind, they came in a group. He reprimanded them, but the boys answered that since two of them had cars, they figured they might as well bring the others with them.

The passing years had brought sweeping changes in the former rebels. Most had grown fat, wore fashionable clothes, and their entire attitude bore evidence of fixed and settled lives. They were relieved when Fabricius told them of the orders to destroy the arms.

They agreed to take the guns up to the mountains in the two cars and bury them away in a cave. Two of the men went in each car, the others remained behind with Fabricius. Conversation was halting and uneasy, but even so Fabricius learned of the changes that had taken place. Bulldozers had swept Erzsébet Colony away, and some of the boys had moved into blocks of flats opposite. With their narrow windows and tiny rooms they were regarded as just as undesirable after 1956 as Erzsébet Colony had been in '51 or '52. Others had bought flats in the city. They had done their stint of army service, learnt a trade and got married—all of this they told Fabricius with a feeling of discomfort. The former commander smiled. He realized that they were afraid of him, or else did not trust him.

The two cars returned at dawn. They had carried out the orders, the guns were now buried at the bottom of a ravine. Should the rain come or some animal dig them out, there would be no clue to the identity of their former owners.

Though they had nothing else to see to, the boys did not leave. One of them opened a bottle of rum and asked Fabricius to drink with them in honour of their final farewell. Fabricius, who knew that with the dispersal of the unit his life would lose its meaning and could not imagine, even in broad outline, what he would do afterwards, accepted the rum.

Since he drank very rarely, the rum went to his head, and his attention slackened, only his sharp sense of danger told him that something was wrong. He wanted to send the boys home, but they patted him amicably on the back and made him continue drinking. Fabricius failed to notice when one of them slipped behind him and took out a concealed knife; he felt the chill of the steel blade only a second before it penetrated the back of his neck. They killed him with the grip he had taught them for the noiseless dispatch of guards.

After getting rid of the weapons and the only witness of

their past, they collected Fabricius's papers too, then left in their cars. For a very long time the affair was buried in silence. It was only the incoherent babbling of a drunk that brought the story to light, years later, when even the bones of the chief protagonist, Father Fabricius, had long since mouldered in the grave."

Translated by J. E. Sollosy

Room 212

BY ENDRE ILLÉS

On weekdays the professor had lunch at the hospital, in his study, at a low, round table with a glass top. This day they put his favourite meal before him, an omelette of four eggs with pieces of green pepper fried with it, on which he sprinkled finely ground red pepper. Afterwards he asked for an orange salad. With it he drank a glass of dry wine.

He had a lovely room. One wall was pierced by an enormous window, from there he saw the snow-covered garden in winter, in spring the trees bending in the whistling winds. A giant Persian rug hung on another wall, a bookshelf behind his desk. Sometimes he even stayed there overnight, sleeping on the couch.

The plates were taken away, and he had just opened an English medical journal when his secretary came in.

"Someone to see you, sir."

The professor glanced at his watch. Two thirty. It was always late before he had lunch.

"Did you tell him I don't see out-patients at the hospital?"

"I did. Neither at the hospital, nor at home."

The professor folded the journal.

"Is some relation of his a patient here?"

"I asked him. He said no."

"His name?"

"He wouldn't give it."

"What does he want then?"

"To speak to you, sir." She added, as though this had some significance: "His wife is with him too."

"Has he been to see me before? Do you remember?"

"I don't think we've ever seen him before."

"Ask him for his name once again." The secretary returned.

"He'll only give it to you, sir."

The professor sat down near his desk.

"What can we do? Send him in."

The stranger came in. He wore a navy-blue suit, with a yellow turtle-neck sweater. His hair was turning a dirty grey, his narrow, pointed beard and the thin moustache above the bloodless lips were the same dirty grey. His wife stood behind him, tired, broken, in dark grey.

The professor looked the man over, his hollow chest, the baggy suit on the thin body, and he could already hear his heavy breathing.

"I was told you'd like to speak to me."

The other two came forward, all the way up to the desk. Then the man spoke his name.

He spoke very softly.

The professor asked him to repeat it. He had been watching him all along, but only then did he take a real look.

The dreaded man stood before him. That dreaded man who only a few years before had held the lives of others on the palm of his hand like the severed leg of a frog, which will still twitch convulsively if hit by an electric current. The man who could know the heart throbs of a bird tight in the grip of his hand.

"You are that ...," the professor faltered.

The stanger stared at him. "Yes, I am."

The professor reached for the ballpoint on his desk and toyed with it.

"What is it you want me to do?"

"I am a sick man. I should like you to have a look at me."

"I think my secretary has already told you, I don't engage in private practice."

The man's eyes grew more rigid still, they were beginning to resemble marbles. He wanted to soften his voice to a pleasing tone but it remained flat and dry, it cracked like dry reed—this voice could not accept any foreign material, any softer overtones.

"Yes," he said. "But I trust only you, professor. I can only trust you."

The professor held the ballpoint tight.

"Why me exactly?"

The man in the navy suit drew a big breath:

"I thought it over carefully, for weeks on end. Because I thought it out ... I thought about it before it all became clear." He spoke crudely. "I never had you investigated, neither you, nor any member of your family. None of them, ever!... Although I could have done so once ..."

He stopped—as though he could not exhale the few cubic centimetres of air which he had just breathed in so deeply a moment before.

The second, third, fourth moment too passed, and the man remained silent locked in a stiff cramp. In this heavy silence the professor asked:

"What could you have done to harm me?"

The spasm finally relaxed:

"I was informed that when a colleague of yours issued a press statement that the recovery rate is better during the winter in the less heated, in fact in the cold wards, than in the well heated ones, you issued orders to keep up the heat! Keep the wards as warm as they had been. Stoke up the fires. I should have had that investigated. What was behind those orders of yours. But I did not..."

The professor clicked the ballpoint and doodled his name

on a white sheet, once, twice, five times—this is how I would have signed my evidence then, he thought.

He looked up.

"May I ask, why you did not pursue the matter?"

The man in the navy blue suit relaxed a little.

"Because I am prejudiced. I like the cold better than well-heated rooms. Those who are prejudiced should maintain their objectivity." He continued in the cracked, splintery voice of the broken reed:

"I am ill, professor. As ill as the others at your hospital here... Take me as your patient, you have got to help me."

The professor stood up.

"If you really are ill... and, as far as I can tell by the looks of you, you really are... I'll arrange for you to be admitted.'

"But will I get a private room?"

"Naturally."

"And you will examine me, right? Just you alone?"

"Naturally. Me too."

"I don't trust anybody else."

"If you want to stay at this hospital, you will have to trust everyone here. Incidentally, where are you employed now?'

There was a moment's pause.

"Are you working anywhere?"

"I am assistant manager at the Costume Hire Company."

"So you are insured." The professor doodled his name on the white sheet for the sixth time, then made his decision. "You will be placed in Katalin Ivády's care. She will be in charge of the preliminary tests. She's my assistant."

"And I'll get a private room?"

"I've already promised that."

"And my wife..."

"Your wife cannot stay here." He picked up the housephone and called his secretary.

"Please take the patient to Dr. Ivády's. I'll ring her right away."

When the man, his wife and his secretary left the room the professor smiled. But this smile could only have been caught by those who knew him very well. I might as well have said: "Take him out," he thought.

Late in the afternoon Katalin Ivády reported:

"Advanced cardiac asthma. I have prescribed Cedilanide and Diaphyllin, and Noxyron for the night."

"Right," said the professor.

Dr. Ivády continued:

"His ECG would even justify Prednisolon."

"Let's wait with that. I'll have a look at him myself first."

"He's afraid of waking at dawn. He says that's when it's worst. He gasps for breath."

"If he can't breathe, give him extra Diaphyllin."

"He asked his name should not be on his chart."

The professor smiled again.

"Open the telephone book, and take the first name that catches your eye."

Katalin Ivády still had something to say:

"He's a difficult patient, he won't undress. Just sits on a chair ... Complains that his window faces the courtyard."

The professor knew how his patient felt:

"Have an armchair placed in his room, with a cushion, and get him to sit in that. With his back to the window. That way he won't see the courtyard."

Before he went home, the sister on duty came to see the professor.

"They brought something to eat for number 212. The person who brought it said it was from home. Shall I give it to him?"

The professor took the lid off the two-tiered container:

pork cutlet with rice and stewed apples, pink sponge-cake on the bottom plate.

"He got the same here. We took it to his room, but he wouldn't touch it," said the sister indignantly.

"He trusts them more at home," the professor assured the nurse. "For now—take him this 'homemade' ... Eventually he'll grow to like us."

The next morning, however, even before the consultant's round, the professor went to room 212 in a state of exasperation, Dr. Ivády and the matron behind him.

The patient was standing by the window, and hearing them enter, turned around.

"Don't do that again!" said the professor in a sharp, raised tone of voice.

"What, professor?"

"Giving ten forints to the boy in the next ward to take your tablets. Haven't you ever heard of adult dosage and children's dosage, and that the latter is considerably less? Haven't you got scruples? You could have poisoned that boy!"

Number 212 looked at the professor for a while, as one who does not wish to answer. Nonetheless, after some time he spoke, very quietly.

"Did the boy tell on me?"

"He did not. You were caught."

The voice of number 212 now took on a bit more colour.

"A strange custom this is, professor, that there are three pills prepared for me in a small cup to go with my breakfast. I have to swallow them, and I don't even know what I'm swallowing."

"That is not a strange custom, these are the hospital regulations!"—The professor was becoming more and more exasperated. "You are at this hospital now and not somewhere else! Did you think we wanted to poison you? We usually give treatment here."

Number 212 defended himself humbly, underhandedly:

"I beg your pardon ... I meant no harm. I beg all of your pardons ... But a professor must also consider his patient's peace of mind as a condition for recovery?"

"Naturally."

"Then let me ask you to please give me a prescription. My wife will pick up the drugs, and the doctor or sister can pick out each time what I should take. That would make me much calmer."

Before the professor could answer, Dr. Ivády's face flushed. She asked indignantly:

"So you really are afraid we'll poison you?"

"I am afraid."

"Are you afraid of me? Your doctor?"

Number 212 did not look up at them, he was examining the linoleum-covered floor.

"I have enemies. I'm protecting myself." He only lifted his head when the professor spoke.

"If you keep this up, I'll have you thrown out of the hospital," the professor said. He turned and walked out. Dr. Ivády and the matron followed him.

In the corridor Dr. Ivády added:

"This morning I had him scheduled for routine tests, X-ray and laboratory, but he didn't go to any of them. We haven't a single report on him yet."

The professor leant to the banisters and thought.

"Let's leave him alone for a day or two. Let him make up his own mind what he wants," he said finally.

On the third day, in the early afternoon, the professor's secretary announced number 212's wife.

"We will leave, professor."

"If that is your decision, no one will stop you."

"Please don't be angry."

"Why should I be?"

"Please believe me ... he didn't want to hurt anyone. It's not in his nature."

"If you say it, I have to believe you." When she was already at the door, he decided to ask:

"Why exactly are you leaving? You do know, don't you that your husband is ill. His illness will soon become worse. What will you do then?"

The woman turned in gratitude, in pain, at the kind words.

"I don't know, professor. ... I don't know ... The problem here was that he got a room facing the courtyard ... He began to be afraid then, right in the first half hour ... Afraid of the courtyard ... Perhaps if you had put him in a room facing the street ... then ... perhaps ..."

She couldn't finish and left.

Translated by Etelka Láczay

Requiem

BY FERENC KARINTHY

The chief physician hadn't planned to attend. He was home for a short two days, a brief respite between a convention in Copenhagen and a ski trip to the mountains. That was when he received the invitation to attend the requiem service in the Coronation Church in memory of Albert Gyulafy, who had passed away in Montevideo on January the 7th. Nothing more, just Albert Gyulafy. No address, no rank, not even a 'Mr.' He promptly forgot it, checked in at the hospital to take care of a few pressing matters, but was immediately syphoned off to a consultation, then signed his name to a batch of papers and letters, at least forty in all. He finished at two-thirty, rushed over to the ministry, had some cold chicken in the buffet, then drove home for a short nap before his two private patients were due that evening. But he had barely closed his eyes on the couch when an old memory unexpectedly emerged from the primeval waters: ruddy-cheeked Uncle Berci, dressed in the special Magyar gala suit, sword at his side, at Ubul Brenner's wedding, as he gave him a reassuring little nod, his way of letting him know that his scholarship to Switzerland was okay. In those turbulent war days that took quite some doing, even for a minister. Actually, he had escaped the siege of Budapest and the battlefield due to this support in the upper echelons, and it was the two years spent abroad that had started him on his career. In fact, he had those same two years to thank for poor Helga, that sad, now irrevocably clouded period of sunshine in his life. He brought her back with him from Switzerland, and it wasn't until later that he realized his wife couldn't acclimatize, she was a flower that couldn't be replanted, her frail physique wasting away in this hot soil... And suddenly, a bittersweet nostalgia, a feeling of gratitude surged up in him, and perhaps curiosity as well. What would it be like? Who would attend? A challenge, a time of reckoning. How much had survived of his youth? The telephone lay nearby. Soon he had called off one appointment, postponed the other, and was driving up to the Castle.

It was cold, crisp winter weather. Dusk fell early. Uncle Berci was his uncle twice removed, his mother's cousin, and so, a Gyulafy by birth. He had been the pride and joy of the combined Brenner, Gyulafy, and Korbuly-Mersich clans, a minister of many years' standing. In private, he was an entertaining gentleman with a Bohemian temperament, an acknowledged hunter and womanizer, a fin-de-siècle anachronism. At least, that was he'd heard; he rarely saw Uncle Berci in the flesh. As a politician he was a liberal, a sly fox, the silent representative of a British orientated policy in the government, and the hated target of the Hungarian fascists. At the time of the occupation, in '44, he was deported by the Germans, that was how he ended up in South America. He was never declared a war criminal at home. Still, it wasn't politic to pride oneself on being his relative.

Several people had already gathered at the side entrance of the Coronation Church. He was flabbergasted when he recognized an obese, porky man as Aladár Zetelaki of Zetelak, or Zaladár Etelaki of Etelak, as everyone called him, wearing a closely-cut coat with frogging, and his wife, Zamália Etelaki of Etelak, in a worn seal coat. Though he hadn't given the old man much thought since God knows when, he could have sworn that the former chief school inspector, the apostle of the "Magyar Goods in Magyar Homes" movement and editor of the Zetelak Young People's Almanac (the Etelak Young People's Zalmanac) was no longer among the living. He must have had a hormone imbalance or something. Bursting at the seams he was, his pudgy, flabby cheeks, small toothbrush moustache, sickly-thick stump of a neck, tiny puffed-up eyes, idiotic, vacuous stare as he blinked in return to his greeting (obviously not realizing who he was), made the chief physician think, the man is a porker ripe for the knife, an open sesame of bacon and lard... And good Lord, Lóránd Korbuly-Mersich, the "butcher"! Uncle Lóri had been deputy police commissioner of Budapest, though in private he was a gentle and softspoken man and an avid collector of insects. Then, in '51, the *Szabad Nép* came out with an article in favour of relocation and published a list of some of the sworn enemies of the state who had already been sent out of the capital to live in the countryside. The list included Korbuly-Mersich, the "butcher" commissioner (or so he had been inadvertently promoted). The family had called this white-bearded, lean old man living on raw food and herbs and fifteen-mile constitutionals by this epithet ever since.

"Egon, dear! So you've come!"

Dear, sweet Babuka. Dear little Baba Kézdy, the orphaned, penniless, old maid baroness who had been like a nurse to him after his mother's death. They kissed. Poor Babu hadn't got any younger either; she was even more diminutive in black, and completely grey. Even her old-fashioned hat couldn't hide that. But it was nice cuddling up to her, and there was the same natural sense of belonging... She had sent the invitation herself, she said, and the chief physician decided he'd stay by her side, hold on to her, and not let go of her reassuring presence.

A ghost came over to him, or rather glided, floated over,

an incorporeal other-worldly shade. And, extending his cold spirit hand, he mumbled something about his wife's cure and couldn't you, old boy, see about a bed in a good sanatorium... He'd never have guessed who the man was, were it not for Babuka whispering: it's Guszti, Guszti Huszár, sub-prefect Dr. Chevalier Ágoston Ladányi-Huszár. Could this man with both feet in the grave be the former Tartar khan of the raven-black eyes and moustache and prominent forehead? The one whose retort to a discussion on the Gulf Stream—"It's nonsense! The brainchild of Jewish scribblers! It's all I can do to believe in America!"—became part of family lore?

Babu quickly supplied the essentials. Guszti is down and out, an incurable alcoholic, and so is his wife. They frequent taverns and bars, drink with bums and do the most distressing things. Last year Guszti fell down the stairs of a pub in a drunken stupor, broke his hip, wore a cast and was dependent on crutches for six months, but made his daily pilgrimage to the pub just the same. He's always the first in and the last out. As for Mrs. Huszár, née Lula Korbuly-Mersich, a once-celebrated beauty, the star of the society pages, she takes up with all sorts of filthy, drunken carters and others of their kind, even now, at seventy, wherever she can, in a ditch, on the road, last autumn she fell asleep in the park and almost froze to death at night, that's what's caused her rheuma... Babu pointed her out in the distance: a shaky, skeletal figure, and even by artificial light you could see the heavy coat of makeup and the ghastly frozen smile on her larva face. The chief physician remembered what they used to say back then, that alongside many of her other scandalous affairs, the captivating Lula had also found time to be Uncle Berci's lover.

They walked into the church. The mass was being celebrated up front, at the main altar illuminated by candles.

The participants sat facing each other on the benches, on two sides of the apse, fenced off by a small balustrade. He was surprised by their numbers, a hundred and fifty or two hundred at least. He moved as far to the rear as he could with Babuka, as he had always done. Mrs. Huszár, on the other hand, sat down dramatically in the first row. And on her right, now, who was the woman so elegant even in mourning, veiled, with flowing ribbons? Could it be Minci Jacobi? Correction. Countess Vayk, after her fourth husband. Yes, indeed, the two Jacobi girls, Trudi and Minci. Had eight husbands between them. Trudi was living now in Canada. She had married the owner of a chocolate factory and supplied her younger sister with clothes, among other things, though Minci would look swell dressed in a sack. To this day, whatever she might have on, her innate elegance was a natural, organic part of her being. What lovely, enchanting women they were! They must have had a secret way with men. Minci, in fact, was still going strong; the tall, thin, quiet Oliver Vayk, also in attendance, was a good fifteen years her junior... The chief physician liked her, he found her bizarre humour entertaining, like the time he had met Minci in town. She was going about some business, carrying a tiny bag in her hand, and in answer to the standard "How are you?" she began to talk in full earnest:

"Just think, Egon dear, the minute I woke up this morning, I found myself all square and covered with polka-dots!"

However, she'd been covering up more of herself lately, that was how she selected her clothes, shawls and hats. The veil must have come in handy; now, too, she was virtually hiding behind it, only a strand of her blonde hair visible, and the flash of her impish eyes. She, too, had been a great friend of Uncle Berci's and Trudi as well, or so gossip said, both at the same time.

And there was the third widow, Mrs. Linger. Her

husband, the famous industrialist millionaire, was carried off in the first confused days after the siege of Budapest and was never heard from again. Gizike had been mourning him close on thirty years now. She spent half her time in church. The other half she used to spend writing to Uncle Berci in Uruguay. She'd been desperately in love with him ever since her teens. Their correspondence became especially lively after Ma Orsi, the old man's wife, died. In a sudden onrush of sentiment, Uncle Berci invited Gizike, and even somehow managed to scrape her air fare together. Mrs. Linger took leave of all her friends, including her spiritual advisers and father confessors, and was accompanied by at least thirty old women to the airport of Ferihegy. But she was back in four weeks. It wasn't hard to guess what had happened in far-off Montevideo; all you had to do was take a good look at this long-necked, hopelessly silly, proud, busybody mother goose stewing in her own fanaticism. They say she had refused to sleep with Uncle Berci even before, she being of the opinion that such things must wait till after the wedding ceremony, and even then should be attempted only with the express purpose of begetting an heir. Otherwise it was lechery... Nevertheless she now laid claim to the title of widow number one. She had already broken into such profuse sighs during the Oratory, mumbled her prayers so loud and wiped her eyes with her black-bordered handkerchief with such emphasis, that anyone could see—she had suffered the greatest loss of anyone here; she was the real widow, the other two mere undeserving self-appointees, unauthorized trespassers.

Behind the three mourning women sat the loose-limbed Vayk brothers, Oliver, Minci Jacobi's engineer husband, and his older brother Jenő, a corporation lawyer. And wedged in between the two counts, the latter's wife, whose various metamorphoses had been followed with great excitement by the family for years. No point in denying it, her dad's name was Sámuel Freund. Following in the footsteps of his ancestors, who were in the leather trade, he also dealt in leather goods and was later founding partner in the Sámuel Freund and Co. leather firm. This was later shortened to Sam Freund and Co., and when her father struck it rich with his war contracts he converted to Catholicism and bought himself into the nobility. On his visiting card, under the five-pointed crown, appeared the name, Soma Freund of Barát. His daughter, elaborating on this, assumed the name of Éva Baráti-Freund, and later under the People's Democracy, when such things were no longer taken so seriously, she became Éva Krisztina Baráthy-Freund, and finally, since her lucky marriage, Baroness Krisztina Vayk Baráthy... There was a story about them that their maid said to a visitor who came to call on them:

"The doctor and the comrade engineer are out, but milady the baroness will see you."

There was nothing distinctive about her. She was rather chubby, but still a relatively well-preserved, energetic woman wearing a short sporty fur coat, cropped hair, and a large gold ring with a coat of arms on her hand folded in prayer. Her twin brother, Chevalier Ferdinánd Baráthy, the respected dog breeder and recurrent sailing champion, cut a more distinguished figure with his crisp moustache and the discreet Maltese Cross in his buttonhole. Ever since Nándi could remember, his main aspiration in life had been to be admitted into the Knights of Malta. But despite all his efforts and connections in high places, in the old world his ambition had remained unrealized. However, he never gave up this aim, not even under the building of the socialist way of life, and persevered until he obtained a visitor's passport to America where, with the help and recommendation of the still-active Hungarian branch of the Order—some ancient gentlemen sans wealth but with impressive-sounding names—for a modest contribution, something like a hundred dollars, he was inducted and initiated into magisterial knighthood. Having thus attained his chief ambition of his life, he returned to his beloved retrievers and hounds as a descendant of Raymund de Puy, the crusader, of Villiers de l'Isle, the hero who defended Rhodes against the Turk, and La Valette, the liberator of Malta.

During the Gospel the chief physician stood up along with the others, but did not cross himself. He caught someone whispering:

"That's Boriska Gyulafy's son. He's a communist."

He glanced that way. Some dark-eyed old women were whispering in each other's ears. He couldn't place them, though. And then, further off, at the other end of his bench, yes, it struck him like lightning, his knees began to tremble, as years ago. Perhaps they even gave way.

Kati Kerecsényi.

How did she get here? He thought she was living in the country, in Kiskunfélegyháza or Kiskunhalas; ever since the relocations, she was a teacher or something down there. Had she come up just for the mass? Of course. She was another of Uncle Berci's protégées, the apple of his eye, in fact, and possibly even his god-daughter. Carefully, inconspicuously, he studied her profile for signs of aging. But despite his scrutiny, he could discover nothing substantial. He found her almost as beautiful and exciting now, the mother of three grown children. Or was it just a reflection of the old glory? Still the clear, well-defined contours of her face, which emphasized the noble curve of the neck, her skin tight and smooth, her blonde hair barely a shade darker, though greying, only her unbelievable, unearthly thinness had filled out ever so slightly... Yet how this woman had fought for years on end, alone, with her children, just to survive. A year after he left for Switzerland she married Pubi Lippai Kreis, a fatuous and lazy lounge-lizard and sports dude. He got her with three children, then, after everything was nationalized and his money was gone, he ran off with a waitress. Later, he died in a car crash in New Zealand or New Guinea. Kati stayed. She refused to become a burden on anyone with her three children. She accepted her fate and first worked in a nursery, then, through superhuman effort, finished the academy and became a teacher, and today she was a school principal, or so they said. And she did it all alone, in the provinces, away from her relatives. The chief physician hadn't seen her in over twenty years, and only knew about her through hearsay.

Babuka was quietly explaining who was who, but he wasn't paying much attention. There were four or five former generals and colonels present, most of them night watchmen and overseers now. And Dénes Antal, a chaplain general. He had held out the longest. He wasn't forced to retire until 1950. He had been appointed prison chaplain in '45 and spent the night before their execution with the war criminals including an army commander sentenced to death at a spectacular trial, to whom—having been absent when they handed out brains—Uncle Dini said the following by way of parting as they left death row at dawn: "My most sincere apologies, Your Excellency!"

A good-looking man of gigantic build in an elegant winter coat lined with fur: Tamás Teleki. The son of Kálmán Teleki, once the owner of a huge estate, member of the Upper House and chamberlain, he was now—Babuka was rapidly giving him the lowdown—a furniture mover; a plain haulier, but with a difference. He had organized a special team with a few friends, all gentlemen like himself. Their specialty was that they never used coarse or unseemly language. Regardless of what they might have to lift or carry, they did so efficiently and with the utmost ceremony, to the great astonishment of their customers: "Go on, dear fellow, a little higher, if you don't mind... many thanks, dear colleague... the back of the chest, if you will..." and so on. Their reputation spread quickly in this rather menial profession, and besides, they were quick and worked with clockwork precision, on the basis of scientific principles. They had more customers than they knew what to do with, and needless to say, they made as much money as they wanted. They all had cars, their own apartments and summer places.

There was an old clipping from *'Theatre News'* among the chief physician's photographs, a picture taken on the beach of Földvár. Some young men making a pyramid in the Balaton, he at the bottom, the two Telekis, Tamás and Tibor, standing on his shoulders, both lanky, sunburnt adolescents. Tibor making a funny face. A few years later he was shot down as an air force pilot... Kati was also vacationing there that summer; he was introduced to her only in passing, which gave him the right at most to greet her along the promenade or the pier, and she nodded back condescendingly. He adored her from a distance. How could he hope to approach the beautiful, spoiled, very popular, tennis-champion, queen-of-the-ball daughter of a fabulously rich champagne manufacturer and stable owner, he, the poor, just tolerated cousin from the periphery of the big family, the medical student son of Dr. Brenner? He thought up all sorts of adventurous ways of meeting her. For example, they get into the same compartment, and the train stops in a tunnel, or Kati sneaks down to the shore at night because she's fed up with the company, and he accidentally comes by, or the girl's horse bolts during the morning's ride, and he appears among the poplars and rescues her, and so on.

Then it all happened, quite differently and much later, just before he left, on that two-day boating excursion on the Danube. He was so nervous just before departure, he almost called it off, but he had promised, and they were so insistent, and the early September was so brilliant, he didn't have the heart. They had decided to go island-hopping. About fifteen of them gathered at the Római beach, and his heart fluttered to see Kati Kerecsényi among them. But rowing up the Szentendre branch, he hardly saw her. There were three girls sitting in a keel, and he was alone in the kayak. They spent the night at the Huszár's villa at Visegrád. Nothing happened, though; Kati didn't even notice him during the hayride. The next day they discovered that the keel was damaged and out of commission, and the girls had to split up. He managed to get Kati into his boat. In fact, through various tricks and machinations, he fell behind the others right at the start, and thought they had agreed to row down the main branch of the Danube and the others made their way towards it, he turned to the right at the tip of the island, back to the Szentendre branch. By the time Kati realized what had happened and he had made his excuses, it was too late—too tiring and long a way to row back and catch up. So they had a full day and thirty kilometres ahead, just the two of them.

They drifted downstream slowly, the weather was heavenly, the early autumn, mist hovered above the tiny ripples of the almost perfectly still water... Gossamers, gleams of sunlight, seductive peace and tranquillity. The fact that he was going to leave in a few days, which he had already told the girl, turned to his advantage; it added a special tension to their words and dissolved Kati's tension. Kisoroszi, Bogdány. The shallow river wound its way among sandbanks and shoals. The dry, white ridges of the riverbed, not visible at other times, and in the distance, the soft outlines of the tree-studded Pilis mountains. At Goat Island, the Danube spread out into a lake, its mirror shining bright in the noonday sun and dotted by thousands upon thousands of wild ducks. As they drifted quietly towards them the ducks took off, clacking, quacking and gabbling in unison. They anchored on an abandoned stretch of grassy beach across from Leányfalu.

How they got to that point is now lost to memory. Kati broke out unexpectedly on her bitterness. She wasn't satisfied with her life, she was fed up with the role her situation and family forced on her, and what they expected of her. She was sick and tired of meaninglessly drifting from one ball to the next, from one cocktail party to another; she'd had it with the petty intrigues, the gossip, the light, superficial flirtations, the same conversations time and again, the incessant pursuit of pleasure, the late night parties. And she envied his work, his career, the fact that he had an aim in life and even a scholarship. She wore a two-piece orange bathing suit. With her tiny waist, very long arms and legs, she represented the ideal woman of the century. On her tanned skin he could spot some scattered, sun-bleached hairs. She lay relaxed in the grass by his side, her eyes closed. All he had to do was reach out. But he didn't even kiss her. He merely squeezed her hand once, and Kati squeezed his in return.

For a couple of days after this, he seriously considered calling off his trip. Once he even called the girl. Had she been at home then, perhaps everything would have turned out differently. As it was, though, he got caught up in a whirl of last-minute errands, visas, offices, school applications. He was living in a rarefied atmosphere. The decision would have had too many consequences. In the end, he didn't even say goodbye.

He discovered many more new faces in the dimly-lit church. Ubul Brenner, sweet, wise Ubul, once the manager of a great estate and lord of half county, today a translator of scientific literature, in five languages, both ways. Miska Gyulafy, stepbrother to the deceased, the "crazy Gyulafy" to the other's "clever Gyulafy", who wanted to prove that the Magyars had originated in Australia, and who danced the Lambeth walk with so much energy. That was the dance in which you had to stop from time to time and jerk your thumb behind your head. Kocsárd Barcza, the "red count", who divided his two-thousand-acre estate in Szabolcs County among his reluctant peasants in the autumn of '44, months before the land reform came into effect. But he landed in jail anyway. And Baron Gorlitz Pasha in a loden coat, Tyrolese hat in hand. Christ, is he still among the living? He must be past ninety-five! His wife, the notorious Baroness Gorlitz, ran an illegal gambling club and house of ill repute. She had paid everyone off, the city council, the police, even the electric company, so that they wouldn't remove the old-fashioned, flickering gaslamps from that part of Bajza Street, to guarantee the visitors some measure of anonymity. And Uncle Ivan, unable to get a divorce, became a Mohammedan so he could marry his masseuse... And many, many others, acquaintances whose identity was now lost to him, and total strangers as well. Who were they, and where had they come from?

When the bell tolled during transubstantiation, the entire row knelt down, except the physician and Kati Kerecsényi at the far end of the bench. Had she seen him? Did she remember him and that outing of thirty years ago? In some way he now felt it important, symbolic, that only they were standing, in this, too, differentiated from the others. A hot surge of emotion gripped him, and he fell in love with her all over again. He had left Kati, or at any rate let her go. They had exchanged a few letters, some rather explicit, but later, in more chaotic times, even this became impossible. And then he found Helga in Switzerland, and Kati met Pubi, that toothpaste-ad windbag. The war handed them a one-way ticket.

Maybe he should have stayed after all? Was that it?... The wounding question, like a dagger pointing at his heart, flashed like a threat through his mind. Although the three years with Helga were unforgettable, could they have been merely a sidetracking, a step in the wrong direction? The dear, frail creature who grew up in rarer air had perished here, in this dense atmosphere; the cause of her illness was never satisfactorily diagnosed. Could that have killed her? But then he was to blame, too, perhaps that was why he lacked sufficient strength to keep her? And Kati... Was this what she deserved? Should he have burst into her life? Rescued her from idleness, grabbed her hand when he had the chance, instead of driving her into the arms of that clown? It was his fault, too, he alone had been in a position to lift her out of her rut.

But maybe he himself was loser number one. He felt a wild bitterness, a choking pain with no relief in sight. Was that the original sin, the fact he left, and did not share the common fate? It was undoubtedly an advantage at the time when the war swept over Hungary; in those two years lightning would have struck around him too, and who was to guarantee that one flash would not have struck him? He sat in Zurich in comfort and security, and it was an advantage in a narrower, professional sense as well, from the point of view of his career as a doctor. But from a wider perspective, if you consider life as a whole, it was a horrible disadvantage, an irrevocable error. That was why he could not really understand things here, why he had always been a stranger, an outsider. He had never gone through the rite of passage! Can a person escape, desert the ones he loves in the time of danger, then dance back in after the storm?

But these *ancien-régime* waxworks, *ci-devant* remnants, archaeological finds and antediluvian fossils, these otherworldly spirit-bodies, he might laugh at them, but they had stayed at home then, and had never left. They all had a chance to slip out, sooner or later, to some country where they could have turned their past and rank to advantage, or where at least these things would not have been a liability to them. Yet they accepted being slighted, persecuted, humiliated, stripped of their wealth, even imprisoned in internment camps and gaol. They accepted everything with true *noblesse oblige* and dignity. They handed over their entailed estates with less reluctance than a fishwife her stand at the market. And though no one bothered them any more, history had broken them in body and spirit, time had laid waste these genuflecting wrecks who would never again straighten themselves, and who probably knew very well that they could expect no recompense... And even if it was fruitless, senseless and of little significance, he too must accept them, yes, fallen as they were, these absolute losers, since he had basked once, however slightly, in the light of their brilliance. After all, their former greatness still discovered itself from time to time in their erect posture and soft voices, in the way they carried their heads, in their handshakes, their glances—a last ray of light from the Eden of their youth.

The tolling and chiming and clinking of bells. Flaming candles cast fantastic shadows on the Gothic arches and pillars. The lamps were transformed into colourful Chinese lanterns, the mournful organ music became a waltz, the hard stone slabs of the flooring melted into parquetry. Servants came and went with soft drinks and champagne on trays, dancing couples floated out of the Béla Chapel. Everyone was bright, young, beautiful, wearing gorgeous clothes, the ladies and gentlemen both bejewelled. Dressed in a flaming red jacket lined with ermine, tight-fitting light blue trousers and soft leather boots and looking just like the time he was photographed on the balcony of the Alexander Palace with the other ministers whenever a new cabinet was formed, Uncle Berci was watching the crowd with pleasure and an amused smile. Ma Orsi stood beside him in seagreen velvet from cap to toe, with a train and diamond diadem. Ubul Brenner in tails came up the aisle with his snow-white bride, under the drawn swords of his fencing comrades. He wore a tuxedo and a white carnation in his lapel. Guszti Huszár of Ladány's long, pointed moustache and Tartar eyes shone black: in a décolletée turquoise ball gown, Lula floated past flirtatiously on the arms of deputy police commissioner Korbuly-Mersich, dressed in a black Magyar jacket. The music turned into a din. With arms outstretched, Trudi Jacobi was doing the Charleston for her own entertainment, Minci with her blonde hair gently pressed against her partner as they danced the tango. In his ceremonial national jacket, Zaladár Etelaki was doing a fast Csárdás, which he accompanied with frequent yodelling. Miska Gyulafy danced the Lambeth walk and jerked his thumb behind his ears. Tibor Teleki was doing the foxtrot in his air force lieutenant's uniform, while Pubi Lippai Kreis, in a dinner jacket, was gliding through the English waltz with Kati Kerecsényi... He came up to them, bowed and asked Kati to dance. The girl nodded, freed herself from her beau's arms and turned to him. They began slowly, feeling each other's rhythm and tempo. Kati wore a strapless orange tulle gown, her long hair flowing free, her arms and shoulders bare. She was light as air: he could barely feel her weight beneath his palm, only the warmth of her skin. Without words they danced past the others, towards the stained-glass window; there, he squeezed Kati's hand, she smiled at him, squeezed his hand in turn, they swam through the glass and out over the Fisherman's Bastion standing silent in the crossfire of spotlights, over the dark, icy Danube, past the Parliament, towards the throbbing city sprawled out below in the cold glitter of the night.

Translated by J. E. Sollosy

TIME PRESENT

The Turned-up Collar
BY GÉZA BEREMÉNYI

It was glorious weather—the October sun shone with a brilliance that brought the summer to mind. And Magda Szukics was not allowed to go to school. Shutters closed against the heat, she had spent the summer vacation in bed with a persistent myocarditis. She had hoped to get well before the autumn term began. Her parents had enrolled her in a model secondary school and had urged her to put up a better show in the future. But her illness prevented her from attending the opening ceremony, and schoolday after schoolday passed until her unknown schoolmates had got so far ahead of her in the curriculum that by October it looked as though she would have to repeat the year. She found the continual, compulsory state of repose difficult to endure. Books covered her blanket; she would begin to read one only to discard it to start another somewhere in the middle. At the time she had fallen ill she had had a dream that continued from one night to the next, but later the dream became jumbled as well. She had no visitors; the fresh linen on her bed every week was the only change in her life. She got well suddenly, when everyone thought she had fallen behind for good.

Still she went bravely to school. Into her bag, following the timetable set for the day, she placed exercise-books with blank pages, textbooks that had never been opened and a ruler for the new, unfamiliar subject, technical drawing, the last two classes on that Monday morning, given by a teacher she imagined would be strict, Dezső Villányi by name. The sun was shining brightly on the other side of the door. Magda Szukics was happy to walk the few steps to the tram stop, happy to be wearing sandals and nothing but her panties under her blue school smock. On the crowded tram only the noisy groups of bluesmocked and capped pupils could catch and hold her attention. She tried to guess which of them would be her future classmates.

Pintér recollected seeing Magda Szukics in the classroom for the first time, but his memory was playing him false. Though it hadn't been more than a glance that had passed between them, their first meeting had taken place on the staircase of the school at the time the first bell had sounded. Pintér was talking to a fourth-form senior and had his back to the new girl who was just arriving. The sunshine, the jostling crowd of pupils at the school entrance and the unexpected semi-darkness that had met her as she went in, a gloom that only cleared on the mezzanine, where the dazzling light streaming in from the large window transformed the shuffling pupils into mirage-like apparitions, had made her dizzy, so she stopped on the first landing, flattening herself against the wall to let the jostling, rowdy crowd pass.

When she looked up she saw a tall, good-looking boy, elbows resting on the banisters, who stood among milling blue shoulders and uniform caps. Many girls would have found him handsome; Magda Szukics did not. But it was good just to watch him standing there, halfway up the staircase, facing her and looking upwards. He was speaking to someone—nodding his head at another boy who stood a couple of steps further down on the stairs. The handsome one was so engrossed in the conversation that he would not have noticed the new girl for anything on earth—not even if she had begun to walk up the stairs and pushed him as she passed. Magda Szukics was curious to see the other boy—what could he have in him to fascinate such a good-looker to the extent that he doesn't even notice a girl nearby? Then suddenly the crowd was gone, a few late-comers ran up, taking two stairs at a time, and with them the clamour receded into the distance. Only the new girl remained on the landing, and the two talking by the banister.

The other boy stood with his back to Magda Szukics, speaking to his handsome friend with his chin raised. His shiny brown trouser-legs stirred restlessly. The collar of his short blue smock was turned up. What a stuck-up thing to do! Can't he think of something better? The two boys laughed, the handsome one facing her doubled up for a minute, the other threw his head back. The first bell went. Its last echoes had died away but still Magda Szukics did not stir. The two boys stayed. The one with his back to her had schoolbag under his arm. A long ruler stuck up out of it, pointing straight at Magda Szukics. The new girl made to move. Just then the one with the turned-up collar changed position and the ruler continued to point at her. And she had a ruler too. A shorter one, one that fitted easily into her bag. And according to her timetable her class would have two hours of technical drawing last thing that day.

At last Magda Szukics started up the stairs, she passed slowly by the still-laughing Pintér with the turned-up collar, who did not see the new girl look at his face. Just glance at it for a minute. Then hurry on up the stairs, her bag pressed tightly to her breast, scuttle along the corridor to find shelter in the new classroom.

Pintér continued his conversation with Pierre, the tall fourth-former, until the second bell went. He knew that

Miss Lovas, who took the first class that morning, was always a few minutes late. He and Pierre had a last laugh together, took leave of each other as the last bell went. By the time he reached the classroom Magda Szukics had already asked someone which seat was vacant in the girls' row, had sat down and introduced herself to her neighbour. When Pintér with his turned-up collar burst into the classroom the new girl took another good look at him and thought that she couldn't really like him as much as she thought she did. She only wanted to see his eyes and to know when he would notice and look back?

Miss Lovas came into the classroom, the monitor brought the class to attention, the pupils stood up from their desks. The white-smocked, spectacled schoolmistress glanced around the room as she listened to the monitor's report. Her experienced eyes rested for a moment on the new girl, then passed on quickly so that no one should notice her thinking. Oh dear, oh dear, she's not going to be easy, that one. Wonder where they found her?

The homework that had been set for the day was a poem by Petőfi.

Everywhere in the school monitors were making their reports. Whistles shrilled in the gym, balls thundered across the floor. The fourth-form corridor prefects were the only ones allowed to remain outside their classrooms. They bawled at the late juniors scurrying along the corridors, checked the toilets to make sure they were all empty, the stamp of their running feet resounded down the echoing corridors; one of them gave a last loud whoop and at last they too disappeared. The corridor-prefects wore blue arm-bands with a big P embroidered on them in red wool by the female members of the parent-teacher association.

Pintér's school was silent. Until the next break. The old building was founded upon tradition, but its weatherbeaten walls had consented to admit the achievements of many new eras. It housed a primary and a secondary school, a consequence of its ample size being that inexperienced children of primary-school age would lose their way from time to time in the labyrinths of its corridors. Which was why the prefects always had a last check after the third and final bell had gone.

At the end of the day the school would release its pupils. In the afternoons there was extra physical education for those who wanted it in the basement gym; study circles were held in the laboratories. The feeble glow of lightbulbs in the corridors would mean parent-staff meetings were taking place in some of the classrooms. Every now and then a dancing class or class party would break the sound of silence with the faraway tinkle of a piano or the loud blare of a tape-recorder. But finally all would be silent and dark in the building once more.

So its days passed.

When morning broke the sunlight would form pools upon the green oil paint of the walls and benches and would settle on the pictures nailed to the walls. Their mute, infinite ranks covered every possible inch of surface. Pictures, each in its uniform brown frame made of plain laths, each under its sheet of glass, all the result of decades of afternoons spent in the woodwork circle. The roving eye would light upon them everywhere in the building. Over the years they had completely inundated the school, becoming so congested in places that the frames almost touched, forming a jumbled tableau; then thinning out again the line would continue, slowing down unexpectedly only when some larger, broader specimen broke the uninterrupted flow that continued around the corners, into niches and hollows, into the darkest nooks; its labyrinthine course mapped out the whole school from the coal-cellar door to the attic. There they hung, as if conscious of the inconsistency, the disregard of chronology and values which had determined their position in the procession-pictures of great moments in Hungarian history, portraits of prominent figures who had distinguished themselves during those moments, portraits of the great examples, cheek by jowl with characteristic paintings from each of the representatives of Hungarian and foreign schools of painting. In a plain brown frame hung Ladislas the Fourth of Hungary on horseback, tending his hand to Rudolph from the House of Habsburg, to whose aid he had gone, celebrating the victory of Marsch Plain; a couple of turns of the corridor and there were the Hungarians again, but the revolting Kuruts armies this time, cutting down Habsburg soldiers in their three-cornered hats, harrying the army that had become strong enough over the centuries to attack those who had once come to its rescue; all this taking place soon after the battles along the frontiers with the Turks, which were represented, in addition to a few paintings in oil depicting the courageous defenders of fortresses in action, by the portrait of the great poet, Bálint Balassi, carrying within himself the contradictions of his age mirrored in his work, to be found somewhere on the second floor, next door to pictures of international revolutionaries. Soviet soldiers waving their weapons in greeting from their tanks, and the crowd greeting them hats off and kerchiefs in the air, which hung facing the photograph of the marble bust of the enlightened philosopher, Voltaire, renowned for his vitriolic pen, followed by a reproduction of the Impressionist masterpiece entitled 'Picnic in May' and a drawing of Attila József, poet of the proletariat, in ink. But in the company of those who sought and found the way out, of those who sang in praise, those who followed and those who were steadfast, a place was found for those who made vain attempts to remain uncommitted and sought refuge in the ivory tower of *l'art pour l'art;* a place was found for the vanguard, for those forced to recognize the contra-indications of ages long become a lesson for today, for those who pointed them out, at them and beyond them, for those who, all in all, in spite of their class limitations, had been progressive in their fashion, who had passed beyond the boundaries of their class prejudices, who had portrayed the complexity of the long-forgotten conditions and tragic problems of their age, problems only resolved by the present—a place was found for the geniuses who, with lasting validity, because with visionary force; the ages which had carried the germs of, the prophets who had interpreted it in their way, and the revolutionaries who had recognized it and created it in spite of transitional regression—a place was found for all of them. Some of the pictures depicted typical scenes from critical moments of history, periods when the course of development was only recognizable with great effort, when ideals were glowing embers under smothering ashes, glowing only in the best minds of the people. The geniuses represented on the walls desired the collaboration of the progressive forces, the standardbearers reached their hands toward the oppressed, and were replaced by others when they preferred death to compromise. The pupils of the school often referred to these paragons when questioned, but seemed to forget them at break, when they would repeat one name, and one name only: Pierre, Pierre.

"Have you seen Pierre?" Pintér heard the arm-banded corridor-prefects shout to each other above the racket produced by the juniors as they ran by them.

"Do you really think Pierre's all there, do you?"

"Do you know what Pierre's gone and done again?"

"Is Pierre going out with Kati or has he still got that platinum blonde bird of his?"

Pintér heard the name repeatedly from the fourth-formers at breaktime. Their classrooms were on the top floor; it was from there that the loud-voiced big boys came down when the bell went for break, to watch over the juniors. They walked in pairs, talking to each other with voices raised against the uproar. When they lost patience they rolled up their soft-bound textbooks and hit the nearest boisterous youngster within striking distance on the head. "Steady on, kid!" Then they continued to stroll down the corridor, because they thought it more important to discuss Pierre's latest doings. From the snatches of conversation overheard by accident Pintér spun an elaboratore web of fancy around the figure of Pierre.

The first-formers discussed him too during breaks in the toilets where they retreated to smoke. Most often it was little Körmendi who began; he liked to draw, and made no secret of it, boasted of it even, and so had been christened Cocky. Cocky Körmendi thought Pierre was like the hero of a penny dreadful; he said Pierre had once bent a coin in two with his thumb and forefinger under the nose of a grey, defeated teacher nicknamed Ficere and had promised to do the same thing to him if he dared plough him at the end of the year. The old, grey-haired teacher has been trembling with fear ever since, as anyone could see for himself—you'd only got to watch him walk down the corridor in his brown smock, staring straight in front of him, his head trembling like a leaf. According to Cocky, Pierre planned to join the Foreign Legion; he spent half the night running in the park so as to be in form for marching in the desert. He played in a band, his father was in prison and his mother was persecuted because of her origins, they had their ancestral estates taken away from them. Cocky Körmendi would take Pintér to visit them one of these days, but first he had to ask Pierre because he was a bit suspicious of strangers. He'd got his reasons for it though. He'd had some trouble with the cops. "Hey Pintér, you really don't know which is Pierre? He just went by. Weird you didn't see him, he even said hello to me. Didn't you notice? If I don't feel like coming to school he always gets me a medical certificate. He's got this doctor girl-friend. She's great!"

Pintér stared at all the prefects during breaks. Perhaps that one in glasses was Pierre. He'd got a deep voice and he was really strong. But he wore glasses. That one there was too fat, he was disgusting. He picked one of them out at long last, a blond one that the girls in his class, by a quick vote, had found the most attractive. Pintér, after he had named him Pierre to himself, followed him everywhere at break. He eavesdropped on his conversations, meditating over the way his companions treated him. But he soon lost interest. Finally he watched his candidate greet Rajnák, the deputy head, and heard Rajnák's reply. After that he wasn't surprised when he saw another fourth-former give his chosen one a friendly thump on the back and say cheerfully: "Don't piss in your pants, man, Pierre's not mad at you. He was just having a bit of fun, you know how he is when the mood takes him."

Pintér took extra gym with Cocky Körmendi. One day they arranged to meet on November 7th Square. Dusk had settled in early that day, the streetlamps were lit and it was raining, not heavily, but in a steady, disagreeable drizzle. Pintér waited for Cocky at the top of the steps leading to the underground station. He wore a leather coat that was much too big for him, and his uniform cap. For a while he banged his gym bag against some railings which sent up clouds of steam into the cold, heavy air. It was the rush-hour, and it seemed as though the traffic jam on the square could not get any worse; as though all the cars in Budapest had converged here on the gleaming wet asphalt to obey the signals flashed at them by the traffic lights. Herds of cars zoomed thundering at the first blink of green, impatiently sounding their horns, spattering the brightly lit trams with mud as they overtook them. Because of the weather Pintér wasn't in the mood to cavort about in the gym, but for some reason the gym teacher was not overfond of him and his good will, said Pintér's mother, must at all costs be won, through paying the fees for the extra gym course and through showing a lot of enthusiasm for the subject.

Cocky Körmendi was late and Pintér, bored stiff, began to examine the photographs displayed in the photographer's window beside him. The simpering children and the smiling women dominated even here by the stern, manly faces of fathers and fiancés' sporting moustaches and clenching pipes, failed to hold his attention for long. He turned instead toward the crowd waiting to cross the street in order to appraise those coming towards him, one by one. The biggest crowd of people the day had seen so far surged across the street in the rain; there was nothing in their faces or their clothes to catch the eye. The crowd flowed around Pintér, brushed by him or jostled against him and he stood in the midst of them, their words an incoherent babble in his ears. By the time the traffic lights had turned yellow they were all on the pavement. On the gleaming, empty asphalt only the cars waited, legitimately impatient, headlights flaring, ready to spring.

And this was the moment that a solitary, perturbing figure chose to cross the street. As he stepped off the kerb the lights turned red for him and justly green for the cars, but that did not bother him at all. He walked sedately, at a leisurely pace, oblivious of the shouting around him; even stopped in the middle of the road, in the glare of headlights, turned to face one of the files of cars and spread his arms wide, stopping them all. "The public is warned," he shouted, but the rest of his words were lost in the din of cars whipping past him. And he punished them for ignoring him, bringing his palms down on their tops with a bang; afraid of a collision, they could take no revenge, and sped on, seething. The other files of cars could not move for the figure with the outstretched arms; people jumped out of the first car, tugged at the jaywalker, almost pushed him under the cars passing on the other side of the square.

We know now that this was Pintér's first meeting with Preston. He could not take his eyes off him; he was drawn to the edge of the kerb, gym bag swinging from his hand, to watch him being dragged off the asphalt. And as one is wont quite arbitrarily to fix a name to a character in one's dreams, regardless of whether the apparition bears any resemblance to the bearer of that name in real life or not, so Pintér was certain that the conspicuous figure in the square could only be Pierre. We know that the delusion lasted a few days only, but it was a characteristic mistake, as characteristic as Preston's behaviour.

After having forced a file of cars to wait for the next green light, and after the rest of the cars had moved on, Preston shook himself free of his pursuers and walked straight towards Pintér. From behind and beside Pintér pedestrians moved forward because the lights had changed again. Preston knew his way around; he too recognized his man in the crowd. He took one look at the boy in the school cap and stopped in front of him. He was tall and dripping wet, only his usual dark blue jacket covered his bare chest. Pintér would have been shaking with cold in his place. They did not say a word to each other. Preston performed one of his characteristic gestures, one with which we were all familiar: he extended his arms and placed the edges of his palms together, which meant "give", or, rather, "give if you want", staring all the while with the unblinking eyes of a priest celebrating mass into the eyes of the honoured chosen one—honoured since he did not ask just anybody and always in good cause. A lot of our money wandered into his pockets this way.

Pintér thrust his hands into his pockets. He had four forints put by to go to the movies. He took out the two coins, discoloured with age, and placed them into Preston's extended palm. Then, suddenly remembering, he silently lifted a forefinger for Preston to be patient. He had a silver five-forint piece in the pocket of his trousers, a rare treasure at the time. He held it up, then dropped it on top of the others.

Preston recognized the distinction between the two gifts. He slipped the two-forint pieces into the pocket of his jacket, then took the silver coin and placed it slowly, ceremoniously into his breast pocket, smoothing the material covering the coin twice to emphasize that it would there be held in esteem. It was a practical trifle—or a solemn promise, hand to breast. Pintér could decide as he wished. With a nod of the head Pintér agreed to join the disciples. In answer Preston performed the rites of initiation before moving on. He really knew how to go about it. As they stood in the square, soaked through, he took hold of the boy's collar and in the tumult that surrounded them gave a shake to the jacket, as if adjusting it. Then he turned up the collar and walked away. A thousand duties awaited him.

Pintér watched him walk away and believed he had met Pierre. He made a note of the light duck trousers and the blue Czechoslovak tennis shoes. At the time Preston did not care for ties and winkle-picker shoes. For practical reasons perhaps? The main thing was that his clothing should be original. We couldn't say a word, he'd invented himself.

For years afterwards Pintér always wore his collar turned up. His teachers often warned him that he would have to leave the class if he persisted in wearing his collar pointed toward the sky; after all, it rarely rains in classrooms. Pintér always took heed of the warning but as soon as the bell went for break, up went his collar again. He wore his coats the same way.

"If that was Pierre you saw then I'm Pierre too. It couldn't have been Pierre on November 7th Square because Pierre was at the seniors' party, OK? He couldn't be anywhere else, there was a bird he's after, at the party. You really don't know where it's at, do you?" Cocky Körmendi underwent an extraordinary transformation every time he spoke of Pierre. As soon as he had uttered the name his whole body began to shake, he humped up his shoulders, his head turned this way and that, and his voice became throaty, guttural, as if he were singing a pop song with a maddening rhythm. He wanted to express a singular feeling, enchantment, enthusiasm, and idealized passion that must be devoutly protected from the whole world. While he was speaking the conductor asked to see his ticket, and Cocky Körmendi, because he was speaking about Pierre, thrust it at him with a recklessly insolent gesture, although he was normally a bashful boy. He even began an impudent dispute with the conductor. "Who asked you, anyway?", just to be true to his chosen ideal. Pierre gave him courage and strength. Occasionally, he delivered Cocky from the glazed look he acquired during class, rid him of his odd grimaces and changing moods, gave him a secret language, a pledged, private code; incited him to make provocative, witty rejoinders. With Pierre's help the fat, bespectacled Cocky Körmendi was able to ignore the gibes and sneers of his classmates, the lectures of his parents; was brave enough to face any conductor on any tram. And this help he tried to requit by measuring up to those exalted feelings which he could express when dreaming of Pierre. His body shook and his voice became throaty even when he was muttering to himself—and not only in front of the mirror. He used the role bestowed upon him with growing confidence, as if within himself; woke with it more and more often in the morning, began to consider it his own, his true self, made it his only pride and joy. He was faithful and unexpectedly conscientious. Pintér jealously watched him tackling the bad-tempered conductor, unperturbed by the interjections of the rest of the passengers, calling him a hysterical, wretched old fool, and knocking his hand away so adroitly that he even escaped a slap on the face. He grudged Cocky Körmendi his Pierre.

The rain did not seem to want to stop. It was still pouring heavily when they came out after gym. Pintér turned up the collar of his leather jacket and mumbled something about a girl he was to meet, in order to get rid of Cocky. He walked a couple of steps in the opposite direction and when Cocky had disappeared around the corner ventured back into the darkened building.

In the school only the landing lights had been switched on, illuminating the first few pictures of the endless procession aligning the walls; the battle-scenes that had made history, the geniuses and other illustrious figures of the curriculum were lost in shadow. Pintér took the stairs one by one, sliding his hand along the banisters as he walked. From around the region of the first floor he heard music and the growing sound of voices singing, the sharp notes of a guitar and somebody screeching. The darkness deepened as he neared the source of the sound. He swung his gym bag in rhythm to the music. The seniors' party was on the third floor, where the lights had been switched off even on the landing and the sound of singing became dangerously loud. An only-just male voice was belting out a song in English in an incoherent falsetto with delightful shamelessness, as though he were crying and did not deem it necessary to control himself, as though, lost to the world, he were celebrating his sorrow, demanding, in an exorbitant desire for immediate satisfaction, more and more from the feeling of anguish, because it was his and his only, because it was a pleasure to lose himself in it, a true experience, an adventure, an adventure that raises one above duty and obligation and achievement and constraint and inexorability and goals and aims to be transfigured, realized, to bloom henceforth only for oneself; to disintegrate and let one's desires wash over one, to celebrate that one is liberated from law and order and their standards, to experience with one's body that one is at last left alone with one's sensual needs. Pintér proceeded into the cavernous depths of the top floor corridor, and when he could no longer see a foot ahead and felt he could not stand the smallest increase in the volume of sound he stopped and leaned against the wall. He stayed there for an incalculable length of time.

The first thing he could distinguish was a green eye. The only source of light was the tiny lamp of the tape-recorder, shining, as it turned out, from within a classroom which had the double door wide open. The desks had been carried out and in their places the white shirts of the final year boys swirled, closely embracing the blouses of the girls who had been invited. The song ended, the bright pieces of clothing stopped and waited for the next song to begin. Then from very near Pintér heard a girl's voice whisper "Pierre!". The voice came from a window recess close by and was at once full of fear, curiosity, reserve and admiration. Pierre must have done something which she was not expecting but would now have to accept reverently. Then she began to pant, and moan a little, softly, but loud enough to be heard above the new English number blared out by the tape-recorder. You could clearly hear her whisper, breathless, full of wonder, "Pierre!". The third time she cried the name out loud. But Pintér strained his ears in vain for the slightest sound that would attest to Pierre's presence; he did not betray himself with a single word. Whatever he was doing he did silently and mercilessly. He was playing with her as one played on an instrument; he wanted to coax his name out of her and that was all.

Pintér drew one of his three cigarettes out of his pocket and lit it. He felt capable of everything. He thought the gesture with which he had struck the match and flicked it away into the darkness had been grand. In a flash, like the sudden flare of the match, it came to him that soon, any moment now he too could arouse the admiration of someone; he too would hold a girl close, feel her body and make his own felt, would find someone to his taste at last, one of those from in there. Soon, any moment now. He was sure, there on the dark corridor, leaning back against the wall again after his last puff while a singer inside, much taken with himself, sang in English, that faceless somebodies had already formed a line, were preparing themselves for an unparalleled, unprecedented meeting with him, and the discoveries soon to be made awakened a feeling of superiority in him. He felt strong and was excited. How will it happen to him? He did not try to guess because it was the uncertainty, the feeling of risk that gave the most pleasure. That they would present themselves incalculably at last, through a superb freak of fortune, and the choice will not be made for him. Not even by him. He will simply be set free.

"I'll be off soon," thought Pintér after the last puff before he threw the butt into the darkness. Then he pushed himself away from the wall, and strolled slowly to the end of the corridor, away from the blare of the tape-recorder and the girl who was still repeating that name.

Translated by Eszter Molnár

Ólmosi-Bleier's Last Work

BY ENDRE VÉSZI

The telephone rang unexpectedly in the sculptor's drapery-darkened, cavernous studio which took up the better part of the dilapidated flat. A rare event of late. Ólmosi-Bleier, going on for seventy-five, sat in the light of a standard lamp with a finely pleated silk shade, sharing the seat of his armchair with his red tabby called Ipsilon, whose fur had black stripes like wire running across it. Although he was still going strong, tall and agile, his heart was as much overgrown with suspicion as a ball of earth just lifted from its pot by thin rootlets. He had not put out a new work for the past twenty-five years: in fact, back in 1958 he had offered the stuff of his early, Cubist and subsequently popular-surrealist period—the works of his prime as he described them—in the hope of a large retrospective, but it was, albeit regretfully, turned down in the spirit of the then current and seasonable campaign against modernism. As soon as he could retire from the Academy on a pension—that was nearly fifteen years ago—he did so in due form. He harboured no resentment in his heart; favourite former pupils of his, connoisseurs of his work, paid him occasional visits, perhaps not so much to encourage him to work as out of gratitude for what he'd done to save them from exclusion and disgrace in those difficult years. He had no battle with phantom enemies; he lived in apparent tranquillity, and though from time to time, he was invited to take part in competitions, these were tasks he declined to accept. But neither his native irony nor his sense of humour had run dry, both of which qualities, he said, exercised one's humanity. He let the telephone ring now for a while with a sense of malicious joy, as if to say, let it have its fill of buzzing and let's see which of us can stand it longer. In the end, however, it was he who gave in. Senescence is not the domain of patience. Dropping the cat Ipsilon down with a soft thud and holding his silver-dipped head high he shuffled to the telephone in a frayed terrycloth bathrobe which could have been the gown of a banished prince or of a high priest of a banned sect. An old man's voice worn thin came from the receiver, the slack vocal bands occasionally giving a falsely high resonance, but in spite of this the speaker's words sounded euphoric. "Have you also had the info, Tibor? We're going to be made an exhibition of, I understand, in the museum in D. The Fifties. Again those wretched Fifties." Ólmosi-Bleier, identifying his interlocutor's voice, felt his breathing quicken, and because he was slightly hard of hearing, something which he rather ostentatiously made no secret of, got the last sentence repeated. "Look, Tibor, please, the thing concerns a lot of us. There ought to be a protest made, and since you're the most respectable of all of us, I suggest you go and raise a stink." Should he undertake to be their spokesman? Is that what this humbug is trying to talk him into? This tightrope dancer of the old *Roman School*, who strolled from the hallowed sphere of blatantly jingoistic abominations of memorials, scarcely making a change in some, right over into socialism? Without making the slightest effort to restrain himself he shouted back: "Don't you use the first person plural. I'll have nothing to do with it. And I'll protest neither on your behalf nor on my own. Whatever's put out on my account, I won't disclaim, but I will disown. And I'm prepared to pay for it on my own terms and in my own way." The man at the other end of the line whimpered and whined trying to stem the spate of his words. "Why are you speaking to me like this? Because I half trusted them, half feared them? Or because that damned summer cottage at Mátraháza was inflicted on me at the time as a gift from the nation? It was about to collapse even then and repairing the bloody ruins is making me bankrupt. No, Tibor, really, you're not fair. You've become a misanthrope. And just in case you haven't noticed I've gone non-figurative since 1956. I'm internationally acknowledged." "Then may I just beg you to go to your own non-figurative hell. And do me a favour and get off the line and out of my life at the same time." Following the prompt click he rested his hand on the receiver for a while. His rage oozed away until he almost began to feel sorry for being so rude to the miserable sod. Who by the way wasn't one of the worst. He drew a corner of the thick curtain aside; the cat, used to the half-light of the interior, noticed at once with his restless, jewel-sparkling eyes the patch of sunlight falling on the carpet; his exquisite body tautened in excited attention and he pounced on it with the swiftness of a beast of prey.

*

The stringy art historian, bespectacled and with the air of an undergraduate, after knocking for so long that she thought it hadn't been worth the effort, finally found herself within the open door. Outside, in the expanse of the uncovered yard, fluffy flakes of spring snow were whirling. She brought in the melted sparkling drops on her thick rust-coloured suit, adorned with an imitation fur collar, and on her boyishly cut dark blond hair. "Who do I have the honour of welcoming? And what have you come about?" inquired the sculptor, almost on the offensive, but since he was rather weak of hearing and could hardly make out anything of her shy murmured introduction, he waved his hand and asked her to step inside. "Oh, I don't think I should carry all this slush into your place, maestro," the fragile woman demurred. "Excuse me..." and with that she stepped out of her moon boots, standing there in her white knitted socks like a child. In the end she lowered herself on a swivelling piano stool in her embarrassment, sitting upright like some freshly-cut plant. No sooner done than she discovered that she's picked the most uncomfortable seat, which she realized was certain to interfere with her work, work that in any case didn't promise to be easy. She was not lacking in self-assertion—some of her friends went as far as to say she was very liable to hold forth—but it was with a certain misgiving that for weeks past she had anticipated this interview, or she preferred to call it, *séance*. The feature editor of the glossy picture magazine had sent her on this assignment to do an interview with the old sculptor who had withdrawn into complete silence decades ago. He had seen two eye-cathing topical features in it. One was that there really was going to be an exhibition of the products (o. k., call them 'creations') of "socreal" in the early summer, and the maestro, willynilly, would have to be included somewhere. The other was Ólmosi-Bleier himself, the petrified legend. And the splendour in the background: the Paris period. But he was reticent about *that,* too. In other words, adamant. But where exactly was the secret hidden? Anyone who was so deliberate in permitting oblivion to bury him was surely fascinating; the old chap had to be shocked out of his complacent hiding. "You know how to pick locks, Karola, and I do think you're the only person capable of getting that rusted lock working again." And Karola had a stratagem all right, a delayed-action explosive device. She would like to do her Ph. D. thesis, without the artist's knowledge, on Ólmosi-Bleier's Paris years. Sitting on her uncomfortable stool, rubbing her feet together, she unwittingly indicated that the studio wasn't exactly overheated. "May I offer you a cup of tea?" A once gallant host stirred in the sculptor, though he could hardly wait to see his visitor gone. "How do you like it? Strong or weak? I haven't got rum or lemon." He diluted the condensed tea with hot water and poured in into bluish transparent porcelain cups. He did all this with the sculptor's sureness of hand, but in the meantime he seemed to hear as if from a tape her words of introduction in the hallway. He shouldn't have let her in: she was a little snooper, a little newshound, a little—he didn't finish the thought. Ought to be thrown out right away. Though putting out a shivering skinny little thing like her? He would give her a quarter of an hour and then he would get rid of her somehow or other, and should she try to be awkward or pushy he would simply boot her out. And because he already had in his hand the smart blue enamelled English biscuit box decorated with pictures of London (SWEET ASSORTED BISCUITS, ELKES BISCUITS LTD, CARDIFF—ORMSKIRK), he had to reach it over to the apparently forever hungry, forever thirsty, forever shivering female, even though in place of the English biscuits there were now only a few pieces of ZAMAT and GYŐRI ÉDES LINZER products of the domestic confectionary industry. Karola's eyes roamed listlessly over the prettily tinted pictures of the tin box, over the glossy emerald, ash and cherry patches of Trafalgar Square against a background of presumably non-existent azure. She picked out a piece of "linzer" despite the fact that she hated it, and began to crunch it with the application of a mouse. The level of complaisance in the sculptor dropped step by step. "Well, what can I do for you, miss?" Karola, warmed by the hot tea, inhaling the aromatic vapours, had lost whatever determination she had felt before, and she'd been apprehensive of, that the interview was not going to be an easy one, was by now made even more difficult by the complications of conscience. She knew more than enough about this old man than to gatecrash as a breezy reporter into a secluded world which had been walled round for a quarter of a century. Her speech became desperately muddled, she offered apologies of every kind, protesting her goodwill and respect, saying, "But, maestro, you were doing the best stuff even in those days"; and the subject of the envisaged exhibition being raised, she went on, "this should not affect you very deeply since as far as I know it was only the Stromfeld portrait that was... er... and it's still... er..." Her pale clean-featured face flushed like an adolescent girl's. The false intimacy of the phrase "as far as I know" made her ashamed of herself, all the more as she could not help noticing the sculptor's growing agitation and his quickened breathing. "Look here, miss, I don't know you very well, and I have no idea of what you do and about what you call your ideology nor about your idols and counter-idols"—he risked a laugh, perhaps a bit too loud, in anticipation, but that could be attributed to his defective hearing—"nor do I know anything either about *the crimes you have perpetrated in the name of aesthetics.*" (The truth of the matter was that he *had* read one or two pieces by the little wench and he'd found himself, by and large, to be in rapport with them. Deny it how he would, he watched developments rather closely.) The young woman sat on the piano stool more stiffly than before, if that was possible, tight rather than frightened, and determined to escape as soon as opportunity offered. "Excuse me for my rudeness, I've become and old, alienated fuddy-duddy, a dodo, even. I didn't mean to hurt you, miss." The reply was more defiant than reconciliatory. "I didn't take offence at all. And as for what I said about interviewing you, I take it back. I admit I am not up to what I've undertaken. I'm gone twenty-six, but when it comes to making plans I'm still as hopelessly scatterbrained as a teenager." She fidgeted, scrambled to her feet, but the sculptor's big horny palm gently pressed her back. "The exhibition doesn't interest me in the least," he abruptly switched back to the subject and began to pace the room. The cat, till then constancy incarnate in his usual posture of sitting on his haunches and holding his motionless head erect, was suddenly caught by his master's agitation. He sprang up and padded softly after the sculptor, rubbing himself briefly against his legs. "What you're interested in, I gather, is the exhibition from *my* point of view; that's what is topical for the lot of you on the paper at the moment. More particularly *those* years." Ólmosi-Bleier paced up and down in the studio—just how many kilometres must be behind him? *Good Lord, I've survived my own death several times over and now this little woman is Posterity. It's better for me to try and interpret myself.* "To put it concretely, I suppose you want to hear about certain portraits. Those that are gathering dust in a cellar along with some of the works of my colleagues. And I also suppose you'd like to ask why I didn't put up any resistance, it was just a couple of years after all. Yes, looking back, it was really just a few years, miss." The cat lunged and leapt into an armchair; he mesmerised the girl with his eyes wide-open with full-blown hatred. "The present of a fanaticized and at the same time intimidated society seems an eternity to the majority. As for *those* portraits, the people who ordered them didn't stand behind me with a submachine-gun pointed at my ribs; no, I can't fall back on any such excuse—I'm not just an artist but a craftsman, a professional. Even though I must say that I was interested in those men in an ambivalent way, I wanted to see through them." He made a gesture of dismissal. "This is again aesthetic blah-blah, psychological salve. So, back to my sitters! A spherically modelled head, a smooth skull, a solid meaty face, flaccid flesh flowing round narrow-slitted eyes, a curving line cut out by a perpetual smile around the lips, whole composition rounded off by the chin. Could this have been the face of state power? Yes, it was—because it had something to say to me. There must have been something amiss with the curve of the smile—the jury didn't dare say it point blank, but somebody whispering into my ear hazarded a friendly opinion: the detail around the mouth is more sinister than jovially paternal, don't you think? There's no denying, the second personage exercised a hypnotic effect. Anyone who claims the contrary is lying. Excellent bone structure, a sharply chiselled, intellectual face, contemporary and mediaeval at once; thick, healthy, wavy hair, a perfect complement to the skull, a pair of spectacles glinting obliquely with the arc-light of laser-keen eyes which question, enquire, interpret, conclude, accuse, and change the finely ground translucent lenses into an instrument of torture. I speak as an expert on this: I'd very much regret it if his head had been melted down. I think even he liked his own demoniac character in the bust—a character that was so complex, combining uncompromising ruthlessness with understanding, something that as a sculptor I was able to sum up analytically, I think. The third one: grey upon grey upon grey, tired, intelligent; the wrinkles of the face and his vulture's eyes had hidden single-minded attention rather than hatred in them. He was the hardest to model because of the covert nature of his real character, his *everyday incognito*. If I had known then how many of his comrades he had sent to limbo as a political commissar in 1919, I think I should have discovered his dominant characteristic, the epitome of his ability: *death rationally organized.*"

Karola listened in silence to the sculptor's words and her childish fascination with empathy had redrawn the features of her oval face, framed by her boyish blond hair, white and shining as if powdered. "But that visage with its plastered down look, even the absence of wrinkles on the face, was cruel. The fourth one to be assigned to me to model, because of a merciful bout of flu and a high temperature, was eliminated from my series of sitters. People will say today that I had the courage to resist *him,* obviously through a conscious political choice. But I would never claim that courage. As likely as not it was my aesthetic revulsion upsetting my stomach, and hence the medically justifiable feverish condition." Karola's face broke into a smile, but even this diminished smile cost her a special effort. She gazed upon this bony old man, opening windows into his past, who could not reconcile himself with himself, and she experienced a kind of pain in her heart. "All this might strike you as funny, miss, but let me point out that this story has one flaw: when it is told these days it becomes completely *retrospective,* and with your leave, miss, I don't for a minute want to pose as an *antedated* hero in séances where some of the spirit-rappers are still some of the formerly enthusiastic zealots." Karola raised herself an inch off the stool, her powder-bleached face exhibiting eagerness. "Nobody says anything of the kind about you. Anyone who knows you respects and esteems you." Hard-as-bone gesture of dismissal. "Let's put it like this: *those who still remember me.*" "But your *authentic* works are still as valid as ever, I think. I do believe you ought to work." Once again the clumsiness of the comforting nurse. This time she caught herself in the act and went red to the roots of her hair. The sculptor suddenly stopped in his tracks. He spoke, but in a subdued voice: "Please spare me your goodness, will you." Karola's face changed back from crimson to the colour of whey. Ipsilon was quick to sense her excitement, and tuning in to it with his whole system, he landed in her lap in one well-aimed leap. The momentum of the landing body caused the girl to lose her balance and topple down onto the carpet below the piano stool. Behind the large mirrors of her spectacles the tears welled up. Ólmosi-Bleier struck the cat's head with his bony fist—this could only be accounted for by the agitated state of his nerves. Ipsilon, propelled by his own anger, bounded to the door and disappeared in the hallway. The young woman sat on the carpet with her white socked feet apart and her bedimmed spectacles. The raw bitterness of the sculptor, the painfully forced explanations about the forthcoming exhibition, the touch of the shimmering sleek fur of the cat nestling in her lap, then the brutal blow—all proved to be beyond what is called the limits of endurance. Ólmosi-Bleier helped her into an elegant rep-covered armchair and even adjusted the spectacles on the girl's nose in his shock and exertion. Now they could not go back to anything, the words having emptied themselves. The visitor had forgotten to withdraw her hand from the sculptor's large palm, then she pulled on her boots and left without saying a word. Ólmosi-Bleier—perhaps to cut himself off from the, yes, the *shock* that the visit had caused him—called Ipsilon immediately, pleading with him to appear, even using a propitiatory inflection in his voice that was not his custom, but the cat failed to present himself. Overtaxing his aching back he went on all fours and started to search the labyrinth of the flat, looking behind and under the studio couch, settee, ottoman, rocking-chair, the frames and stands and the heavy wings of draperies. Finally, the sight of the kitchen window aslant indicated the cat's route of exit in the swing of his acrobatic body and oversensitive heart.

*

Dear Karola, if I may call you so, I am obsessed with the idea of having to express my apologies to you in writing, but I do not feel even this form a proper atonement for the kind *(what kind?)* of insult I exposed you to and for having let all my bitterness come crashing down on your amiable and fragile being. I may have my reasons for doing so, but I had no right whatever to do it. I have to say that it'll soon be a quarter of a century that I've been living with this sense of bitterness, but up to now I've managed to keep it bottled up. *(Too literally, rephrase it.)* I feel myself under an obligation to you, and to you alone, to give an explanation. The purpose of my withdrawal, let's say, voluntary exile, was *not* to pull myself out of the world of my fellow men, commonly called society: I simply had to realize something that I'm telling you now, and nobody but you. *(What's the use of these repetitions?)* Many years ago when I had come to terms with the realities of the world, I started to work in almost complete illegality. It sounds idiotically romantic, but as it turned out is was a necessary measure of precaution. I wanted to return to the source of my youth, the world of my prime manhood. Back to where in the studios of Léger, Zatkin, Brancusi (I went to the lectures of Léger too) I first learnt about the meaning of art, the purpose of expression, the importance of the simultaneous presence of substance and sculptor. I wanted to return to the richest austerity: plastic art on the small scale, to the easily available substances of the richest austerity: that is, lead, zinc, aluminium, wood, and the more valuable chippings thrown away by tombstone stonemasons. I tried my hand at the chisel, the hammer and mallet, the plane, the welding-gun — my hand worked surely, and I felt in full possession of all my strength and powers. The creations of long and lonely months lined themselves up: the plummeting bird, the miner's hand reaching up from falling rock, the exquisite feet of Madame Bisse, Irene's clean forehead and Assyrian nose—in short, they convinced me of my successful comeback. This was some ten to fourteen years ago. I cannot describe the euphoria which took possession of me, the elation of a clandestine bomb thrower. *(On rereading he struck out these two sentences as too exhibitionist.)* I called up S., a former pupil of mine, a genius who had become a great painter, and who has been dead now for several years. I knew we still had something to say to each other, so I could count on his affection as well as his merciless rigour: his taste was bold, his outspokenness fearful and I knew he had kept his fingers crossed for me, desiring—now, how to put it?—let's stick to the pompous word—my resurrection. "You can come," I told him on the phone, that being agreed code phrase: there was something to show. "Right away," he shouted into the receiver; it was about midday, and before midnight he knocked me up. He didn't get me out of bed, I'd been at the ready since noon. He had a drop too much, as he had done at all times of day for the past few years, but that only made his judgement the more precise, the working of his brain the more target-oriented. He asked for a drink, naturally, knocked back two glasses of brandy, which helped him get hold of himself just as a surgeon gets ready for an operation on his way to the operating theatre. Forty-two statuettes of mine were waiting for him in the studio; he examined each of them slowly with his narrow Asian eyes, proceeding from piece to piece, now and then returning to one or another. Then he sat down on that piano stool you also know. He whirled around once as was his habit. "I'm going to say something nasty, Tibor," he began. It was his way to start off with a summary. "It's pretty good stuff, appealing, presentable and the snobs are certain to go wild about them and all that, and there's money to be got out of them too. But you're exactly *where you were before*. Donkey's years ago. You haven't made one inch of progress. Art has long since assimilated, stored up this stuff, and made history of it; let's add, majestic history. But innovation is something quite apart. I'm sorry, old boy, you're a bit like the fashionable moderns who think they've set the world on fire. Was I rude?" He had another two glasses and went his way. And after doing some soul-searching I melted down the zinc, the lead and the aluminium. I chopped up the wood and crushed the marble: Madame Bisse's exquisite feet.

The letter, which he wrote on a piece of old yellowed paper, Ólmosi-Bleier read over a few times; later he added a few parenthetical remarks to these already there, but in the end felt like an old man stood in a busy square, his naked body exposed. He had neither the strength nor any inclination to rewrite the letter, because in the meantime he had received the invitation to the exhibition. He tore the yellowed paper into shreds and threw it into the lavatory bowl.

*

The fact that he had written the letter and destroyed it was the conclusion and at the same time the beginning of something. What followed could be called in Biblical parlance the Week of Preparation. He went to a special shop and bought a paint spray can (ALBATROSS KG 127), he stirred the nitrate bronze paint very carefully and filled the can with it. He worked with a pleasurable anticipation. In the meantime there were quite a few calls from the people concerned, painters and sculptors of his age group, all of them former participants or 'accessories'; people buried in oblivion, and those who by renewing themselves had just managed to slip through into the present, more than that, had obliged themselves with an advance promise of the future. Crooks and honest men; zealots and dupes. Even an old lady, thin as a stick, with a trembling head of puff-ball hair, a widow you would call respectable, called on him and asked him to vindicate the integrity of her husband, who had died five years before, because she said *in those times those works,* such as *Rice Fields in the Sun, Comrade R. among the Apple-pickers,* etc., etc. had been important and creditable achievements. And she added that the later works of her late husband (still-lifes, amorous scenes in the folksy tradition) were still much sought after in America and Japan, where people had become disillusioned with all these impossible what-d'you-call-'ems, thoroughly fed up with modernism. Ólmosi-Bleier acknowledged all this with what is called a placid smile, with what seemed the calm of flagging down life functions. For instance, he proffered the contents of the English tin box twice and went so far as to ply her with bonbons as well. "The Fifties". He read again and again the title of the exhibition catalogue he'd cunningly laid his hands on in advance. Yes, inescapably: "The Fifties". And the opening address, inescapably again, would be delivered by Professor Gyula H. Kovács, yes, by who else, and how could it not be 'delivered' by the man than whom no one was better qualified, a Ph. D. in his own discipline, who had written *the* monograph of the past thirty years on the fine arts in a meticulously analytical chapter of which, entitled "The Personality Cult and Naturalism", he put in correct perspective that peculiar period which it was customary, not unjustly, to place between 1949 and 1957. Ólmosi–Bleier relished this thought gloatingly, as with the pleasure of someone crunching salted almonds, in the first-class carriage of a presumably *decelerated* train that fell grievously short of even the most modest parameters of public transport. Needless to say, he was bound for the inauguration of the exhibition in D. He was afraid that his arrival would be delayed because of the frequent stops, but he hoped nevertheless to arrive in good time, at least as far as his own business was concerned. Firing rockets at a rabbit ("THE FIFTIES")—he carried on a dialogue with himself—all right, so be it. He himself hated that rabbit which had been, in its time, a hyena to say the least. But that one who had beaten down everyone (currently a professor and Doctor of Art History), the implacable official of the former highest authority in matters artistic, the chief critic of reviews and dailies—that this man should now be attempting to blast to pieces what history had done anyway—well, there was something extraordinarily humorous in all this, enhanced by historical amnesia, apparently not to be dispensed with nowadays either. All right, he said to himself, if this be humour, let there be laughter, too! And he lovingly stroked his capacious, bulging briefcase with the intimacy of a good relation, experiencing the thrill of satisfaction felt by the clandestine would-be assassin, as he had done when getting ready for his new period in the seclusion of his silence. (See letter to Karola.) At long last the train pulled into the station of D. three quarters of an hour late—something unavoidable, it seems, for a national means of transport with an express destination. It was getting dark and silver-and-black rain was coming down in buckets. His thick overcoat was drenched by the time he entered the hall, lit by crisscrossing striplights in an unnatural (almost supernatural) manner. He was met on entering by the sight of a television crew, *multitudes* (a *de rigueur* cliché) of visitors, critics and journalists and a corpulent man (Professor and Doctor of Fine Arts) of about sixty, though his thick hair was still not turning grey, standing on the austerely decorated rostrum. The speaker, perceptibly moderating his irony, diluting his otherwise caustic wit (tact!), was describing the particular period and the works inseparable from it now on display. He kept repeating that all this was today *incredible* and that the exhibition was the reflection of a 'warped' policy of the arts ("Comrades, you're still fixing your eyes on Paris"—this was an allusion to a famous Hungarian poem welcoming the French Revolution) and in the context of today's world all this looked horridly *grotesque*. ("Yes, the best of our artists have found their way to the people, to the simple men and women, lifting themselves by their own bootstraps from the morass of bourgeois ideology.") Of course, that was the way to talk now, and the inner man reared on dialectics also claimed a voice: there were, he said, fine works born despite the age, some of them even of enduring quality, and he listed some of them. Those excellent masters put their own personalities into their creations in the face of every attack. ("Comrades, there are many who still inhabit their own paltry private worlds.") It was at this moment that Ólmosi-Bleier stepped out of the background in his heavy coat dark with wet and approached the speaker's platform. He produced from his capacious briefcase that paint spray-gun (ALBATROSS KG 127) and carefully observing the prescribed distance of one foot he pressed the button. He worked with careful and economical movements, covering every inch of the personage before him with a coat of glancing bronze; first his plentiful hair, next his benevolent face, then his broad chest, finally the hands half covering his notes and the paper itself. All this, let us repeat, he did unhurriedly and without flurry. The work done he surveyed the result with the assessment of a master, then with a nod of satisfaction he walked out of the hall in his heavy, drenched coat.

Translated by László T. András

Illatos Street 5, Budapest
Childhood Memories of a Housing Estate
BY ESZTER ANÓKA

The A, B and C blocks of Illatos Street (Fragrance Street) 5, in the ninth district of Budapest, were built between 1938 and 1939 to an English design, on the occasion of the International Eucharistic Congress. They were meant as model accommodation for workers, partly for the inhabitants of the old Mária-Valéria housing estate, partly for those who had previously been living in even more wretched conditions. The flats, thirty metres square each and consisting of one room and a kitchen, came with a twenty-five-year guarantee. They are dry and airy. There is a lavatory and a tap for every two flats, and on each floor (depending on the size of the block this means thirty to forty flats) there are two bathrooms and a laundry room. There is a loft which is excellent for drying the washing, a well-constructed, insulated cellar and an air-raid shelter. These blocks, with their four hundred and twenty flats, were a showpiece of the Horthy regime, meant to demonstrate its progressive attitude towards the well-being of the workers, and so on. The construction of such an estate in 1939 did represent a step forward, and was in fact a good thing. Nonetheless it was a clever piece of propaganda, nothing whatsoever to do with any genuine social policies. The estate is known as the "Jumbly", which probably comes from the word "jungle", and its inhabitants are known as "Jumblies".

I am not a Jumbly by birth. I can thank my stars for having landed me there, in that proletarian and lumpenproletarian quarters. My parents got divorced, my mother, who was training to be a nurse, lived in a hostel, and we three children were sent our separate ways. This meant to an institution or to a kind relation or, in my own case, to live with my father and his new wife, my stepmother whom I hated with or without good reason. It was because of me that the army got this flat for us, which was typical of the housing situation in 1952. We were given it as a service flat, because mother worked in an army hospital. At that time I stole one thing after another—sweets, dried apples, my classmates' coloured pencils—and my stepmother in her wisdom denounced me as a thief, a degenerate and a lost soul in her letter to my mother, and this compelled her, already softened by my own pleading letters, to ask the hospital's political representative to find a solution to her family's problem, i. e., a flat.

In those days the kitchen was not separate; the floor of the living-space was rotting boards, the kitchen area pitted concrete. Yet this flat meant everything to me in more ways than one; it rescued me from being unloved; it meant family, mother instead of stepmother. At the time of my parents' divorce I was seven years old. I already had many treasured memories of family warmth, and I longed to experience it again. It was autumn, pouring with rain, the house was noisy and smelly because every kitchen door stood open onto the corridor, allowing all sorts of sounds and smells to escape. The paintwork on the grubby walls was peeling, our door was rotten and had been bashed in (apparently the neighbours had swapped it for theirs when the flat was uninhabited), and the windows didn't close properly, but we had our own kitchen equipment and our own furniture (what we could fit into the available space, that is), there was a cooking range for me to light, a floor for me to scrub, and jobs to do; "We're going out, love, cook the pasta, and fry the bacon-fat to go with it." I was at home. I hummed happily, like water bubbling in a pot. I didn't even notice that the flat was small, the ceiling low (2.25 m), the walls were covered in a salt deposit, and an army of bugs lived in the cracks, I only began to notice and be affected by these things as my delight wore off. Right now I had other matters to attend to.

I knew that all sort of people lived in the block. There were gypsies, alcoholics, prostitutes. The majority were unskilled manual workers. A child can feel at home under any circumstances if its mother is there too, consequently, if it finds itself in a harsh world governed by Draconian laws, then it adapts to the Draconian laws. I don't deny that at first I wanted to shine. I was a good scholar, and was better educated than the other children of my age. I even had had piano lessons once, but that didn't count for anything here. Quite the reverse: I was paid back for it in scorn, the children calling me "Baroness Lulu". At the same time I was stunned to realize that my best friend Sima Simakova (she called me Anna Ivanovna), who was the model pupil, was beaten to shreds by her mother because she hadn't made the beds up, hadn't lit the stove, and hadn't brought kindling from the timber yard. So I began to discover the system of values that operated here, and to get a grasp of it. Before I did anything else I instinctively made a place for myself in the class and among the local children. Sima Simakova was respected by all the children; she was our leader, my protector and fellow-sufferer, the first to judge my actions, and my teacher. The next thing I had to do, like it or not, was to learn to fight; to fight, to curse, to yell. Power, independence and personal freedom could only be won that way and anyone not learning how to fight, like, for instance, my little sister, soon became everyone's prey.

I had my first real fight over my little brother who came

home bloody and bruised every day until my maternal instincts were finally aroused, and I asked him to show me who had been beating him up. Then I, a mere ten-year-old, gave the four big lads such a pounding that from that day on my little brother had only my hand to fear. I just couldn't accept the fact that he was a coward, incapable of fighting. In fact he wasn't a coward, he'd suffered too from the divorce, but in a different way, that's all. Mother had carried him and given birth to him during the war, so from the very beginning he was a slow child, difficult to handle. She always tried to keep him near her; she cosseted him, and so he became a real mother's boy. I was the one who wouldn't have him put in a class with the backward children, I charged into the headmaster's office and yelled, banging my fist on the giant of a man's desk, that my brother was completely normal, and should be put into the proper class. And so they did. When I did this I was ten years old. And when I talk about all this, you can forget the cosy reminiscences of the good old days that old ladies exchange over their coffee cups. Only five years ago a woman from the estate overturned a table on top of a housing official because she hadn't been given a flat.

Punching, provoking fights and brawling were the natural means of self-expression here, the simplest solution to a problem. We children would fight over the smallest difference of opinion, the adults would fight with each other and beat their children, but other people's children only occasionally, because by and large they kept to the principle of "if you don't feed him, you can't beat him". Mother didn't beat us, at least not wholeheartedly. She was influenced by her surroundings though, and a clever relation of ours also urged her to do it, and then, slowly, fate took matters out of her hand. She hadn't enough strength to cope with her work, the three children, the surroundings and the grinding poverty. Because we were really poor, as was half Hungary at that time. If mother slapped me, I would feel sorry for her. If it was brother who got a beating with a wooden spoon after a long chase round the kitchen table, then the four of us would huddle together and weep for ourselves: how low had we sunk?

I was used to gentleness; when I was eight I kicked my teacher on the shin because she rapped me over the knuckles. There was no point in hitting my brother either, the poor child was terrified enough by a raised hand, a beating had little effect on him. He became underhand and deceitful. Neither could mother get anywhere with my little sister, either with beatings or with kind words. Only one thing had any effect on her; that was when we huddled together on mother's old, badly-sprung bed on a Sunday morning or on those evenings when others were fighting (which was often), and we sang together.

One of our neighbours, a woman whose nose was eaten away by syphilis, sold bootleg booze and herself into the bargain. Once the drink was in them the men would need little provocation to fight. The blows would rain down, the boots thunder, the bed break, they would smash chairs over each other's heads. Gross obscenities would penetrate the flimsy wall, as well as inarticulate shrieks of rage and sheer fatigue—on occasion someone would have arranged an orgy, with one or two prostitutes to four or five men. They would take it in turns to mount the women, some beating them up, some, with their various perversions, depriving them of their last vestiges of humanity. They would snigger and cackle and pant, and give a running commentary on who was doing what, why, and for how long. We would huddle into mother's clammy warmth, shivering and afraid. Mother would cry, or tell stories, or we would sing. We loved to sing with mother, it offered us protection, and even if it didn't give us security, it certainly gave us a feeling of being different, of being a cut above the rest. The songs we sang were the folksongs that Bartók and Kodály had collected, while the songs the Jumblies sang were either popular songs from pre-war or wartime days, or were lewd and vulgar. Yes, despite all the adjustments we had to make, we still managed to preserve a feeling of separateness, of being different.

I used to swear like a trooper, just like all the others. But at home it was considered shocking to say something like "silly fool" or "moron". Our mother never swore, she never even heard obscenities, they just rolled off her like water off a duck's back. I could argue and get into a slanging match like the rest of them, but let anyone refer to my mother, using even the most commonplace of insults, and I would lash out in fury; the idea of motherhood was as holy and inviolate to me as was the Virgin Mary to the Catholics. My mother was not like the other Jumbly women. She was good. She was good for goodness' sake, she was good because good was beautiful. Her good nature was the reason why our mincer, our frying pan, our walnut and coffee grinder all ended up at the neighbours' on permanent loan, because they forgot to return them and mother didn't like to ask for them back. To this very day I know who's got what of ours, if it hasn't moved even further afield. My mother was peace, a blurred shadow of my distant childhood. The divorce, you see, had really messed up my childhood and with the move to the Jumbly it ceased completely.

As a newcomer I had to face and come to terms with things way beyond my childhood, things that defeated the powers of a grown-up newcomer, Mother, an adult being less flexible than a child. I never got used to life there, and the more my eyes were opened to what was going on around me the less I was able to bear it. What's more, I remember times when my ability to adapt collapsed completely, and I just couldn't bear it at all. The difference between myself and my desires, and the Jumbly surrounding me grew so acute that I couldn't face it. I avoided it, which, in the eyes of the Jumblies, was a bigger sin than to have opposed them and their ways directly; that would have been to have recognized them at least. Human relationships were the direct opposite of everything I had previously experienced as normal. It was common knowledge that brothers and sisters were living together as man and wife, that sisters swapped husbands around, that a father was having sexual relations with his daughter, that many of the girls were tuppenny whores, that the men and boys visited prostitutes and stabbed each other, that the men would beat their wives, and that their wives give as good as they got.

In 1952, therefore, at ten years of age, I adapted myself to it, rather than accept it, because my survival instinct was strong. Perhaps it was also because the general poverty made it easy; our family's standard of living was no higher than the others'; we all suffered together. It was this 'together' that magically transformed some aspects of Jumbly life into a sort of game for me. I convinced myself that I was an enchanted princess; that one day events would take a fairy-tale turn and I (we) would escape from there. Having to look after my helpless little brother and sister made me feel like a mother to them, and as my mother herself would cry on my young shoulder until she had exhausted her tears, and expected my fledging powers of comprehension to understand her adult woman's problems, my new role was reinforced. I became head of the household, substitute father. This threefold consciousness meant that I could dare to face it, and was able to bear life in the

Jumbly. Then after less than a year of it mother had a breakdown and I was sent to an institution (though we never used that word). By that time I was a sneaky, servile little creature, a child no longer. I already knew that there was a life other than that which they were preparing us for, where values and standards were different, and more important, the conditions and possibilities were different.

Those conditions were as follows: just enough money to stop us starving or freezing to death. I didn't even have a winter coat, three times a week we ate potatoes with potatoes, and at the end of the month we often didn't even get that. In the depths of winter the tap would freeze, in the summer it was hot enough to boil blood. We were packed together like sardines in a tin, a constant hum of noise, the anger of people crushed against one another, turning on one another, attacking one another without provocation, driven to it by their wretched conditions. Drink, which brought oblivion and a release from the pangs of hunger—in those days alcohol was unbelievably cheap. Noise, noise, noise, radios on at full volume bawling out "La Demoiselle de Paris". The gypsies holding a wedding feast and singing their strange songs at the top of their voices well into the night; mothers shouting above the row as they called their children. Babies crying. Women quarrelling. Men arguing. A thousand adults and three thousand children.

Incredible skill and extremely modest requirements were necessary in order to survive on the money a family received. This skill was partly the job of the children. We had to go to the timber yard for woodshavings, stuffing a sack bigger than ourselves till it was full to the brim and we could hardly carry it on our backs, and all this for one forint. It was the children's job to steal bark from the timber yard. The yard wasn't fenced in, but it was guarded; somehow we'd sneak our way in with our sacks and chisels. Within seconds our sharp eyes would spot the big logs with the thick, easy-to-crack bark, then quick as lightning, noiselessly we'd strip them, picking out the cracks where we could break up the bark with our chisels. We would often find fat, thick, white worms crawling around underneath it. Once it was off we'd cram it into the sack, keeping our ears pricked for the guard all the while, like wild animals. If we caught sight of him we'd whistle to warn the others, because if he caught us we'd lose our sack and our chisels, and get a beating at home as well. If it had been raining, we had to tug the dry logs out from the bottom of the carefully stacked piles. It was also the children's job to get coal from the shunting yard. Off we'd go with our sacks, balancing on the sleepers and collecting the coal that had fallen from the wagons, heaven knows how. A poem by Attila József comes to mind, where the labourer "accidentally" kicks a log that then rolls down from the pile and falls onto the road. I suppose the coal fell off bit by bit. If we were in dire straits and the winter was long we would steal from the coal heaped up at the junctions. But we only did that now and again because we could be seen by the men way up in the signalbox. If they caught us they would thrash us brutally, because they lit their fires with stolen fuel as well, and so they were blamed for anything we took. (Fuel had to be stolen in those days simply because it couldn't be bought. There was a chronic fuel shortage in Hungary. Sometimes it does no harm to think back and remember those times.) Another thing the children had to do was to sidle up to the doorway of the grocer and pinch the paper sacks and the cases that jam came in. We used to call the chemically coloured, over-sugared, stiff synthetic jam "Hitler ham". Further afield they called it "Stalin salami". It was also the children's task to go to the market-place nearby and scavenge amongst the rotting vegetables. We'd take our knives with us to cut away the rotten bits from the carrots, cabbages and pumpkins that we found there. We would rummage through the mounds of potatoes, braving the sickly-sweet stench as we looked for any that were still edible, or we'd pounce in triumph on a split water melon, until the porters would snarl at us, "the market guard's coming", when we would promptly decamp, clutching our loot. We kids would swim across the Danube to Csepel Island to pinch stuff from the market gardens. We'd bundle up kohlrabi, tomatoes and green pepper in our shirts, and in the evening, when our exhausted mother would begin to cook the supper, she wouldn't ask where we got them.

Children had lots of other things to do as well, work that was hard or heavy. We had to fetch coal and wood from the shop, if we had enough money, that is, and if there was any for sale. We had to chop the wood, rake out the stove, light it, clean the flat, mop it, scrub the dirty pots, and do the shopping. The official working week was forty-eight hours in those days, but the workers were forced to volunteer for extra work, overtime for which they weren't paid. The public transport system was at least three times worse than it is today, and travelling took a long time. We got many a slap in the evening for having wasted time playing. But even if the mother did not go out to work, the children still had to do all these things, because there would be five, or nine, or maybe eleven children to raise, and the family income would be even smaller. There were those wretched creatures who had become incapable of work because they were alcoholics and depended on their wives, their shrunken or swollen-bellied, rotten-toothed wives, broken by work, who looked after them and their dozen or half-dozen children, although the children would also help to look after their father.

But in addition to 'coming by things' we would manage to get hold of money too. We stole iron and copper from the local factories, sold it to the scrapyard and won awards for it in school. We were 'Outstanding Iron Collectors'. We also collected paper, but not from the estate, because we used it ourselves as fuel. Then there was a lot of money to be made by collecting rags. We'd walk to Buda, where we felt no shame in ringing the doorbells of the smart villas, one after another, and pestering the inhabitants until, in a bid to get rid of us, they would hurl a few odds and ends of clothing at us, or some piece of unwanted junk, or a bundle of old newspapers. They did not hand them to us because we were dirty and infested with bugs. We washed daily to no avail, the smell of poverty, of boiled onions, smoke and our own selves ate their way into the cleanest of garments. The houses had the same stink. Even if the newly washed clothes dried outside on the gallery, they would still soak up the same smell. We had fleas and lice too. Once I was queueing in the milk shop when a juicy fat bug slowly and calmly made its way from my coat sleeve on to the counter. If a garment was at all wearable then we wore it out, until it was well and truly a rag fit for the rag and bone man.

Our mothers were always at the washtub because we only had a few bits and pieces, and they were constantly patching and mending because our clothes were terrible, made of cheap, shabby material and worn to death. I vividly remember something that happened in school a little later, in 1953. The whole country stood still for one minute when Stalin died, and we stood to attention in the great hall, lined up in our groups, while the Stalin Cantata boomed out, "The land and the sea...... the name of Stalin". After (or was it during?) that moment every factory, engine, and ship sounded its siren or horn. Even the sirens from the wartime air raid shelters went off. Something on me itched, but I didn't dare scratch. Silence descended, and we stood there numbly and then the headmaster spoke. "May I ask all young comrades to wash daily, as there is an unbearable smell in the classrooms, especially those rooms used by the seniors, who seem to think that a sprinkle of perfume can replace washing. Cleanliness is halfway to health. 'Progress!' "

What was the point in telling him, living as he did up is smart Buda, that we did wash every day. And I've never undestood that remark about perfume. Who could have afforded it? Unless the seniors were on the game and got it that way. I can only remember perfume at Easter, and even then we were sprinkled with soapy water more often than not. Sima Simakova and I nudged each other, and doubled up in a fit of uncontrollable laughter, it appealed to our sense of the grotesque. But not much to our class teacher's though. He gave us a black mark for laughing on the solemn occasion of Stalin's death, and we were lucky to have escaped so lightly. Our class teacher, by the way, was another one who thought we smelt. He didn't like us to get too close to him. We hated him for being so fastidious, and took no notice of the black marks he gave us. We just got the notes signed at home, or if the atmosphere there was tense and we were afraid we'd be smacked for it, then we forged our parents' signatures. Our mothers never remembered how many black marks the teachers gave us; school in general was of secondary importance. If we got a beating at home because we'd been given a black mark, of course it wasn't really because of the black mark. Learning didn't count, it was cleaning and mopping up and lighting the stove and 'coming by' this and that and so on, i.e., trying to make this unbearable existence bearable, that was what mattered.

I first read about the smell of poverty in one of Gyula

Illyés' books. Even today all you have to do is to walk from Wesselényi Street to Váci Street, and you can smell where the bigger and better flats are, and where the more fashionable people live. Or try walking from Pest to Buda, from Nagyvárad Square to the János Hospital for example, and smell the difference in the standard of living. Even if a person washes six hundred times a day, he won't be able to wash away the kitchen smells which, in these one-roomed flats, eat into the skin, and clothes. Whenever he hugs his sweetheart he can tell what his future mother-in-law cooked for lunch that day. And in the Jumbly there were no walls to separate the kitchen from the living area. There would be any number of people, five, eleven, fifteen even, including grandparents, children (some married already) and grandchildren, all squashed into thirty square metres. And indeed, from autumn to spring we were in no rush to let in the fresh air, for the smelly warmth was better than the clean-smelling cold. And in summer every door and window was flung wide open, and we all breathed in the same air. Of course we were less smelly in the summer, as towards nightfall there would be a gentle breeze from the backwater of the Danube, which would blow in through the open doors and windows and clean the air. The flats would cool down for a few hours, allowing us a few peaceful hours of sleep on the bed which two or three of us shared, curled up top to tail, that is if the fleas and bedbugs left us alone. Sometimes in summer the scent of flowers would drift in on a wind, from the hills of Buda perhaps, or from the gardens on Csepel Island. When I was sent to the institution, I was full of lice. Later, when I went to grammar school and we had to wear our own clothes in the hostel, it was no consolation for me to have arrived in September with freshly washed, neatly ironed clothes in the required quantity. They smelt. I had to wash the whole lot again because I couldn't stand my own smell. When I put on clean underwear it would turn my stomach.

But the Jumbly is on 'Fragrance' Street after all! The street, however, wasn't named after the stink from the Jumbly, but from the factories round and about. These were the Animal Protein Products Factory (this was later moved to the country), which we called the bone works, the Sulphuric Acid Works (now the Budapest Chemical Works), and if the wind was blowing in our direction, the smell of frying or burning crackling, fat or suet reminded us that the slaughterhouse (today's Budapest Meat Products) and gut-dressing works were also in the neighbourhood. We would open our windows to let out the smell of wretchedly poor human beings, which would then mingle with all these stenches. Sometimes they would be so unbearable that despite summer temperatures of over 100° F we would rather sweat behind closed windows, in flats made even hotter by our own body heat and the cooking ranges, than let in the choking foul air from outside. Although some of these disgusting smells weren't dangerous to the health, merely unpleasant, there were others which were poisonous; the sulphuric acid and hydrochloric acid fumes pouring out of the Sulphuric Acid Works scorched the leaves on the stunted trees, burned the sparse grass growing between the houses, attacked our mucous membranes and gave us long fits of coughing. These horrible smells even ate their way into the wood of the furniture, seeped into the pillows and the quilts. We stank, and although things are somewhat better today anyone with a keen nose will still be able to notice a faint odour clinging to us. Despite my rigorous efforts to keep the flat well aired, the first thing I do is to fling open the windows whenever I arrive home, especially if I'm coming from the fresher air of Buda. At least then I have the illusion of fresh air if not the reality.

Let us stand in front of the open window now and take a deep breath. It's been raining, it's early summer, late afternoon, and the air is fresh. We needn't be nervous about breathing it in. So what if the neighbour has just cooked stew and I've been boiling cabbage? Let us forget about it, digest it, deposit the waste matter in the communal W. C., pull the chain and forget the smell. Let's look at the view instead. Just what do my windows, our windows overlook?

The estate on Illatos Street consists of three blocks. As well as its nickname it's known as the 'six houses'; this isn't a contradiction in terms, it's a description. It's as if six identical buildings were standing parallel in a line, but each one slightly overlapping and partly obscuring the next. A staircase joins the buildings together in pairs, but each pair counts as one block: A, B and C. As the estate stands on the corner of Illatos Street and Gubacsi Street, so that Illatos Street 5A, with its 'façade' overlooking Gubacsi Street, could also be Gubacsi Street 91, should anyone happen to want to address a letter to one of the residents. A and C buildings are smaller, having only a hundred and thirty flatlets; B building is bigger, it can boast one hundred and sixty flatlets plus twenty converted formerly laundry rooms.

Why did I put quotation marks around the word 'façade'? Because this façade is a dirty bare brick wall, into which are set three dreadfully regular rows of windows, one above the other. Looking towards Gubacsi Street from here, we can see a macadam road, and two pairs of tram lines. The tram stop is right opposite the house and the bus stop thirty metres away, opposite the (real) façade of the MEDICOR medical instrument works, now a faded grey. It was restored, only to be devoured, eaten away and made filthy by the polluted air. Anyone interested can look further into the distance from the upper floors and see the Budapest Chemical Works, or the Ferencváros loading station. Those with windows in the façade of A building and the back of C building have the best view of all. The latter can see Soroksár Street, the suburban railway tracks, the yards and workshops of the building equipment repair works, the Ferencváros shunting yard and Csepel Island. It's also possible to see the great firework display on Constitution Day, on Gellért Hill, and, in good weather, Hármashatár Hill. But to see these you have to lean out of the window and thereby encounter the (entirely justified) accusations of the inhabitants living in the next building partly blocked by this one: you peep into their beds, even into their mouths.

We live on top of each other not just because every door and kitchen window opens on to the same corridor, and we count ourselves lucky if we have ten metres between us, but also because the back windows of one block look into the front windows of the next, and at best there is fifteen metres between them. That's why the view from the windows at the front of A building and the back of C building is thought to be good, because they don't look right into the private lives of the other inhabitants. Instead the view is of the factories, works, railways, depots, etc., that this particular, distant corner of the city contains. No inhabitants of a remote and isolated village or small town are such easy prey for each other's curiosity as are those who live in this estate. Suppose I am not concerned with what my neighbours are up to. What choice do I have? I'm not blind! Whether I will or not, in the few seconds when I open my window, I can see that the Horváth's have still another baby, that the youngest Gólik boy is growing a beard, and that he's busy with his studies, and that Auntie Lizzy, the local council member, is watching me from behind her nylon curtains.

Whether I will or not, I can hear when the neighbour comes home, blind drunk or just a little merry, whether he gambled his wages away on the horses or at cards, and I can hear my other neighbour calling me a lousy whore simply because my life and my work rhythms differ from those of the Jumblies. And when we all open our windows in spring and leave them open till autumn (these brick walls retain the heat, and so we feel we're melting away), then all summer the noise and commotion of several thousand lives can be heard within, to a greater or lesser degree. Even the calm of the night is disturbed by a crying baby, the occasional drunken singsong, asthmatic or consumptive coughing fit, the strident sounds of a quarrelling slut, and loud snores. Exposed as I am to all this noise, it's a miracle my hearing is so good, or rather, it's a curse. For, you see, the neighbour's parquet squeaks, the occupant of the flat below talks in his sleep, and if I turn the radio down as far as it will go because there are people trying to sleep after ten at night, the four walls just act as an amplifier. So there's no point in trying to listen to Ella Fitzgerald or the Bartók String Quartet after ten o'clock. If one of the neighbours is watching late night TV and it happens to be a programme that no one else is watching, then shouts telling him to turn the volume down will be heard, after which we still have the privilege of enjoying the film through to the end.

There are those who say that this was all in the past, and it is of no importance now. And it's as if they're trying to prove it with their own lives; having left the estate they don't come back, even if they've left their best friends, their cronies and relations here. What a praiseworthy forgetfulness it is, the amnesia of progress. But if I want the present to be better, and know it is, then I have to talk about the past and I have to talk about the bad side of things too. Although much has changed here already, and there is fairly steady progress, the past cannot be wiped out. It has left its mark in the consciousness and nerves of the people who live here. The standard of living has risen, thanks in part to the efforts of the Council's maintenance office, the flats now have gas, gas stoves instead of the old-fashioned cooking ranges, a wall and door separate the kitchen from the living room, allowing for some division of function between the two rooms, the use made of the flats is more thoughtful and civilized, the kitchen floors are tiled, the living rooms have parquet floors, all doors and windows have been replaced. (Though the flats still have no bathrooms or WC, they are as cramped, and privacy as scarce, as before.) All this, and the effect of TV and radio, has visibly raised people's expectations of life, has brought them more in line with the lifestyle and standards of morality of the average citizen.

Translated by Gillian Howarth

Sea with Gulls

BY SZILVESZTER ÖRDÖGH

So they have finally set off. It's all one now. Off into the unknown. The frontier is already behind them. 'Go on, Imre. Show Etuska the sea!' Vince Árendás had talked him into it. At first he had thought Vince was only pulling his leg. 'What the hell do we want to see the sea for? It's only water. Why should we stare at the water?' 'But Imre, it's still the sea, isn't it? Etuska has never seen such an enormous stretch of water. Go on, take her to see it. After all, what have you got a car for?' 'To carry the slops to the pigs.' Etuska really stung him with this comment. Well if that's how we feel, let's go then. Out into the wide world!

It's daft. What else was he supposed to carry the slops in? Couldn't take that much on a bicycle. You'd have to make three or four trips. No time for that. Not on top of three shifts. But then who cares? Let the woman see the sea. Now she would really be able to see it for herself. Now that they have finally set off.

They can think of nothing to say to one another. The woman scrutinizes the foreign signs. Squinting, as if making out the letters would help her understand. 'But how will we make ourselves understood?' Etuska had complained. 'Well you've got hands, haven't you? You can gesticulate.' – Vince had just laughed. 'Just like the deaf and dumb, eh?' Etuska blushed, perhaps with shame. Or perhaps she felt insulted. 'Well ...' – Árendás simply went on laughing. 'We really shall look a right pair.' He too had to say something. 'Gesticulating on the beach like a couple of fools.'

No way. They'd rather not speak at all. They wouldn't mix with people. Wouldn't even go to restaurants. They'd cook for themselves. Vince's wife had said there was a kitchen. They brought potatoes, fat, onions and the like with them. After all they were bound to be able to point to bread and meat. These they couldn't take along with them. They would go. They'd get by somehow. At most they'd stand and talk to the sea. Surely with the sea they'd be able to make themselves understood. After all, that's what they'd gone to see. To look it in the eyes, together.

They still have nothing to say to one another. The man keeps his eyes on the road. He is aware of the cramp in his hands. What if you have to drive differently on those foreign roads. What if the signs are different, the signs and everything else. Of course he'd take the slops at home by car, but driving abroad? He would never have dreamed of it. He wishes he had already arrived, longs to be done with the whole affair. He's terrified that the fear in his hands might creep up to his eyes. But he says nothing: it is better not to speak of such things. After all they are on holiday, going to the sea. Going away together for the first time in their lives. He could suddenly say: this is our honeymoon. After thirty years. Nevertheless he remains silent.

Of course they hadn't wanted to go. Not alone. 'Why don't you come too. There's plenty of room.' 'We're going somewhere else this time. To Vienna. They say you can get a lot of nice things there. Only everything's so expensive.' 'It's expensive everywhere.'—Etuska had said to Vince's wife as if speaking from experience. 'True ... but we'll have to have a look all the same. It'll be worth it just for that.' The Árendáses are going to Vienna. That's their business. They had goaded the others into this trip to the sea. There was no way they could have backed down. It would have been cowardly. Anyway Etuska had never seen the sea, so why not let her. If only they were already there. If only they were already on the way back, unharmed.

"Maize," the woman gestures to the fields with her eyes.

"That's right," says the man casting a glance in the same direction. "And over there, potatoes. Do you see?"

The woman nods. They can't cheat her with potatoes. But what about room prices, or at the butcher's and baker's? She'd ask everything five times, syllable by syllable. She'd get them to write it all down. She'd rather be despised than cheated. After all, it happens at home too. These days you never really feel secure anywhere. Who can you trust, who? No one thinks of anything but money, and the more the better. Nobody cares about honesty.

The man swallows. He should really tell her after all: do you realize that this is our honeymoon. Thirty years late.

It's daft. Etuska's bound to know anyway. Of course she knows. Perhaps that's why, after all the pondering and persuading, she had simply said: 'I don't mind.'

There are more and more cars on the road. The man clasps the steering-wheel still more tightly and even slows down a little. What would become of them if, God forbid, they had an accident? They didn't have enough money, couldn't speak the language, nothing ... How would they get back?

They hadn't wanted this trip. It merely spelt trouble and worry. The Árendáses are different. Vince has even learnt the language a bit back in the days when they had been captured. He always was one for mixing with people, so no wonder he liked all this to-ing and fro-ing. They didn't envy him the world, but had simply faltered when Vince had kept on saying: 'Come on, Imre, Etuska deserves that much, doesn't she?' 'Give it a rest, Vince. I've got by till now without the sea and I can carry on quite well without it.' 'But that's not the point. Up until now you had neither the means nor the time. But now? Now you've got a nice car, everything ...' 'But what about the garden, and the animals?' 'Imre has just got rid of the pigs, and your son will feed the chickens. Maybe he'll even water the garden, if he has to.' 'Oh he's got too many other things to do!' The boy had just come in and the Árendáses immediately told him about the idea at once. 'Well, at long last! I'll look after everything. You two just get yourselves up and away.' So the boy was on the Árendáses' side too. They couldn't really think of other excuses. They'd simply have to risk a trip to the sea.

It's daft. A peasant going to the sea.

The woman sits and looks at the foreign world with pursed lips. 'One day I'd like to go to the mountains. To the peace and quiet of the mountains.' She betrayed this secret to no one. She retained it with a stubborn faith, just as the first communicant guards her vow. Without knowing why, she longed for the mountains and not the sea. After all what could she do with the sea? She wasn't going to swim. Her legs throbbed with pain. Warm medicinal water was what her body needed. No, she felt no longing for the sea whatsoever. The mountains were different. It was there, perhaps, that she could really be alone. Alone, as she imagined in her dreams. Among sweet fragrances, within an arms' reach of the clouds.

"They're picking the potatoes." It is the man who speaks. It was the potato season. Would he ever have dared to think of driving to the sea during the potato season? Perhaps he should also ask Etuska if she remembered all those other summers, those other Augusts? The first summers, of '42, '43 and '44? But why pain her with that? It was no good to remember those days, let alone to speak of them. Now they should speak of happier things. They were going on holiday: this was their honeymoon.

The woman gazes at the land, at the bending peasants disappearing into nothing. There they had stood in the courtyard, the cart loaded with about forty hundredweight of potatoes. When she had opened the gate there was even something of a smile upon her face. Then suddenly she had put her hand to her mouth. 'Jesus!' There she had stood, staring in disbelief, pawing the potatoes with her fingers. 'Jesus Christ!' Her eyes had filled with tears. The man said nothing, only led the horse to the stables, giving it water and fodder. Only then did he come over to the cart and lean his elbow upon its side. 'Mole crickets and weeds.' The woman shook her head. 'We can throw the whole lot away.' 'I can't do anything about it. It's the bloody soil. Mother earth.' The co-operative had given them the land as a household plot. It would do. More than an acre, after all. Out of the forty hundredweight of potatoes thirty were useless. Impossible to sell, fit only for the pigs. The woman had cried. 'Don't cry. Crying won't help.' In the end they just sorted out the potatoes in silence. One by one, into three piles—those to be sold, those for their own kitchen and those for the pigs. Night fell.

"The peasants still own their own land here."

"What, didn't they ever have the reforms? Didn't they ever form co-operatives?"

"It doesn't seem like it."

Again there is silence. They have no idea what to say to one another. Although now would be the time to talk. They could talk about everything, right from the beginning. After all, they are now completely alone together. Locked up in their nice car, on the way to the sea. To see the sea. After all, this is their honeymoon, thirty years after. They should talk. There is time to talk, and little else to do,

'Etuska'—'Imre'. To say even this much would suffice. It had sufficed for thirty years. Or just to reach out and touch one another's hands. Only lightly. Just enough to know that they are there together, side by side, with one another. But the hands of the man simply clasp the steering wheel more tightly. The woman's fall asleep in her lap.

It no longer befits them. They have grown out of love. Pain has made them indifferent. But even so, wouldn't it be worth a try? What if? 'Etuska, do you remember?' But then, what should she remember? Nights, days? Joyful moments? Had there indeed been joyful moments? Even the children had already flown. Like wild geese. And this is how they always see them, way up above in an autumn twilight. Gaggling as they disappear into the clouds. Only the smallest had remained with them. And his departure fills them with fear.

Still, they could have done without the sea. It wasn't for them. They were better suited to the home. From kitchen to courtyard, to garden, to pigsty. From the house to the corner of the road. For them it was better to watch television before falling asleep; merciful to their fatigue. Why should they gaze at the sea, at each other? They had never wanted that before. Nor now. They are beyond everything. They curse nothing. Blame nothing. They have no strength for either. At some point one must learn the lesson of silence. One must make friends with silence when the time comes. And the sea is icy cold. Their joints and bones ache endlessly.

They proceed at a slow and lordly pace: why should they provoke life? Life treats them well. Better than at any other time. What was there to complain about? Soon they could stand ashamed before the sea.

"Isn't our soil better at home?"

"God knows. You'd have to try it."

The soil. Since leaving the co-operative how should he know what the soil was like. That was more than eight years ago. All he knew now was that there were three shifts. From six in the morning until two, from two to ten and from ten to six in the morning. That was all he could judge nowadays. Not the soil. Did he miss it? The man shakes his head.

"What's the matter? Do your eyes hurt?"

He had to force himself to blink.

"There's more traffic. You have to concentrate harder."

"Are you tired?"

"No."

'Etuska, do you love me?' — 'Imre, do you love me?' From where do these words echo? From what evening, from what quiet? Where are the acacias, and where is the acacia blossom? Where are the dewy dawns? Are these their voices at all? Are they really theirs?

A fine mess the Árendáses had got them into. 'At last you've come to your senses.' 'Lost them, more like.' They had looked at all the forms and passports, had run their fingers along the road-map. 'It'll well worth it, you'll see. Just think of the women you're going to see. On the beaches. There's even a nudist beach.' 'And what is that?' asked Etuska. Vince's eyes twinkled. 'Where people sunbathe in their birthday suits.' 'I suppose you've been there yourself?' 'Well I had to give it a try while I was there, didn't I? I was just curious.' 'My God, what a world!' Etuska turned away, and Vince continued to wink at Imre. 'Phew, you can't imagine what you're about to see. You'd better pull your socks up. Some birds! I suggest you keep an eye on Imre, Etuska, they'll take up all his attention.' 'If they want it, they can have it. It's none of my business.' 'Well, well, you are soon rid of me, aren't you!' Imre wanted to joke too. 'I don't need other people's goods. Never have and never will, you know that.' An irresolute silence passed between them.

Women. Dafter than the sea. After all, he'd seen the sea, he knew. When they had been captured they had been driven there one Sunday in spring: a special occasion. They had stood around on the beach. Some had howled against the roaring of the sea. Others leaped about, dashed into the water. He had just stood there and picked up a few shells. He would bring them home as souvenirs. Souvenirs of captivity. By the time he got home they had all broken in his pocket. And so he had just stood there, looking at the great stretch of water. 'The sea, the sea,' he had repeated to himself. But what could one do with it? Even his eyes had started to ache. He liked to look at the land. At the windswept corn, at the rows running together. This great mass of grey water was unfamiliar to him. Even though he saw seagulls and the foamy crests of the waves, he could not feel happy. The seagulls made him think of his pigeons in the attic, the foam reminded him of the brindled horses' mouths. It was all in vain. That was the way he was. Even so, he had given the sea a long open-minded look. Well, that was how he had seen the sea then. Etuska's absence, the absence of the child. Everything that was far away at home. Soil, horse, plough, everything. Why should he have shouted for joy at seeing the sea? He looked at it in vain. He saw nothing.

"It's clouding over," said the woman leaning forward to look up.

"You'll see. There'll be clouds over the sea."

"Then why did the Árendáses say that the sun would be shining the whole time? Well, that'll be lovely, won't it, if we can't even get out." The woman was frightened that she might not see the seagulls. She didn't know why, but suddenly she longed to see seagulls. It was because they were snow-white.

"Well, maybe the sun will be shining, and there won't be any clouds over this sea. But there were clouds over that other one."

The woman's gaze loses itself upon her husband. She had heard roaring and shrieking. Darkness had rushed over her eyes. In her nose was the smell of the musty cellar. 'Over that other one ...' Then, as the silence settled, the sickly cry of a child. She wanted to silence him. 'Don't cry now. Don't cry.' She was frightened the little boy might give them away. That orphan cry. She was almost pleased when the bombs began falling again, and the child's voice was lost in the commotion. But soon the planes passed and the silence of ruins was upon them again. The little boy cried more and more. 'Perhaps the child can sense something.' The rosary beads froze in her mother-in-law's hand. She almost went mad. 'Stop it, stop crying. Don't cry, my little one!' She rocked him, hugged him, covered him up. But the poor little soul went on ceaselessly. She was crying now as well. She bit her lip and whimpered. 'Be quiet now, my little love. Don't cry. You mustn't. Don't you hurt me as well. My darling little boy.' She shook the little body. Her mother-in-law's face was crimson. 'Listen, he can sense something.' 'Oh, come off it.' And she saw Imre. The way he rose from the table, took his knapsack and went out of the gate. She began to sing. 'Hush now, baby, sleep and dream of angels.' She sang louder and louder. The child continued to howl. His face was purple. Her mother-in-law brought tea, but it was no good. 'Please, please, stop crying. I beg you.' The tears sizzled down her cheeks. She offered her breast, but it had no milk, it was completely dry. She felt dizzy. She couldn't hold the swaddling-clothes. It was night. There was no way to get a doctor, nowhere to call one from. 'I believe in the one and only God ...' 'Please mother, don't say your prayers out loud, or I'll go mad.' 'At such times one must make one's prayer loud, my girl, loud!' All the same she quietened down to a whisper. The child was whimpering, hoarsely. In the morning, in the little light that filtered in they could see that his cheeks were already turning blue. She could bear it no longer. She picked up the child and held him tight. 'Please, don't cry, please! Your father's alive. Everything's all right. 'All she could hear was the child crying. To her the crash of the bombs was no more than the momentary buzzing of a nest of wasps. Her mother-in-law laid the rosary beads on the swaddling-clothes, the icon of Mary. 'This will help. I'm sure it will help. The Virgin Mother will help little Imruska.' 'Take them away!' She must have gone mad to have yelled like that. Again Imre's face, the knapsack, the gate as it closed. The little boy's face was quite blue. The sobbing shocked up from his throat. 'Why can't you be quiet? Why? I'm here, my little baby. I'm here.' She had no more tears. They had all dried up. Her mother-in-law closed her eyes in the corner of the room and swayed: 'Oh, Virgin Mother, help Imre and little Imruska ..."' And then suddenly the bombing stopped. Silence seeped in, heavy as mud. Only the baby was crying. He had hardly any voice left. Only as much as a well-sweep caressed by the wind. The woman fell asleep. Three days later she collapsed altogether. As if she had seen her son's purple face in snow-white glory. And then nothing. The boy fell fast asleep too. The crying must have tired him out. He had fallen asleep without milk, without tea, without a lullaby. The mother-in-law tried to revive him. 'He's up there playing with the little angels now.' And then she saw that Imruska's face was no longer purple, but snow-white. A motionless seagull. The beads of the rosary rattled together. 'My first-born son ... sleep tight ...' She did not know that she was only moving her lips. She had no voice. In the graveyard Russian soldiers were resting and eating. A tiny white coffin. The neighbour had carried it in his careful arms. The grave hardly deeper than a potato pit.

Over that other one there had been clouds. Over that other one.

But here the sun shines. Gulls fly through the air. Snow-white.

Something needs to be said.

"I forgot to tell the boy which dough basket to put the eggs into."

"He'll find out."

"I put fifty aside for the pastry. I don't know what I'll do if he mixes them up."

"Does it make any difference which eggs you use for the pastry?"

"Of course it makes a difference."

She can't understand how she had forgotten. She'd written down everything else. She'd left the list on the sideboard. What and when he should eat. What there was in the larder, in the fridge. When to go shopping, and what to buy. He would have to fetch the milk. On Saturday he should sprinkle the grave in the cemetery. She had forgotten the eggs. Now what?

It really was a shame to have come. It wasn't for them. The Árendáses were different. They didn't have any children, didn't have animals or a garden. 'Etuska, that blue water! That crystal-clear water! The streets and shops, and shop-windows!' The woman had kept on thinking of the seagulls. That's why she had agreed to go to the sea. Because of the seagulls. There were no seagulls in the mountains. But she confessed this to no one. She was counting the foreign money, calculating.

The man was suffering inside. Cramp in his hands, anxiety in his eyes. At least they shouldn't just sit there like that. Completely silent. Now that they had decided to set off they might as well have a bit of laugh. Or at least smile. He would say it. He would say it, after all.

"Do you realize that this is actually our honeymoon?"

"What are you talking about? After thirty years."

True. It would have been better not to have spoken. 'Etuska, you are beautiful! I love you. We will be happy, won't we?'

"I suppose it was Vince Árendás who put that idea into your head. Very nice. Absolutely tasteless. Two fools make a pair."

Of course Árendás had mentioned it. He had meant it as a joke, but it was true all the same. 'You can be all on your own with Etuska at last. You're still young enough after all.' He had simply given a dismissive wave of the hand.

He clasps the steering wheel. 'All the pretty chicks in bikinis on the beach.' That Vince, that boy Vince! It's easy for him. He's different. 'Imre, you do love me, don't you? You'll never leave me, will you? We belong together, don't we?' From where does he hear this again? Had they ever said such things? As if he was seeing that twilight. That secret embrace and the hiding away. Night and day. How greedy they had been. How thirsty, how hungry!

"Look out!" the woman shrieks.

He hadn't noticed the lorry. That it too was overtaking. He wipes his forehead.

"They drive like animals." Fright presses the cry from her throat.

He ought to admit that it was his fault. He hadn't looked in the mirror.

"I told you this kind of driving wasn't for me. They drive differently in all this traffic."

"It's too late now. If you'd have stood your ground we wouldn't even have left."

"But I also wanted you to see the sea."

"Well, we'll have to get there first, won't we?"

What will become of them? Five days, a terribly long time. Doomed to inactivity, shut up together among foreigners. What could they say to one another, what could they do? They'll sit on the beach and watch the sea. The seagulls. They'll listen to the roar of the waves. Thirty years. But what will they see in the sea? The surface will reflect nothing.

"Have you got the address?"

"What address?"

"The one that Árendáses gave us."

"Of course I have."

'You are beautiful to me. Like a seagull.' Would the man ever have said such a thing? 'Have you ever seen a seagull?' Would this have been the woman's voice? 'No, I've never seen one. But they say that seagulls are very beautiful. Because they are fragile and snow-white. Because they are faithful to the sea.' Would he have said this? 'All right, so I'm a seagull; what does that make you?' Would Etuska play with him like that? With words? 'I'll tell you what, you be the sea.' 'Then I am strong and powerful. Unbeatable.' They must have laughed. Must have. And kissed too. It is not possible that they hadn't kissed.

He notices the clouds.

"The sea will be over there."

"The sun's shining."

"You'll soon taste it. The water will be salty."

"Then what do I want to taste it for?"

"Just to know what it's like."

The woman waves her hand dismissively. All she wants are the seagulls. Nothing else at all. 'It'll be unforgettable,

Etuska, you'll see. Unforgettable. All these towns and shops.'

The traffic is really heavy now. They drive slowly. They come into the town.

"It's so clean everywhere." The woman begins to look at the signs again. "Butcher's."

"Where?" The man does not take his eyes from the road.

"There. And a jeweller's too."

"Then let's go down to the sea. Vince said that the house was down towards the sea."

"You two discussed it all."

They are pulled along by the caravan of cars. It clearly pulls in the direction of the sea. The woman licks her dry lips. Yes: shops, nice clean houses, streets. The man sees only the clouds even though the sun is shining. Suddenly a wide square and a promenade. The vast stretch of water trembles before them.

"Is that the sea?"

"Couldn't be anything else. I'll find somewhere to park."

He backs into the car park, feels for the address in his pocket.

"I'll ask the way ... it must be here somewhere, according to Vince."

The woman says nothing. She winds down the window. She watches the sea carefully, but cannot hear its roar.

"That's the street over there. And there's the corner house. Vince was right."

The woman sits stiffly in her seat, blinking as she watches the sea. She is looking for seagulls.

They stop in front of the house.

"This is it. We've arrived." The man smiles awkwardly. Well, here they are. The two of them. He might say: 'Etuska, my dear Etuska, look: the sea! Would you ever have believed it?' He can almost hear their laughter. He can almost feel the way they hold hands so spontaneously. And then squeeze a little. Just until it hurts. Until tears come to their eyes.

He looks at the woman. His smile breaks apart. He opens the door and gets out. Only now is he aware of the pain. In his back, in his legs, his stiff hands.

"Come on then," he says in a gentle voice.

The woman shakes her head just a little. Her gaze is still riveted upon the sea.

"What's the matter? Don't you feel well?"

The woman freezes. Beyond, a seagull flies up from the asphalt. It glides off into the infinite obscurity of the sea.

"It's not white. It's grey."

"What?" The man is impatient.

"Nothing. Nothing at all." The woman opens the door of the car.

Translated by Richard L. Aczel

Mother Is Dressing

BY ERZSÉBET GALGÓCZI

The metallic clatter of the mail train, the cooing of the turtle doves in front of the window, the swaying street lights on the wall, joy coursing like blood in the head, under the ribs, around the belly—the old woman awoke to find herself still alive. Twice already had she been brought back to life by the doctor's injections in bright daylight: clean night shirt, identity card, soap, cutlery, glasses, ambulance, hospital—o, my God, never again! On leaving hospital she had been told to move about a great deal, even if she had to force herself, because bed is death itself for someone of seventy-seven if she spends more time in it than on her feet.

She had been lying on the bed since seven the night before—and not the other way round—yet it was she who was crumpled, and not the bed. Her hands felt like sticks, the vertebrae were rusty at her waist and the blood faltered along the channels of her varicose veins. The bed was pulling her back, it would have had her float there till the end of time. It was as if she were dragging a full sack of wheat, this half turn towards the reading lamp. By the light of the opalescent bulb the corner of the room came to life: a tiled stove, a wardrobe half covering a door leading to the adjoining room, a scarlet rug by the bed with a footstool and shoes on it. On the bedside table under the small circle of light a book with glasses in it and next to it a lyre-shaped mahogany pendulum clock that had to be wound every eight days, without its glass; it did not matter where the hands pointed, for her it was good enough to set it by the mail train which passed at three every morning. Her engineer daughter had bought it for their golden wedding—it was the clock that reminded her of her husband every morning. She was no longer irritated as she was while he was alive, nor missed, as she did for one or two years after his death, the snoring, coughing, hurrumphing and catarrhal throat clearing from the other bed, to be followed immediately by the scraping of the match being struck and the stench of his first cigar. Her husband had been older by seven years. She did not want to count the years, but her grandchild, born on the very day of his death, skipping about from morning till night, was a constant reminder: she had so far outlived the deceased by six years.

She balanced herself with her hands into a sitting position, dragged out her swollen feet from under the eiderdown, let them dangle and tried to draw the footstool nearer, but only her big toe could reach it. She raked her false teeth from under the pillow, removed the circular comb from her sparse knot and smoothed the scanty, knotted strands of hair. (After her second stroke she had called to her daughter-in-law: "My teeth...? The children ...? My money...?") She had had a bath the evening before and in the clean nightshirt and with her skin refreshed she felt almost well now, if only she were not so heavy, like so much mud.

She was the youngest of three hundred pilgrims when she went on a pilgrimage to Maria Zell at the age of seventeen. They marched barefoot under the gold-embroidered, deep fringed, shining banners and the crucifix; hymns welled up all along the long procession, undulating over the June meadows; the chant snaked to a different rhythm from that directed by the choirmaster, even the words were changed; it was neither the text nor the tune that evoked devotion, but the joy of forgetting oneself, singing as part of the multitude of people. On the carts which brought up the rear there were bundles containing provisions as well as the crippled, the epileptic, the aged and the footsore. She could still see the seven-spooled well; they camped there one afternoon, drank its water and washed their feet. When the gaping villagers only spoke German it was clear that they had left Hungary behind—Hungary still belonged to the Monarchy at that time. An Austrian innkeeper and his plump, sad-eyed wife wanted to adopt the late-August-born girl, this chit of a young thing, a barefoot little cricket, whom they had only seen for an evening. They were charmed by her nimbleness as she came and went, taking dinner to the weary-footed elderly. She often wondered, when she was burdened with cares, and one worry would bark awake seven others at night, what her life would have been had she stayed with the innkeeper's family. The Mother of God embracing her Child in the church which rose on the summit of the awe-whispering mountain, the knee-bending gratitude, wonder, high clergy robed in rustling splendour, the dazzling vision of the church interior floating in incense and hallelujahs, like an enormous Christmas tree covered with a million candles warmed the memory and turned into an irrepressible wish to reach the true source, Jerusalem! The Holy Land!

She inched her way out of bed, leaned her palms against the tile stove, and shuddered with joy: it was warm. Her joints crackled like a cogwheel clogged with sand. The neatly folded clean clothes filled the shelves of the linen closet. She looked for underwear to go with her just-washed nightgown.

The old woman lived in one room and a kitchen, the rest of the house being occupied by her son and his family. It had been built with three rooms in the thirties—the largest in the street—her daughter-in-law, however, finding it small and impractically divided, had changed it beyond recognition as soon as she had felt sufficiently at home; had the old man come back to life he would not have been able to find his way home from the cemetery. For her a bathroom was also necessary and a pump costing twenty-five thousand forints because the village had no drainage. Now her daughter-in-law had taps in her kitchen, by the well and in the former stable, where the coal and oil were stored and the ducks fattened—only her own kitchen had no tap. "You can get your water from me, Mother," her daughter-in-law had said, after all both kitchens opened on to the same veranda. But what for? The tap in the yard or in winter the one in the stable was good enough for her. In any case she was alone all day and even though her daughter-in-law had pointed out many times where she kept the keys she would never be able to bring herself to open a locked door. Why was the tap left out of her kitchen only? Of course, as soon as she dies, they will be able to add this minute space to their room. She complained about this only to her eldest daughter who came to see her every week, laden with a bag packed with wine, pastry, smoked sausages and coconut chocolate; in one way or another her daughter-in-law had got wind of this, but was quite brazenly lying to her face: "But Mother, it was you who would not let us install the tap there. You were afraid you'd have to pitch in two thousand."

She sank down on the footstool and with a lengthy effort managed to pull up the chosen fleecy lined knickers she favoured over her varicose-swollen feet and well-fed hips which had preserved their man-teasing curve. Warming her back against the tiles she could forget herself on the footstool: it was only after her husband's death that she had had the courage to speak aloud of the dream that she had nursed for fifty-three years, since Maria Zell: the Holy Land! Since they had joined the co-operative and her dominion had shrunk to the flower garden in front of the window she had taken up reading; her daughter-in-law, knowing of her longing for the world of the ancient Jews and early Christians, kept supplying her with the Bible, the *Jewish War, Ben Hur, Quo Vadis? Joseph and His Brethren, La Gerusalemme liberata,* half a dozen lives of Jesus by different authors, the *Catacombs of Rome*—so many emotional attacks brought to the surface an obsession which had turned into a goal.

And what happened? Her daughters, sons-in-law, sons, grown-up grandchildren and daughters-in-law betrayed no shock, they neither rebuked her, nor waved deprecatingly: Israel? It was practically on the doorstep, and the travel agency would take care of everything. Mrs. Garam went by herself to Japan last year to see her son; she flew via Moscow and Vladivostok, and for a change decided to come back by a route she had not travelled yet, namely India and Turkey; although she only spoke Hungarian and that with a pronounced Tósziget-Csilizköz accent, nothing had happened to her, except when she lost her way in Budapest trying to get from Ferihegy Airport to the Eastern Railway Station. Her engineer daughter would have gone with her, the twenty thousand forints in her mother's savings account would have covered the expenses. Yet she had hesitated: her husband needed a tombstone. A new cemetery had been opened recently and although the first row had not yet been completed in the direction where the wood lies, her eldest daughter and son, as heirs to the family prestige, succeeded in having a second started for their father's body. Her husband now lay at the head of the second row, directly in front of the mortuary, almost in a place of honour, where not just any monument would do. This was what she wanted to devote her twenty thousand to. And yet there they were, just an arm's length away, the Mount of Olives, the

Sea of Galilee, the Temple in Jerusalem where the twelve-year-old child had spoken to the scribes, the tomb of the Virgin Mary... After many months' hesitation she still could not make up her mind until history did it for her: the Arab-Israeli war broke out.

Her son had vacuumed the rugs the day before, so the old woman shuffled to the window in her bare feet and looked into the November dawn. She was curious about the weather, about how many underpants, bodices, slips, skirts, vests, pullovers, coats and overcoats should swathe her sensitive body, but also noticed the plaintive cooing of the wild doves. It was she who told her grandchildren that the wild doves were mourning Christ—the poor man was killed, killed. The sound was coming from the top of the fine, tall pinetree standing in front of the window; she twisted her neck in vain, the street lamp revealed neither the nest nor its inhabitants. What could they be wanting? Not food; just like with her hens, she took care of that with the maize.

She slipped down on the footstool, pulled on her black stockings and her fur-lined lace-up shoes. Her grandchildren never got tired of lacing and unlacing these big shoes. They pushed and shoved each other in their excitement, and got the laces so tangled up, it was more work untangling them than if they had not touched them in the first place. Her shoelaces seemed longer than a sleepless night. From time to time she went faint and pressed her back against the tiles.

The reading lamp lit up more of the room—had the darkness outside softened? Above the beds were two Munkácsy reproductions: *Christ before Pilate* and *Christ on the Mount of Olives*. She had bought them during the war for half a pig from a refugee lady from Transylvania; the lady's son, a major, had been drowned in the industrial canal the very next day. Before moving in, her daughter-in-law had had the two empty rooms whitewashed, without a frieze, so that she could decorate them with her own things. She put back those two works of art on the snow-white wall as a wedding present—after all she herself had received from her mother-in-law a Virgin Mary, and a Head of Christ as well (the sunlight was eating away their colours in the loft). But, before the new bride had even changed her dress or the lorry finished unloading, she had taken down those pictures and brought them into her room: "Don't be offended, Mother, but I would go mad if my child had to stare from his cot at a man being whipped and crucified. He'll have enough time for suffering, for other people's too, when he grows up."

And so she had hung the walls with fancy homespun, rugs, glazed plates, church etchings, gay calendars and Egyptian queens dangling on chains. She placed brick-red statuettes among the books. The shelves, laden with pots of cacti and vases, might crash down on the children's heads at any time. The old woman had thought that her daughter-in-law would forbid her to make the children kiss the blue-mantled Virgin Mary statue, or to tell them the story of Holy Christmas. But that did not come to pass. The children's capacity for stories was like the appetite of the man in the folk tale who could consume one hundred and twenty plum dumplings at a single sitting. The young woman complemented the tales their father remembered from his childhood with adaptations she found in books of collections from Hungary, Transylvania, Moldavia, the Banat, Baranya and the Csallóköz, while their grandmother was free to recite the life, death and resurrection of Christ. "Go ahead, Mother," her daughter-in-law had said encouragingly. "I shan't be the one to deprive my children of the timeless values of culture. When magnificent creations such as Bach's *Passions,* Dante's *Commedia,* Leonardo's *Last Supper,* the churches of Lőcse and Bártfa or the *Confession* of *Saint Augustine* call out to them, I don't want them to stare back blankly, but to become their echoes, and meditate on them." They banished the Munkácsys. They never went to church. Who could understand these young people?

Groaning, the old woman struggled from the footstool and again rummaged in the wardrobe. She put on two warm petticoats and a shaggy white waistcoat over the yellow flannel night dress. She tied the strings of the petticoats tightly round her waist. Then she tottered to the window; the window of the house opposite was lit up, so it was already past four o'clock; Miska Süveges always left by the five o'clock train for the wagon factory. Her gaze strayed to the ground. From the spring to the early frost she had been digging, setting out, hoeing, weeding and watering; and since they did not keep animals any longer, when the herd passed by and no one was looking she had often sneaked into the road to scoop up the cow dung and throw it over the fence—to pamper her little garden with stolen manure. She had planted the pine fifteen years ago; there were evergreens for the edges and each season was hailed by a different kind of flower, from the March violet to the chrysanthemum. No garden in the whole village was richer, except Bözsi Sós's plantation of roses, carnations and gladioli, but those went by the bundle to the market on the back seat of the Skoda.

Several coffins were removed from the old to the new cemetery together with their tombstones, but none could be better than that of her husband: it was red marble, the finest work of the Pilis stonemason, a cross resting on a squat foundation stone. On the smooth plate, under her husband's name, was engraved: "and his wife Gizella Ráckevi 1895–".

There had been a singing in her ear for ten years, a kind of buzzing. Sometimes she could not even make out what people were shouting directly at her. All Saints' Day while she was arranging the wreaths on the grave, her engineer daughter had whispered to the elder one: "What a barbaric custom: she's fit, has never been ill, knows influenza only by name, and yet has her name with her date of birth engraved on her tombstone as if only the final figures were needed to seal her fate." "What do you mean, barbaric?" exclaimed her fifty-year-old daughter, herself a grandmother. "You and I and she will die, as surely as the sun sets. Look round: old women prepare for death just as they did for childbirth in their youth. Have you ever seen a young expectant mother who was not getting ready with swaddling clothes, nappies, little dresses and bonnets? Look around this graveyard: if the wife dies first, the husband's name is never carved on the cross. Only old women are pregnant with death, men never."

She squatted down once more on the footstool. The warm voice of a man filtered through the door which was hidden by the wardrobe. Although the words were not intelligible she knew that is was five o'clock, her son was up and had switched on the radio. She hurried to extract her green and brown check flannel dress from the pile on the sofa; by the time the ringing tread of studded boot heels reached her door and the sharp raps reached her ears, she was already smoothing the stiff, thick material around her waist.

"Good morning, mother dear!" and even the air resounded. "There was a frost last night."

At one time she also used to wake up the family with a weather report: "Every two froze into one during the night."

In his right hand a small bottle holding about a third of a pint, in the other a glass hardly bigger than a thimble; he poured it full of spirits and offered it to his mother.

"Good morning," returned the old woman. She did not

reach for the glass but arranged the dress over her hips and thighs. Her son placed the bottle on the carpet and squatted at her feet, one of his hands pulling down the hitched-up skirt at the back. "It's November. Why shouldn't the nights be frosty?"

She wetted her lips with the spirits and handed it back immediately. "Thank you." In hospital they had also ordered: no wine, no spirits.

Her son searched her face: no, it did not seem to be ready for the grave yet.

He drank up what his mother left.

"Mother dear, would you feed my ducks? They have not digested their last feed yet." His voice was like a flute.

How did her son know? He had not even had time to step out the house. Shining boots, grey breeches, light polo-neck sweater, that was not how one dressed if one intended to go near ducks splashing about in the dirty stable.

"Of course I'll feed them." Her face was serious and serene. And immediately she began to look for her shawl. Her son turned lightly—"Goodbye, mother dear!"—and she was pleased to have work to do. Her daughter-in-law also let her get on with jobs that demanded no hurry, but required skill and a great deal of trouble and could be done sitting down. She cracked the nuts for strudel, spent a week stoning the sour cherries for preserves, stirred the sugar and raspberries for two hours, plucked the slaughtered ducks, put blue patches on the knees of children's red track suits and red ones on the blue, boned the chops with matchless skill, sorted the potatoes for sowing, husked the maize for the squawking mob of chickens, threw the wormy plums and overripe apricots into the starting tub, picked peas for soup, banished mud from ten pairs of shoes; sometimes did things on her own with exasperating, disastrous results. Her daughter-in-law had scattered grass seed over the yard;

to her it appeared to have become overgrown with weeds, and remembering the Hungarian curse: may God give you a weedy yard and a bad neighbour—she got a hoe and flung herself into the work. Her daughter-in-law recoiled at the sight: her crippled mother-in-law sweating profusely added nothing to her good humour. "But Mother, grass is no longer a sign of poverty. We are not poor, only no longer have animals to trample the grass." The old woman thought it over, went out to buy seed and after the first shower sowed it surreptitiously. The others thought the grass, which had been imperfectly hoed out, had simply recovered by itself.

With an apron over her warm clothes and thick scarf on her head, she went again to the window. She opened it to see if she would need any more clothing for feeding the ducks. The turtle dove was cooing on top the pine while its mate paced and searched among the dying flowers. "You little fool! You don't think there are still worms there? The earth is frozen now." The bird listened attentively to his mighty patroness, who to him was as much part of the yard as the well was. The patroness also knew that they were unmistakably hers, no matter how many other birds raided the yard. Just as she could pick out her own broom, preserving pan, clothesline, basket or flower pot from among a hundred others: she was in touch with all organic and inorganic beings and things in the house, drawers, barn, yard, and in the small and large garden. Her daughter-in-law even accused her: "Mother can tell her own rainwater from others."

One Sunday, as she was sitting here on the footstool, lacking courage to switch on the light so early, she heard her engineer daughter's faltering voice from behind the half-hidden door: "I've been home for a week now and see that mother takes three whole hours to get dressed every morning. I wonder if there has ever been a time in my life, whether at seventeen, thirty or forty, when I would have put up with this three-hour torture every day, this self-resurrection each morning, merely for the sake of keeping alive. Never! We are nothing, but shoddy copies of Mother, she is the original."

"Life is never merely," the old woman muttered; she put on her greasy but back-and-waist-protecting fur-lined jacket, went out, looked about her on the stairs and became at once with herself again. The great acacia tree, higher than the draw-well, the chimney or the television aerial, had been the reference point of her dominion, defining the space. Its vast crown gave ample shade to the yard, which was the size of a football pitch. For fifty-eight years she had been able to forecast the weather from the trembling of its branches. The shock reverberated through her like a siren: the great acacia was gone! Even fifty-eight years ago when she herself had come to live here, with her mother-in-law, it had been the great acacia and not just any tree in the backyard. Now she began to remember: her son felled the half-dead tree last Sunday, and the electric saw had been sawing it up for two days, and its logs took up half the barn. In three of its hollows they found birds' eggs, desiccated nuts, a small pair of rusty scissors, a copper curtain ring, and in the fork of the thigh-thick branches over the barn there was a pigeon's nest as big as a plate.

See, the homeless pair of birds now live there, and one can see they would spend the winter in the pine in the small garden, but what would they make their nest of? Since the threshing of the corn had been done by combines the birds had not been able to find a single intact blade straw either on the threshing floor or the road or even among the sweepings in the ditch. That was why they complained all the time. It looked, though, as if there were a few scraps of straw under the disused, decaying cart (which not even the co-operative would take over) in one corner of the barn. Her son did not overlook any rubbish, but luckily the handle of the broom did not reach there. Wearily she got down on her knees, groveled under the cart, pressed in further and further, and with her fingers raked together a handful of long, shiny, crisp straw. She slipped out into the flower garden, placed the straw carefully under the whispering pine, moved back and lingered until one of the birds swooped down to pick up a straw.

Translated by Peter Szente

A Winter's Tale

BY SÁNDOR TAR

Hermán, the railwayman, called out the stop for the third time, but no one got off and there was no one waiting to get on. The train hummed black and dirty against the white, snow-covered countryside; from time to time faces appeared at its frosty windows, eyes peeped curiously through the breath-clouded panes. High above, among the snow-heavy clouds, crows slowly circled. Come on, what are you waiting for?, the driver shouted, aren't you going to let me go? The bus hasn't arrived yet, called back Hermán and looked anxiously around. The driver swore, his words lost in the growing rumble of the engine. The train jerked impatiently. Hermán shrugged his shoulders and signalled. All right!, he called out unnecessarily, and with a discouraged flip of the hand started off to get back inside the station. As the last carriages passed the station building, a battered old bus pulled shakily in; the doors swung open and a boy jumped out, hastily deposited two cans of milk by the wall and dashed off after the train. Hey, stop, shouted Hermán. András! András! You'll go under! He looked on horrified as the boy caught the bar by the door of the last car but one, swung himself on to the steps and waved back cheerfully. Damn it, said Hermán to himself, and shook his head in disapproval. He lifted the cans and took them inside; Szikszay, the carter, would come for them and take them to the creamery. Turning to see the last of the train he shook his head once more.

András stuffed his cap into his pocket and leaned far out to let the wind tug and ruffle his blond curls, then drummed on the door. Two boys grinned at him from inside, gestured to him, then struggling through the crowd on the platform dragged the door open and pulled him up off the steps. Hallo, hallo, they said, you were nearly left behind! Good morning, said András loudly, and looked around him, proud. What about the last time, then, when I jumped on at the bend? His cheeks were crimson, burning from the cold and he was panting happily. On the platform, cold and stuffy from the smoke of many cigarettes, the passengers stood squeezed close together and silent. András looked around. Is Vera here?, he asked quietly. She's wandred off inside, answered one of the boys and took out a packet of cigarettes. András's face clouded over; the other boy was shuffling a pack of cards. Want to join in?, he asked András, who shook his head dejectedly. She could have stopped here—like you. Don't bother your head about it, the first boy said to console him and blew a great cloud of smoke up high into the air, put his foot up on the doorhandle; a broad aluminium cross swung on a chain from his belt down to his groin; let's play, he said, and his friend began to deal the cards on to his knees. They played without speaking, squinting into the smoke, stopping now and then to look at each other and burst into laughter. The loser would then shake his head and fish for small change in his jeans. The train rattled and rocked monotonously; in the dim light strange shadows flitted across the faces; someone would move to ease a limb gone numb and the rest would stir and yawn, then suddenly there was a commotion among the crowd, someone shouting: Let me through! I have to go to the toilet!

András listened to the indignant quarrel which followed with a weary lack of interest. Oh my God, came a woman's voice, do you have to squash me to death! It's terrible, she said, squatting by the door, terrible. She was breaking off large pieces from the cake she was holding in her hands and stuffing them far back onto her molars, opening a gap-toothed mouth wide. It's terrible, she said again with her mouth full; beside her chickens clucked in a basket. In front of the communicating door a very bent and thin old man in a heavy black coat stood slumped against two old women, his waxen face indifferent, almost lifeless, it seemed he wasn't even breathing, do you call that living, asked the gap-toothed woman, turning to him, now tell me, can you call that living? Crumbs spattered her thick fur coat. The old man did not answer, just stood staring in front of him with half-closed eyes, we're taking him to the doctor, said one of the old women, though... She left the sentence unfinished and made a discouraged gesture with her free left hand. The gap-toothed woman stopped her chewing to look through screwed-up eyes at the old man.

He's ready, she said finally, that's a man who is ready. You can always tell when they're ready. No use taking them anywhere. You know the worst thing is that he lets himself go completely, continued the old woman from behind her thick scarf, and you can guess how hard it is for us to carry this heavy body. The gap-toothed woman nodded and stuffed another piece of cake into her mouth, Oh God, she said, oh, my God. The other old woman stood silent and smiling, her face red and puffy, tears trickled slowly from her inflamed eyes, look at him, continued the first woman, just take a good look at his legs, see how he's got them spread out, he isn't even standing on them, we're holding him up, well, so tell me... You should have gone inside, someone interrupted, he would surely have got a seat inside, a sick old man like him.

Yes, came other voices, why don't you go inside?

Oh, dear me, we wouldn't be able to get off in time! Why, only the other day the train took us on to God knows where because of the crowd, goodness, said the gap-toothed woman, goodness gracious me!

He won't even walk, continued the old woman, you have to carry him like a child.

The chickens suddenly began to cluck frantically and flap their wings, the woman pushed them back in the basket, shut up, she said, come on, give us some peace now, and once more the platform was quiet except for the clatter of the wheels.

András looked out of the window, gaunt frost-covered trees and bushes flitted by; those in the distance seemed to be following the train. Drowsily he felt the sausage in his pocket flatten with the pressure of the bodies around him, but there was not enough room to draw away. There's nothing really the matter with him, he heard later, except that he's lost the will to live, now my sister there is really ill. Seriously ill. This one, she said, pointing on the other old woman, why, only last night she threw everything up, everything. The woman in the fur coat got up, groaning, Jesus, my back! She swept the crumbs off her coat and adjusted her scarf. I never take chickens home from the market, she confided, to someone, never. In the end I sell them for what I'm offered. God knows the diseases they'd pick up from the other stalls, I'm not going to take them home to the others. I bought two hundred off the hatcher this spring and what I sell's my spending money. She sucked her teeth loudly, then yawned. Dear God, she said, goodness gracious me.

The train reached the suburbs, the rattle of its wheels quietening to a rumbling murmur as it passed tenements and derelict warehouses. András yawned and tried to stretch his cramped limbs. We're there, he said. I was just about to drop off on my feet.

One of the boys wiped the window and looked out. Oh no, we haven't even reached the depot yet. They put the cards away to be ready.

Would someone please help us, said the old woman. We can't lift him off by ourselves!

There's plenty of time, someone said, the train's still moving! Voices were raised and there was a rush for the door as the train hooted and the brakes gave an ear-splitting, strident shriek. The boys tore the door open, jumped off the still moving train and made for the subway, see you, András called after them, I'm stopping here a bit longer.

People rushed by him, he stood anxiously stamping his feet on the asphalt, the trains were still squirting out their load, a milling, swarming mass that surged towards the subways, scurrying, loitering, carrying boxes and bags, shouting to friends, in the middle of this mass, a short, dark man without an overcoat on sauntered, hands in his pockets, a lighted cigarette between his lips, frozen drizzle glistening on the bare wood of the violin he carried under his arm. From time to time gusts of icy wind tore through the crowd. After some time András saw Vera with Rudi Keszszel. He called out her name, Vera, Vera, jumping up; the girl saw him, waved, and called back, see you there!, and drifted off laughing, among a group of women carrying bundles on their backs, Rudi Kesszel followed her holding his briefcase high above his head. For a few minutes longer András stayed where he was, confused and angry, then the thought of being late shocked him into movement, and he dashed down the stairs, pushed his way through the jostling noisy crowd, ran out through the station building to the bush, which he just managed to catch, one of the last to get on, get off me kidneys, someone grunted from inside as he shoved hard to allow the doors close behind him. Just then the Waggon Works' siren sounded, quarter past, he thought relieved. He had to be in at the workshop by half past five.

At half past five the workshop was cool and silent, he was the first to arrive, he switched on the lights and the drying kilns and turned on the steam for the vats. The tall, cross-eyed foreman came in a few minutes after half past five, deposited his things in his cubicle, put on a white smock spattered with paint, and came out to shake hands with the boy, his hands were freezing, his lips purple from the cold, he inspected the preparations and nodded. Rubbing his hands together he took a quick look into the dyeing cabins, then together they opened the doors of the drying kilns.

All right, said the foreman, let's warm ourselves up a bit. They sat down on one of the racks in front of the kilns and a little later, as the warm air enveloped them, almost simultaneously, their heads nodded drowsily. Portulácska, the gammy-legged charwoman found them sitting there every morning when she arrived with clinking buckets. The foreman would clear his throat, his face surly and dour, and András, yawning, would go down to the washroom to begin the day's chores. We should come to work earlier, the foreman had once said to András, and have a real sleep for once. András had laughed but the foreman's face had stayed serious, almost dreamy. Look out for the crane, he had said later, it keeps jamming at the turns. András had watched him go in some bewilderment.

The last to arrive was Esztike, called the Scooting Skeleton, an incredibly thin woman. Portulácska was waiting for her, all excitement, just think, she said by way of greeting, they took Géza the very first thing this morning. Esztike said good morning to the others and opened her drawer. Géza who? she asked finally, fixing her enormous eyes on the charwoman, my husband, of course, replied

Portulácska, disappointed. Something to do with politics, she added later. He never could keep his mouth shut. That's just what I need, him put away for two years right when prices are going up and all... Esztike, the Scooting Skeleton, was no longer listening to her; she was taking her emery cloths and buffers from her drawer, opening the tap and waiting, her head turned, for her tank to fill. Her hand, like a bent and broken twig, rested on her hip. Should I tell the foreman?, asked the charwoman. What do you want to tell him for?, was the uncomprehending reply.

Portulácska looked at her, disappointed again, don't you understand? she asked, her voice tremulous, no, replied Esztike, and she really did not.

The painters began to drift in one by one, greeting the women, opening their cabins, setting up the trestles and pieces scheduled for the day, the paint-mixers droned, the hum of the air-conditioner became louder and louder and in the cabins hissing beams cut across the pale rays of the wintry sun straining through the mean little squares of the paint-splotched windows. András liked to watch the painters at work, spraying coloured streaks on the plates first horizontally, one under the other, then, turning their stools, vertically; the colours would glisten; fresh and clean, and the painters would whistle or sing as they worked, they each had their favourites. Mister Bánát, for example, preferred "Proud castle of Krasznahorka"; Galambos, not long out of the army, sang marches, "Hey Schoolmiss" or "The Battery is off", and even Mister Venyige sang, though he was the duffer of the team. The foreman himself never sang, but he sometimes stopped in front of Mister Bánát's cabin and listened to him sing, with solemn face and crossed arms. The portly lady in charge of wages came in at half past seven, her smooth, sleek face sporting a never-fading smile, she would go and greet everyone in turn, good morning, good morning, she would say, radiating the immaculate freshness of the purely and serenely fat; she always shook hands with András, hallo, beautiful, she would say, and lightly caress his cheeks, in the radiance of that rapturous gaze András felt truly beautiful, strong and vigorous, and for this he loved the woman in charge of wages, but he loved her also for whistling "Hey Jude" all day like a man, and for smiling, just smiling as she whistled.

András liked his own work too. Everyone had to pass the door of the washroom and it stood open all day. Placing the fittings and plates into one delubricating vat after the other —alkaline bath first, then rinse, ferrodite bath, rinse again, phosphate bath, hot rinse, and finally the drying kiln, he could listen to the whistling of the woman from wages. He had a little overhead crane for lifting the containers from one vat to the other; the job was clean and easy, just running up and down the platform, standing in front of the vats, and he was left in charge of it all. Lye bubbled in a steaming vat by the entrance, he used this for boiling the paint off fittings the painters had botched and which could then be repainted, the floor and the walls were covered with yellowish tiles, running water washing down the splashes the chemicals made into the drains. He used a trolley for taking the clean fittings to the cabins and those to be cleaned back to the washroom, and so the day would pass, the only thing that vexed him was that he could not whistle "Hey Jude" himself; it was the foreman who had told him he had no ear for music, he had said, András, do you mind if I tell you not to whistle, you have no ear for music. And if you don't stop whistling we'll all go mad. All right. András liked the foreman and minded his words. Another time, the tall, stooped man had said to him, son, you could be a real good painter if you tried. If you want to I'll make a painter out of you. András had thanked him but did not say anything more. They were in Mister Venyige's cabin at the time. All the painters' cabins had graffiti scribbled on their walls, most of them said MINE FOREVER, usually in red above the spray guns, but Rudi Kesszel had TRINK TRINK written on his wall and I WANT YOU in English. András copied that one down, but first he asked what it meant. He would have liked to have graffiti on his walls too, but the water would have washed the tiles clean.

Vera came up after eight o'clock with the first load in the goods lift, she had spent the time on the ground floor buying breakfast for the fitters, András arranged to be there to meet her at the end of the corridor while the fittings were in the rinse. Hallo, he said, as if passing by accident; he was terribly in love with Vera, so you've come, he said, pulling off his mask; the girl's black mane shone in the lift, Vera, Vera, András said and put his hands on her shoulders, but she just laughed at him, she was stunningly beautiful, going around the painters and polishers for their breakfast orders; she'd always be laughing, after breakfast she would sit shivering by the drying kilns, I'm cold, she told András, my hands are always cold. Before breakfast she did the shopping for the shift, after breakfast, she was one of the polishers, András would gladly have rubbed the plates with emery cloths for her all day, dipping his hands into the cold water, but he had his own work to do, so he used the short breaks to hold her hands in his and blow on them to make them warm, — that's so good, said Vera, oh so good. I'd do it forever, said the boy, blushing, and caressed her water-withered fingers with his lips, and Vera laughed; behind them the drying kilns purred away and the air-conditioners hummed softly. András would have liked to touch her face but Vera was so beautiful that he was afraid of her, afraid to touch her, though they were standing behind the big trestles where even the painters could be found in company every

269

now and then at lunch-break or when they ran out of material. András would sometimes hear laughter or whispers as he passed the trestles and it would always make him hurry back to the washroom, ashamed of himself; there he would take the hose and, lifting his head, would squirt a thick stream of water on his mask for a long time, the water drummed loudly on the plastic and trickled down his rubber apron to the tiles below his feet. What shall I do, Mister Pap?, he asked the lift attendant, a dried-up old man who spent the day smoking bleary-eyed in the dark den of the goods lift. He was the only one who knew that András was in love with Vera. Dear me, the old man would say in his worn-out voice, shaking his head, dear, oh dear, and such a strong young man too. But even he couldn't say more. He'd ask for a cigarette and pay for it, I don't want nothing for free, he'd say, you know I mustn't buy a whole pack, I'm a chain-smoker and I'd have it gone in two shakes, I never know when to stop. My poor wife used to tell me, Alfred, she'd say, you never know when to stop. Never had a bite of food or a drink of water over what was enough, did my wife, then she up and took forty sleeping tablets and died. I'll never know now why she called me Alfred when my name is Gábor. Leaning back on his tiny chair, he thought it over for a while, forgive me, he said at last, after a long period of silence, forgive me if I've offended you in any way. András blushed. Of course you haven't, he said, of course not. He helped the old man load the heavier stuff; he usually tried to help everyone, but he never knew what to do with the coins the old man gave him for the cigarettes, please don't, he said, holding them in his palms, ashamed of himself; of course it never bothered Rudi Kesszel, Mister Pap, he'd say, I don't want this money, and he'd throw the coins into the bubbling lye where they'd be boiled down to nothing with a hiss; another time he broke a fifty-fillér coin piece in two and gave one half back, saying, Mister Pap, that's all it cost me. Mister Pap was not really interested; once he had paid the money he'd always look away somewhere far in the distance and once he told András that they would be coming to fetch him soon in an aeroplane and take him far from here at last. He asked András not to let on to anyone else about it and asked him for a cigarette.

Rudi Kesszel knew a lot of tricks, he could throw a coin up into the air, then conjure it back out of different places, just reaching out for it and there it was. András envied him terribly and wanted to learn the tricks because Vera liked them so much, even the foreman had stopped to watch one time, though he had said it was all a swindle. Portulácska had been spreading wet sawdust on the floor so that she could sweep up without raising the dust, and she came over to watch too. Géza's sure to know how to do that one, she said, because he's been in prison, he's there right now only I don't know how long for. He was in the Szabadság restaurant when they came for him, she explained to Esztike, they said he had already got up on the table, he always wants to stand on the table when he's drunk to make a speech, but it's a bit difficult for him as he's had a leg cut off. Rudi threw the coin up in the air, everyone followed it with their eyes, here it is, said the freckled boy, laughing and pulled it out of Portulácska's ear. Dear Jesus, said the Scooting Skeleton, wringing her bony hands, I can't believe it, it's scary. The woman from wages wasn't really interested; she was stacking papers in her cubicle and whistling "Hey Jude" beautifully, smiling at András every so often. András smiled back and in the end started to laugh and decided that there should be someone to whistle "Hey Jude" everywhere, someone you could smile at, on the train even, everywhere. He told Vera about it at breakfast when everyone was there and they opened the door of one of the kilns, even the foreman would come to eat with them though he never said anything, just munched away at his thin slices of bread and butter, he always looked older at breakfast. They offered him some of the tea they shared between them but he never accepted more than a small cupful. Mister Pap never left the goods lift, just opened the door and sat facing them, nibbling bits of bread from a plastic bag; if they spoke to him he would nod his head slowly and serenely, his eyes closed but he never said anything in return. The painters were given milk as a protective drink, András too because he worked with acid, the polishers didn't get any but András always gave his milk to Vera, she never had anything else, just tore the plastic milkbag open at one of the corners with her tiny teeth and drank the cool liquid down in small slow sips. András usually had sausage or salami or hash for breakfast; he would have given some to Vera but she never wanted any, she was as slim and as supple as a young willow, her waist so slender you could reach round it with your two hands.

At half past twelve Mister Venyige dropped his spray gun into the paint and got his mouth full of resin. He wiped the acrid, stinking mess sticking to his tongue and teeth and palate with a cloth and everyone went over to him to have a good laugh. Vera laughed so hard she had to lean on András and so he could put his arm around her waist, he was so happy that he wished Mister Venyige would drop his gun into the paint every day. In the end Mister Venyige rinsed out his mouth with some thinner and that put an end to it as far as he was concerned, but they were still laughing when they went out into the street, and even when they got on the thirty-one bus which they took to go to the station. Rudi Kesszel played the scene again, retching, his hand in his mouth up to the wrist. They still had some time to spare before their train, Rudi Kesszel asked Vera to come and have a drink with him in the milk-bar but Vera said she hadn't any money, of course you have, Rudi said, throwing a coin up in the air; they watched it soar, even Rudi, here you are, he said, taking it out of her hair, you see you do have money after all. They laughed and strolled through the waiting-room a couple of times and even András did not put on his cap though his ears were freezing out in the street.

An enormous crowd droned among in the waiting-room, long queues stood in front of the booking-office, the newsstand, the snack-bar, everywhere, the loud-speaker boomed continually and as the trains arrived and left, hordes of people packed the doorways; a noisy, happily munching bunch of students had occupied the area around the vending machines, a determined-looking little boy stood by the telephone booth, guarding a great heap of packages. Vera began to play with the time-table indicator while Rudi Kesszel bought a ticket to Tiszacsege from the slot-machine, though that was not where they were going, he gave the ticket to Vera who said that it was a stupid thing to have done and that they should take it to the booking-office and get the money back, but Rudi threw the ticket up into the air and everyone looked up to see where it went, the ticket had disappeared, it stayed up in the air, said Rudi, and they laughed. How do you do it, Vera asked, Rudi Kesszel looked at her and said, I'll tell you if... and there he stopped. If what? asked the girl, Rudi leaned over to whisper something in her ear that made them both blush, András lingered by them dejectedly, we'd better be going, he said, the train'll be in soon. They started walking towards the exit, Rudi did a few dance-steps in his high-heeled boots, then threw a coin up in the air and cried Hey Presto! pointing after it with his other hand; those nearest to them, then almost the whole crowd in the waiting-room stood looking up, pointing, asking questions, Rudi pivoted around and took out the coin from between a railwayman's buttocks, the people standing by them laughed loudly, Vera laughed with her hands pressed tightly to her breasts, then the signal went and the loudspeaker began to announce departures and stops, Do let's hurry, called out András, we might still get a seat! They ran down into the subway.

There were no seats free but they managed to find a place to lean against on the platform. Rudi Kesszel was the only one who did not lean against anything, he told stories, play-acting all the while, did you see that, he said, I fooled the whole station, they were out of their minds! He twirled the end of his long scarf, I'm going to buy a radio on Monday, he said, a Pluto, it's only just come in, it's a portable, a radio and telephone in one. How'd you mean, a radio and telephone in one? Vera asked. A family got on the train, husband and wife and two ten-year-old boys and a little girl of about four or so; she was sitting on her father's shoulders, a red pompon on her bonnet, they were loaded up with packages and looked uncertainly for places to sit, they too settled down on the platform. A paper boy hurried through the carriages shouting out titles, fresh crowds of passengers arrived while others wandered from carriage to carriage. In the throng András tried to stay within touching distance of Vera, but Rudi Kesszel was also pressed close to them and he had twice whispered in her ear and they had laughed. At last the train pulled out with a jolt and the little girl sitting on her father's shoulders let out a peal of laughter. There were people running after the train, András watched them through the window to see whether they'd catch it or not but they didn't; then they passed one of the benches and sitting on it with his head lolling was the old man of that morning, the talkative woman beside him holding a handkerchief up to her eyes, a bit further on the other old woman sat strangely stiff and lop-sided, her face covered with a scarf. She's dead, said András, surprised, why, I saw her only this morning! Who's dead, Vera asked, but Rudi Kesszel whispered something in her ear and putting his hand on her shoulder moved even closer to her. I came up on the train with the old woman who... András answered half-heartedly, but Rudi Kesszel interrupted in a loud voice, is it you who stinks of cows, he said, and, wrinkling his nose, leaned to sniff at his hair. Someone laughed, András looked at Rudi, then, without thinking, slapped his face. It made a loud crack and a strange silence followed; Rudi Kesszel's face turned blood-red, the pale imprint of each finger standing out. For a moment it seemed as if he would hit back, but then his eyes brimmed with tears and he turned away. András blushed too, he was terribly ashamed of himself for hitting someone smaller than himself. Vera turned away too, then the connecting door opened and an old man with a violin came in, said good afternoon, and tucking his instrument under his chin began to play and sing "Mother, dear lady". Slowly the uproar died down, inside the compartment a middle-aged woman stood up and sang the song through, stern-faced; beside her a drunk slept with his head dropping on to his knees. András looked out of the window with a sinking heart and by the time the song was over Vera had disappeared.

His sullen mood lasted through the evening, at home he hardly spoke, finishing his chores in silence; he said he wasn't hungry and went to bed without any supper. His mother woke him up at half past three, get going, she said roughly, the light from the hall shining into the room. The boy dressed drowsily in the cold and dark; they kept cows and bulls and pigs, his mother set off across the courtyard with clinking pails and lighted lamps and the boy followed her. Inside the stable it was steamy and warm, the air stuffy and pungent. His mother hung the lamp on its nail and coughed, András began mucking out, brought in fresh straw, mother, he said suddenly, I have something to tell you. What's bitten you then? his mother asked without turning round, she was washing a cow's dugs with warm water, I want to get married, András said. And I want to leave here. I don't want to stay on the farm. What, his mother said, slowly turning her head, you want to do what? I'm going to leave, said the boy. I want to get married, I can't be doing this forever, can I? You are going to do what, his mother said again, getting up from beside the cow. I'm going to leave, said András, his voice choking a little, I'm going to leave! He did not stop shouting it out when his mother slashed him with the whip, I am going to leave here, he cried, shielding his face with his hands as the whip cracked and cracked again. They stood glaring at each other and she called him a dirty tramp who'd leave his widowed mother for some hussy or other, your blood's on the boil and there's a bone in your leg, isn't that so, you scoundrel, you blackguard, you good-for-nothing, you!, shrieked the woman, infuriated beyond measure, and not caring where the blow would fall, down came the whip with each word, I don't care, I'll still go, shouted the boy, then, when he could no longer stand the pain, he ran in to the bulls where his mother did not dare follow him. I'll see to you, just you wait, the woman screeched after him, I'll have your brains out, but I'll not be mother to a villain? The bulls snorted, pawing the ground, nervous from all the shouting, they tugged at their halters, moaning, saliva dribbling from their mouths and one of them, in a burst of fury, pitched into the manger with its horns. András kicked him on the nose, whoa, he said, whoa, and kicked him again. He was trembling with excitement.

He washed quickly and left the house without saying goodbye to his mother. He walked past the cans of milk set down at the gate, but he hadn't gone ten steps when he turned back for them and, picking them up, ran towards the bus-stop. He only just managed to catch the bus and had difficulty finding room for himself and the two cans, inside it was full of smoke, and the radio was on. He did not speak to anyone but as they neared the station the usual excitement came over him; stuffing his cap into his pocket and gripping the handles of the cans he waited, tensed-up for the bus to stop. He saw the train pulling out of the station, the bus stopped with a jerk, the doors opened and he started to run in the snow that came up to his ankles, stop, stop, he heard Hermán shout, throwing down the cans he broke into a run again and caught up with the train, grabbing hold of the bar by the door of the last car but one, he jumped up on the steps, and waved back to Hermán. He panted a little, then leaned far out to let the wind tug at his hair and drummed on the door. Inside someone was standing with his back to the door, it was Rudi Kesszel. He knocked again, shaking the latch, but it was locked from the inside; Rudi Kesszel was fidgeting about and as he lifted his arm András saw Vera, she was laughing, you could see they were talking to each other, then Rudi Kesszel took out a coin and threw it up in the air. Vera looked up and András saw from outside that the coin was still in Rudi Kesszel's palm, held tight at the base of the thumb and forefinger, of course when he turned down his palm you couldn't see anything, so it really was a swindle, thought András bitterly, he just pretends to throw the coin up! The train was going faster now and an icy wind tugged at his coat, a cloud of minute snow-flakes stirred up by the wheels whirled into his face as he stood sadly holding on to the bar by the door. He didn't knock again.

Translated by Eszter Molnár

Looking for my Brother
BY ZSOLT CSALOG

It was in 1944 that I lost touch with my brother. I haven't seen him since. Since '44 I've heard nothing of my brother at all. Not a word.

First my father died. They took him away and executed him for hiding four Russians. The Germans found them, took my father off and shot him. A month later they took my brother away. As he was a boy scout the Germans sent him off to drive cattle. He managed to escape, but by that time we were nowhere to be found. By that time there'd been raids on all the gypsies. They'd gathered them all up and taken them to Dunaszerdahely to do away with them. I escaped with my brother-in-law's mother, but back at home we only found an empty house. No furniture, nothing. The flat was completely empty. It was then that I saw my brother once more. But after that my uncle took me under his care. He brought me across to Hungary—and that's how I was parted from my brother. And I haven't heard anything from him since.

We lived in Ágyalla, which now belongs to Czechoslovakia. My father made troughs. Before we had a house in Ágyalla my father would gather all our bits and pieces together, sit us up on the cart and off we'd go to wherever he was able to find work, wherever there was room for making troughs. Then, if we couldn't get some kind of farmhouse from the landowner, my father would either build a mud hut, or put a tent over the cart, so we could stay wherever he was working. And this was how we lived, always on the move. I liked this life of wandering. After all I was a child, and what does a child know? Whatever my mother and father did was fine by me. And there were always all these troughs; large ones, small ones, round ones, great big salt troughs, washing troughs—all kinds of troughs. That's what my father made. I liked to watch him working. I'd always go and peep at him carving up those enormous trees. I'd catch the shavings and put them on the fire when my mother was cooking. I liked doing that. Once we'd got the house we didn't always go off with my father. He'd leave us there in winter and go around the neighbourhood making troughs on his own.

In '44 my father also stayed at home. It was wartime, and the front was getting closer. Then one night four Russians came. My father knew how to talk to them and they asked him to hide them away. We had two double beds, so my father tucked them away there. My mother put up a bit of fight:

"My God," she cries, "don't you care about your own family? We'll all be shot if they're found."

"No," says my father, "it'll be all right." And he hid them away in the beds.

Then, at about nine o'clock the next day, the Germans came looking for the Russians. They found them in the beds and brought them out with their hands up. They took them away, and what they did to them God only knows. Then my father was taken too, along with our neighbour's son-in-law. They were taken off to the village hall, put on a truck, which left. These were Hungarian hangmen. Arrow-cross men. One of them had a long white beard, I remember. When they got to the end of Ógyalla they pushed my father and the other man off the truck and told them to run. They began running down at the bottom of the garden. It was there that the bullets reached them.

That's how they shot my father. He just lay there dead. Shot through the back of the head. I saw him as I see the soil in front of me now. The most they allowed was for us to bury him.

My elder brother was seventeen and already married. But he was a scout, and so had to go off to drive cattle. That's how he survived, because a week after the Germans took him away the raids started. We had to collect three days' food and blanket, and they rounded up all the gypsies. Masses of them—Hungarian gypsies, trough-makers, Wallachian gypsies. They rounded us all up and drove us on towards Szerdahely. I escaped with my brother-in-law's mother during the night. They held us in a big open space, but we managed to hide among the tanks. Behind the last tank was a farm. That's where we ran when the soldiers weren't watching. A Hungarian man and his wife hid us among the corn, and we stayed there for two days while the others were driven to the banks of the Danube and killed. They shot the lot of them. My poor mother, my two brothers and five sisters, my brother's wife and her father and brothers and sisters, and a whole lot more, hundreds more. They murdered them all there on the banks of the Danube. They destroyed all my people.

Then I met my brother for the last time. It was after he had escaped from the Germans. We just leaned on each other's shoulders and cried. Then he went on to Dunaszerdahely to look for his wife and our mother. But all he found was my three-year-old sister at the water's edge. My little sister shot dead. He took off his winter coat, wrapped her up in it, and buried her at the foot of the dam. A little pit had to serve as her grave, because gypsies weren't allowed in the cemetery. Then he came home and handed me over to my uncle. I never saw my brother again.

I wanted to stay in Ágyalla where my father was buried, but that was out of the question. I was alone, without anyone to look after me, just wandering about. I would stray into farms and tell people my troubles—who I was and what had become of me. They'd give me something to eat and I'd go on. It was a miserable life. Then my uncle took me out into the wide world to make troughs.

My uncle also dealt in troughs and that took us around the country. But he treated me badly, really badly, like a dog. My life was miserable. His wife would tie me down and beat me like a little girl. I couldn't stand being with them, so I ran away. I was taken in by a Hungarian household, and it was they who brought me up.

That was in Kerekegyháza. Trough-making had taken us there around '47 or '48. The man who adopted me was called Ferenc Spanyol. He was a good man. He treated me just like one of his own children, even though he already had three daughters and a son. They bought me shoes, boots, scarves, a winter coat, a spring coat and yards of material. They had a sewing machine and Mariska made me dresses. I had all kinds of clothes at that time. I did anything they asked, just as they wanted, and they liked me for that. They loved me very much in that house, I spent three or four years with them and it was from there that I got married.

I was seventeen at the time. Their daughters were older. Mariska also got married at that time, but Veronika and Teruska were still at home. A Hungarian boy from next door had been courting me. The parents were against him at first and wanted to stop him seeing me. But he kept on sneaking back, courting me so assiduously that they just couldn't stop us seeing each other. And that's how we got started.

My husband was a peasant boy. He had a few acres of land, but after a while took up delivery work and became a private delivery man. He treated me badly because he was always drunk. He was a good-for-nothing drunkard, and I was always just a gypsy to him. He'd always curse my gypsy mother for making me like this or making me like that. He kept on telling me that I had nothing, he kept battering me with words. He came from a kulak family. All his forebears had been kulaks. He'd rather drink than see to his land, so I was left to work with the horse. But it was a wild horse and scared me stiff. I was always in tears, always going off to complain to the neighbours—by then we weren't living in Kerekegyháza. 'If only my brother were alive,' I kept groaning to myself. I had no one in the world, that was what hurt. No one at all to tell my troubles to. If only I could go and complain to my brother, how good that would be. Or just sit and remember our parents together: have a good old natter about my father and mother or something like that. But just to complain to strangers... who couldn't help me anyway, and wouldn't even want to. Maybe they'd believe my troubles, maybe not. Maybe they'd just laugh at me.

In the end I wasn't good enough for my husband. I had to leave him because he drove me away. And I was three months pregnant when I left.

Then I went into building. I worked my way round Sarkad, Gyula and Békéscsaba. With my three-month belly I signed a contract for the whole year and worked on a building-site. The company found me a room and paid the two hundred forints rent for it as well. I got all kinds of benefits there: one thousand four hundred forints maternity, seven hundred from the trade union, six hundred for the lying in, and some for food. I got all this from the company because I was ready to work myself to death. I gave birth to twins in Békéscsaba in '53. I didn't hand them over to state care. I didn't want just to dump them on someone else's doorstep, so I kept them at home while I went to work. I got three months' leave, and after that they let me go home from the site every three hours on a company bicycle to nurse my children. I stayed on at the site and carried on work.

In '56 one of my sons, little Józsi, died. The boy was ill. First he had little lumps on his lungs which they managed to cure. But then, because he was so thin, they gave him injections to fatten him up, and when he started putting on weight he kept getting attacks of nose bleeding. And that's what took my little son. He died of nose bleeds. He was three years old.

It's better to be among Hungarians. Among Hungarians there's no real poverty. It's different when you've got land like the Hungarians, because you've always got work. Or if you haven't got land then you've got a vegetable garden, which means food for the winter. You've got everything. And because there's no poverty the cleanliness is different too. Everything is different among the Hungarians. But then, because my first husband was a Hungarian, and because he was such a drunkard and treated me so badly, I never dared marry a Hungarian again. I could have had other Hungarians, though. I could have had plenty of them on the building-site. But after my first husband I never dared start anything with a Hungarian again.

And then the man I live with now came to Csaba. He came to work on the building-site. He's a gypsy, a Wallachian gypsy, so he speaks the language of the gypsies. But not like us, because we always spoke Rumanian or Hungarian at home in Ógyalla, and so I couldn't understand him at first. Somehow we got to know each other. Then he told me that he had a wife, but didn't want to live with her any more. He asked me to give up my job and go with him to Túr. Since I had nobody he would look after me and support me. He would support the child too.

To this I said:

"Look Pali, I don't want to be the cause of any family row. I don't want to get you into arguments and fights at home. So just leave me in peace."

"Only listen," he says, "I'll look after the child as if he were of my own. I'll support you in every possible way. I don't have any children. So it's easy for me. Easy to divorce too."

I didn't want to marry him at all, but for two years he kept coming to see me. After living with that woman for ten years he sent her packing, and brought me here to Túr, eleven years ago now. And we've been together ever since. All the time. During these past eleven years we haven't been apart for ten minutes.

I might have had a child by him, but we were working on machines at the time and I collapsed trying to lift a sack on to his shoulders. I couldn't go on working, and had to spend two and a half weeks in hospital. And because of that I'll never be able to bear children again. But to tell you the truth I can't say I'm really sorry. Because after my other accident I don't think I'd have the nerve to bring up another child.

My accident happened when we were on the way to see my brother-in-law, that is, this man's brother in Üllő. His brother came to meet us with a horse and cart at the station in Monor—he collects rags and bones for the Waste Material Trust. On the way back from the station a big lorry smashed into us. The fact that we had lights on didn't seem to help, the lorry caught the righthand side of the cart, throwing the three men into the fields and me into the middle of the road on my back. The ambulance took me to St Stephen's

Hospital in Budapest, where they had to operate on me. I wasn't conscious at all, just covered in blood, and they had to cut the clothes off me. I spoke all the time during the operation—in Hungarian, Rumanian, and Romany. I kept calling my brother, crying for him in vain. But I didn't know any of this was happening, they only told me about it afterwards. Then I was put into the Mezőtúr hospital for three and a half months and even after that the doctor would come and see me while I stayed alive on five or six different drugs. And so I survived. But my nerves have never been right since then. And I'm always nervy now.

As soon as I was a bit better I went to the courts saying that I wanted to sue. After thirteen hearings in Monor I won the case. But even though it was the other man's fault, I only got a thousand forints. I simply wouldn't accept this, and asked them to take the case to Pest. The Pest Supreme Court sent me an extra nine hundred forints. And there you are, that's what a person's life is worth: one thousand nine hundred forints.

The man I'm with now is a good man. He works in the brick factory like my son. But he always brings his wages home and never checks me on what I spend the money on. Even so, I always give him an account of where it goes. I haven't been able to work since my accident, but my man wouldn't have me work anyway—that's one thing about gypsies; they keep their wives in comfort. We can't paint the town red or buy knick-knacks or what not off the two sets of wages, but we have enough for what we really need. The first thing we have to think of now is a place to sleep, because this house is about to fall on our heads. We haven't got any furniture at the moment because my father-in-law died last autumn and we had to sell everything to give him a funeral. We are hoping to pull this house down in the spring, if weather permits, and live in a tent while we build a new one. My daughter-in-law is expecting a baby in autumn so we'll need a roof over our heads and a place we call our own. That's what we're working towards now. That's what we're struggling for.

This man of mine is really a very good man. He takes care of my son as well. He even wanted them to give the boy his name. But even though they agreed to give it to him they still slapped mine back on when they gave him his identity card. It's because we're not married—that's the trouble. I would have liked it if my son had had the other name.

In '64 the boy's father, my first husband, came to see the child. Since '53 it had never entered his head to come and see his boy. Only now that someone had gone through all the difficulties of bringing him up did he get the idea of coming. Up till then he hadn't spent even five fillérs on the child, but now here he was with a packet of sweets. He talked to the boy, asked him his name and how old he was, gave him two forints, shook his hand and left. Then he went to the courts and asked for custody of the child. But I told the court and my man backed me up—that I hadn't struggled to bring up the boy since '53 just to let him be taken away from me. Why should I let him go just when he's beginning to work, to earn money and be of some use to me. No, I didn't let the child go.

The boy didn't want to go either. Not a bit. He always clung to this second father of his. Even to this very day he doesn't recognize his Hungarian father. If someone asks him:

"Who's your father?"

"Pál Rafael."

"But he's not your father. You don't even have the same name."

"But he is my father!" It's because he loves him so much. He's the only father the boy will admit to.

I even went to the police looking for my brother. They said to come back and see them again if I had time. So I went there three times in all, but they never paid any attention. They didn't even write down my complaint. The officer would only say, "Well, he must be either dead or alive, mustn't he?" And that's all they ever tossed at me. About a year ago a Hungarian moved down here from the county of Veszprém. He's a bricklayer, but he knows how to write quite well. I asked him to write a letter for me to the Red Cross. The letter was written, but so many things got in the way, with my father-in-law being ill at the time, that I let the whole thing drop and then lost the letter altogether. Anyway I can't expect help from the Red Cross either.

I'd love to have some news of my brother. To know whether he's alive or dead. He was still alive when he handed me over to my uncle in '44, but after that we lost touch and I've heard nothing of him since. His name is Rudi or Gyula Kalányos. Rudi was his real name but we called him Gyula. He was my oldest brother, and I loved him best of all. But we all loved him, my mother and father and all the children. Whenever he was on day work or with the scouts he would always come home singing, and we'd run to meet him, leap into his arms and kiss him. We loved him very much. I don't know, I really don't know if he's still alive. Being a man he might have died somewhere in the war. The one thing I always wonder is, with all the place I've been to, and with all the people who've come towards me in the street, how is it that I've never come across my brother? Or perhaps I wouldn't even recognize him if I saw him?

I've often thought of taking out my passport and going to Czechoslovakia, to Ógyalla, where my father was buried.

Maybe I'd find my brother there. But still I daren't go. Not because of the money, and not because of my illness either. But because I'd prefer it if he came here, to my own place. After all if I did go over there and see that part of the land again I might very well not be able to come back ever again. And even if it did turn out that my brother was still alive, and came over here to see me, I'm not sure if I could really bear it. If he suddenly appeared now, introduced himself and showed me his identity card ... or if he was just sitting here, like you are sitting here talking to me now, and simply said something like: "Well, well, Mari, well, well"... I'm not at all sure I could even bear that.

Translated by Richard L. Aczel

Babylonia

BY BULCSÚ BERTHA

"And the passover, a feast of the Jews was nigh. When Jesus then lifted up his eyes, and saw a great company come unto him, he saith unto Philip, Whence shall we buy bread, that these may eat?... One of his disciples, Andrew, Simon Peter's brother, saith unto him, There is a lad here, which hath five barley loaves, and two small fishes: but what are they among so many? And Jesus said, Make the men sit down. Now there was much grass in the place. So the men sat down, in number about five thousand. And Jesus took the loaves; and when he had given thanks, he distributed to the disciples, and the disciples to them that were sat down; and likewise of the fishes as much as they would. When they were filled, he said unto his disciples, Gather up the fragments that remain, that nothing be lost. Therefore they gathered them together, and filled twelve baskets with the fragments of the five barley loaves which remained over and above unto them that had eaten..."
The Gospel According to St. John 6, 4–13

I was late leaving for Bábolna on the M1. I drove fast enough to get there on time, though I suspected it to be hopeless. The people coming in the opposite direction also seemed to be late, like me; there was hardly any other explanation why we all raced along the M1 like madmen. There was no way I could make up for the lost time, only by beginning the whole trip from scratch. But man is an optimistic being. Perhaps ... with a bit of luck ... if the car holds out ... if they start the programme a little late, if those who expect me also get there late. A car is hardly a place to think things over calmly, particularly when you have to overtake, and are in turn overtaken, in a series of risky manoeuvres. Yet you can think, even if disconnectedly, intermittently. That is how Jacques Piccard came to my mind, who said at the symposium at the Stevens Institute about ten years ago that he rather doubted that mankind would survive this century, since there are risks other than the threat of nuclear war: worldwide pollution contaminates the air we breathe, the water we drink and the soil we cultivate. According to Piccard, the whole of our technology is to blame. Arthur C. Clarke, who worked in the Twenty-first Century Science Institute fifteen years ago, promised us, on the other hand, that before the year 2,000 we'd be using artificial brains, we'll have decoded the language of the whales, we'll have landed on other planets, opened mines under the seas, changed or modified our notion of time, and will have introduced Cyborg (Cybernetic Organism) into our lives, or rather society, to complement our bodies and organs. Afterwards, in the year 2,000, the planets will be colonized. Comparing the two forecasts, I wondered whether to rejoice or lose heart. Society expects a positive response from me. But what's a positive response? All I know is that an instant before the temporary cooling occurred (when the traditional energy carriers were almost all exhausted), mankind discovered that nucleic acids, proteins, lipids and polysaccharides constitute the chemical material in which life's characteristic processes take place and set about to create life, man in a test tube or a swamp from the discovered components. Mankind has so far been able to accomplish everything it has had enough time for. And now it will either have enough time or not. It's a fact, however, that half of all the people created with the ancient, say primitive, technology suffer from malnutrition, with millions starving and, in less prosperous years, dying. Between 1785 and 1900, twenty-six million people starved to death in India alone.

Hundreds of thousands and millions die of starvation in India, Africa and other places even today. The birthrate has fallen in recent years in Europe, the United States of America, and even in China and India, due to radical measures introduced by the state. Even so, the earth's population increases by some 200,000 daily, and six to seven thousand million people are expected to 'celebrate' the year of the millennium. In 1976, the world produced 360.2 million tons of wheat, 292.9 millions tons of corn and 323.2 million tons of rice. This is an immense quantity, but what it is for so many people? It isn't even enough for the four thousand million people, let alone for the two to three thousand million to be born up to the turn of century. Those starving in the world are most affected by the lack of proteins, animal protein in particular. But in order to obtain one kilogram of animal protein in the form of chicken-meat, four kilograms of vegetable protein need to be used as fodder. In the case of pork six and in the case of beef twenty to thirty kilograms of protein-rich fodder are required. In such a world situation, every ton of surplus in the cornfields of professional meat production is of vital importance.

According to the system of large-scale mechanized maize production elaborated at Bábolna, the member farms headed by Nagyigmánd have produced 50 per cent more maize in the last five years than before. They produce broiler chicken, layer-hybrids and eggs by the million, all in keeping with international standards. Three airlines, eight charters a week, 440–460 charters a year, transport poultry and eggs to Algeria, Lebanon, Jordan, Saudi Arabia, Kuwait, Iraq, Iran, Austria and Yugoslavia. The more important business partners include the Soviet Union, the German Democratic Republic, Czechoslovakia and Great Britain, as well as the German Federal Republic, Italy, France and Spain. In 1976 the production value per capita was 644,945 forints, while the net income was 43,511 forints at Bábolna. That is why I set off towards Bábolna with impatient curiosity, trying to understand something of the modern operating structure of food production. I failed, unfortunately, because I'm a mere writer with no agricultural training. But I did manage, at least, to sense something of Bábolna's atmosphere, its own world of laws, hallmarking the opportunities offered to socialism and socialist man. I learnt that something that had seemed a Utopia ten years earlier was now possible. And possible it was here in Hungary.

I must admit that despite my curiosity I approached Bábolna with a certain suspicion, an indefinable unease. Bábolna was not to blame, only its prestige. I have observed many times in the last fifteen years that factories and co-operatives which are frequently visited by the country's leaders, or what's more, foreign heads of state, maybe even kings, have begun to behave as if they were no longer factories or agricultural stations but kingdoms, displaying huge photographs of the kings or higher-ranking and more authoritative visitors to their units rather than talking about their production. On such occasions it always comes to light that they haven't the faintest idea about the difference or similarity between a politician and a writer. I have had occasion to see for myself that guests are received democratically at Bábolna. Or rather, normally. This is due either to the management policy of the plant or, more simply, to the fact that it is impossible to determine seniority among the multitude of visitors, as it is difficult to know what each one wants. In the worst case he is plain curious, but he might wish to buy, help, offer co-operation or sell something useful like a machine or an idea.

I got to Bábolna around ten o'clock. The neat village, the

concrete road, the trees, the roomy, marked-out parking spaces, the cleanness surprised me. The building of the agricultural complex stands in an ancient, well-kept park. As far as I can remember there was no sign on the fence round the park to indicate the complex. If there was one, it must have been very modest and that is why I didn't notice it. The building, the entrance, the corridors, everything was of an established good taste, built predominantly of fine building material, which had nowhere been replaced by plastic in the course of renovation. Later I came to discover that there were no nameplates or numbers on the brown stained doors either. I was expected at the reception, where I was given a key to a guest house where I could leave my things. A lady suggested that I drive in through the side gate to arrive straight at the guest house. All this was done in a matter of seconds. In the meantime my arrival was announced and by the time I reached the guest house, the lady I had met at the entrance was already waiting for me and told me that Dr. Róbert Burgert, the director of the complex, was engaged in talks with a foreign politician in Budapest and therefore someone else would show me around the plant. I got my things out of the car and went to my room in the guest house. It was a big room with a couch, a settee, a radio a refrigerator, a telephone, a hall and a bathroom. Prompted by curiosity, I opened the refrigerator to find a cold platter, some wine and mineral water there. I washed my hands and went downstairs. In the entrance hall I caught sight of a marble tablet, informing visitors that the building had been designed and built by Ferenc Beke in 1915 under the professional guidance of Baron Gyula Podmaniczky, ministerial councillor. From the courtyard I could see the back of the central building with its huge terrace, and on the two sides the stables and outhouses stretching as far as the guest house and even beyond. In the round, well-kept circle in the middle, horses were exercised whenever guests were present or auctions were held. The statue of the faithful Arab horse stood in the centre of the track, amid all the flowers. The Napoleonic troops had driven away with the stud, but one Arab horse made its way back, and the statue paid homage to its loyalty. On the two sides there were horses neighing and pawing the ground with their feet in the stables. It suddenly struck me that Bábolna was a horse-orientated farm living of poultry.

A car drove up. Gábor Nagy, director of Agrária, invited me to accompany him on his supervisory tour and offered to show me various things on the way. The Bábolna agricultural complex has independent foreign trade rights, which it exercises through the Agrária Foreign Trading Company. We left the village rapidly and drove along a well-kept private road through woods and clearings to arrive at one of the big poultry farms. *Babylonia* was the name I read at the entrance and I turned questioningly to Gábor Nagy.

"Our very first export went to Iraq, consisting of one million eighteen week-old pullets for the city of Hilla in Babylonia."

A fence surrounded a log cabin, housing the office of the premises as well as the common rooms and other facilities. Somewhat farther away eight long, windowless, aluminium-covered buildings in a row, with fodder-mixing or regulating towers at the end. Concrete roads, everything orderly, plants along the fence, outside the woods. Gábor Nagy informed me that 55,000 baby chicks were hatched and with an 8 per cent loss approximately 50,000 hens were reared in each building. A big board on the first building gave all the data.

> 1974 investment: 82 million Ft
> Pullet production: 1 million a year
> Places for the chicks: 400 thousand,
> two and a half cycles per year
> Henhouses: 8
> Technology: 5-storey "Salmet" battery
> Staff: 15 persons

Bábolna needs fifteen persons to look after the one million Tetra-SL hen-hybrids every year. When we entered the first house and I looked at the pullets through the glass, I realized that it was only possible because the compound was well-equipped and the feeding regulators were all automatized. All the staff had to do was to control the equipment and the installations. Transporting the hens (picking them up one by one and placing them in other coops) was practically the only physical work that might tire them out. Although I was greatly impressed by what I saw, I couldn't help wondering how the chickens felt in such a *Salmet battery*. The manager put my mind at rest, saying that the hens were always kept at the required temperature and were fed satisfactorily and at regular hours. Everything was taken care of, they didn't need to run after insects, grains and other pickings in the field. All they had to worry about was how to strive for the perfect embodiment of the Tetra-SL prototype.

Gábor Nagy guided me in an apparently friendly manner, yet I kept sensing some kind of formality behind the uttered words. To put it another way, I detected the mental aloofness and unfailing attention of a manager used to guiding people of different outlook and rank. Another thing I didn't fail to notice was that he had other things to attend to and his restlessness grew by the second, as if he had been receiving news from somewhere, which was constantly modifying the acual situation. I thought that we entered the doors together, but many times when I looked round for him, he wasn't by my side. Later on I found out that Bábolna has its own short-wave radio circuit, which enables the managers, the director, the secretariat and the different units to keep in touch within a hundred-kilometre radius. Some of the radios were in the office and cars, while others accompanied people (in the hand or tucked into a deep pocket) wherever they went. While accompanying me Gábor Nagy was worrying about two things: a possible visit to Bábolna by a foreign government representative and an impending Algerian tender worth 2 million. Driving back to our starting point he confided that they had another poultry-farm in Bikarét, producing 325 thousand hens annually. Their other well-known products included Tetra-B, Tetra-SL, Tetra-L and Tetra-S, the latter being not hens but pigs. They also bred over 50,000 sheep, almost a thousand horses, out of which some 360–380 are racehorses. They have two stables at Kerteskő and Diópuszta full of English thoroughbreds and two stables at Bábolna and Széphalma full of Arab thoroughbreds. Breeding horses has been a tradition at Bábolna, they have the same number of horses as before, and horse-breeding is still lucrative.

"Tell me," I asked Gábor Nagy, "why must you disperse your breeding plants so widely among the woods and fields? Surely the distance causes great problems."

"It's better this way as far as epidemics and overall hygiene is concerned. If a disease starts up anywhere, we are able to close off the plant, disinfect it and, if it comes to the worst, burn it down."

Gábor Nagy invited me to have lunch with him in the canteen of the complex. On the tables there were white tablecloths, wine, soda-water and bread-baskets. We were served a good soup and stew. There was a photographer from the

Hungarian News Agency and two "horsepeople" (a trainer and a jockey) seated at our table. The horsepeople had just returned from Vienna and were complaining about the race. At another table a Hungarian and three foreign gentlemen wearing meticulously ironed shirts and ties were discussing something in English. The entrance-hall was covered in marble and so was the bathroom. Everything was well-ordered and spotless. The crisp white loaf came from the Bábolna bakery and the soda was also produced on the premises. In the afternoon I learnt that besides its own bakery and soda factory, the agricultural complex had its own design and construction section as well, which, on request, even erects similar henhouses in the Arab countries. Bábolna has its own computer centre which looks after breeding selections as well as book-keeping and payroll accounting. Bábolna has, furthermore, its own printing house, its own machine designers, its own permanent exhibition and, most of all, its own brain. When we went to see the former-hen-house-turned-computer-section after lunch I asked Gábor Nagy why they needed to have their own design office.

"Because of time," he said. "If we get a contract unexpectedly or something crosses the boss's mind at night, we have to design and execute it at once."

"What do you mean by at once?"

"Two days, at most a week. International business allows for no slow orders, correspondence, six or more months of planning, because by then the offer will long have been given to some fast, flexible foreign enterprise. If the boss says that there should be a poultry-farm right here between these two woods on this clearing, then in two months' time (including design and construction) the poultry must be in the houses."

"Forgive me, but there are two things that I don't quite get, and both have to do with finances. Have you any kind of capital that enables you to invest and to adapt to the requirements of the international market?"

"No, we have no capital; we rely on state credit."

"People have to work with much greater precision and discipline in closed, large-scale maize production systems and meat-processing than as a rule in other branches of agriculture. I suppose you pay them better than other places."

"We pay the same wages as other farms. We employ 4,266 people in the complex, out of whom 162 have university degrees, 610 have finished their secondary education, and 2,920 are skilled workers. The average monthly salary is 3,464 forints, which is complemented by 4,682 forints of profit sharing at the end of each year."

"What is labour discipline like?"

"Our employees do what they are required to do."

"Any drinking problems?"

"That's impossible here. We'll have no drinking on the premises whatsoever."

Gábor Nagy would have been quite happy to lose me somewhere between the computer centre and a henhouse, but as neither Róbert Burgert nor Miklós Erdélyi, deputy manager, had returned, he had to take me along to his office. On the wall of his office I discovered the photograph of Dr. Sándor Kotlán, vet, and professor of parasitology. Upon further inquiries I discovered that Gábor Nagy had originally been a vet himself and that in some crisis Burger had appointed him director of Agrária.

His colleagues reported to him in a relaxed atmosphere, though the great tension of the Algerian deal was still in the air. Gábor Nagy explained:

"Our Arab contacts began in 1965–68 within the range of a few thousand dollars. This rose sharply in 1973. The oil profits had piled up and they had many hungry mouths to feed. State programmes were launched and private capital invested as well. Transporting the goods costs more than the products themselves in Budapest. Now we're expecting an excellent deal shortly."

A telephone call, a telex, colleagues rushing in and out. I could catch the words but couldn't make sense out of them. First they calculated how many fillérs they could afford to knock off the price for the deal to continue to be feasible; then they began to favour the idea of a guarantee by a French or West German bank. They talked of letters of credit and called the National Bank in Budapest twice. Then there came a call from a Ferihegy Airport dispatcher, informing them that one airline was refusing to take the seats out of the plane. I would never have known how to handle such a situation had I not heard immediately Gábor Nagy's sharp voice. In ten minutes the dispatcher was on the line again, this time to say that the seats were being removed. In the meantime a letter had been written in French for the Algerian partner. Gábor Nagy crossed out two sentences, one at the beginning and one at the end, before authorizing it to be sent by telex.

Although the workday was practically over, Burgert had not returned to Bábolna. Deputy manager Miklós Erdélyi asked me to stay in or near the guest house if possible, as Burgert wished to speak to me that very day. They were kind people. I, too, wanted to speak to Burgert, that was why I had gone there. If it hadn't been for Burgert, I wouldn't have gone to Bábolna.

It's such a strange place, this Bábolna. The bosses are always in a state of readiness, expectation and tension. This seeps down to secretaries and close colleagues as well. But the atmosphere around the stables and henhouses is calmer than during the reign of Joseph II.

Bábolna was founded by Joseph II in 1789. First it was

part of Mezőhegyes, but became the independent military stud-farm of the Crown in a matter of years. Having spent the afternoon wandering around the place, I found that a stallion called Obayan, bought in 1885 from a Syrian Bedouin tribe, had a tomb and a memorial tablet in the courtyard. His descendants are still around today. I also learnt of a colonel by the name of Mihály Delallah el Hadad who had arrived in Hungary with his horse as a stable-boy and had ended up as manager of the studfarm. The case of Colonel Tibor Petkó-Sandtnel was just the opposite: he had been manager of the Bábolna studfarm in the years 1932–1942 and had subsequently become King Farouk's master of the horse in Cairo. Bábolna first established contact with the Arab countries through horses, and now these relations continued along the poultry line.

In the afternoon I went round the stables, had a look at the permanent exhibition, entered the stable-boys' quarters without permission or supervision, saw the names of those who fell during the Second World War, as well as of the commanders of the Bábolna stud-farm carved in marble, and felt Bábolna to be a unique place, a place that reveres tradition, takes seriously and cherishes the continuity of history while at the same time making a name for itself in the world with the most up-to-date agricultural technology and production that is outstanding even by international standards.

Burgert had some normal-size and some miniature books printed in Bábolna's own printing house: two treatises by him, one on his study-trip to the United States and the other on the Bábolna maize industry (both are now virtually text-books); *On Horses* by Count István Széchenyi; an abridged version of *On Peasants* by Gergely Berzeviczy, and a letter Emperor Joseph II addressed to his officials. Let me quote some points from this letter: "1. Examine my former orders. 2. My orders have hitherto been carried out literally rather than according to their meaning... Though their aim is different... 4. Pursuing interests other than those of the state leads to corruption... 6. Office-bearers should not only report back but should also reflect on how to improve the state things... 10. Superiors must always bear in mind that favouritism has no place in the service, only merit... 12. Saving time is an important aspect."

I could see from the courtyard and from my window that the stable-boys lived a merry life. Gyms had been built and ping-pong tables set up for them in the big barns. They enjoyed playing games, and later on also listening to music.

When dusk fell Yugoslav, Italian, West German and American cars drew up in front of the guest house. Fatigued businessmen got out of the cars and hastily retired to their rooms. At seven the next morning only my car was still outside the house, the rest had gone.

I sat by the telephone until one at night, waiting for Burgert to return. The phone remained mute. While I was waiting I began to wonder what human factor made the complex run so smoothly in the absence of large capital and a special system of wages. What I did feel was that the managers were highly motivated, ambitious men, but I failed to work out how this inspired the poultry-keepers commuting day in, day out to work in the farthest section of the whole farm. I also managed to sense that a central will dominated, and whenever Burgert was away, his spirit was still present both through his deputies and his radio contact. You could never be certain when his voice would suddenly be heard in order to supervise something. Anyway, I believe that to produce chicks in great numbers in the second half of the twentieth century is not only a scientific achievement of organization and technology but is a generally humanitarian action as well.

My phone rang just before six in the morning. Miklós Erdélyi (who, incidentally, died of a heart attack before I could put down my impressions of the visit to Bábolna on paper) told me that Burgert would see me at seven in the morning in his office. During the night I had jotted down some pertinent questions which I wanted to put to him, but I never got round to it, as Burgert towered over me like a thinking giant, leaving me speechless. As a matter of fact it turned out to be a fortunate encounter, as I was interested neither in Burgert's tie nor his office-room, only in his thoughts, and for some reason or another Burgert was worked up enough to be willing to talk. With sufficient perseverance I managed to get a word in edgeways:

"Where is the point of departure from the norm in our society?"

"Look, this is a cruel game, but I still consider it a game. It's all relative. To what do you compare a farm to determine whether it's good or not? To its former self? Former conditions were of a Balkan level. If we compare it to what we have achieved, we'll immediately become conceited. No one can help becoming conceited if he compares himself to his former self, and this will show in carelessness as well as idleness. That is one side of the coin. Compare yourself to others? The drive to do better than your neighbour is one remedy for idleness. But I never look at what others say or expect, or how they manage. I am constantly aware of our potential and judge what we achieve in the light of that. The biggest problem is that opportunities appear much faster than we managers can possibly handle. There is a growing discrepancy here. If I judge Bábolna in the light of this... My enemies could attack me on this account, but fortunately you don't need to present the account of your potential assets, only of the money in your hands. It's all a question of recognizing your potential.

So what have I done within the given potential? That's what I ought to be expected to give an account of. But even if no account was required, at least people should bear the need to do so in mind. If this is the shoe you put on, you fee the pinch day and night. There's no way you can get rid of it. This is a relay race. Our farm is 180 years old. Many people have carried the baton shorter or longer distances, and I would also like to run my part of the race, so as to be worthy of the team and even to improve the result. And now I can see more of an opportunity for this. That is why I support the principle of socialism. I have been to the West many times and have seen what they have there. Hungarians need some kind of roots. I would perish in the United States; people there live on conveyor belt. You cannot experiment or play in America as you can here. This society gives you more and more opportunities to discover new things, but I also feel the growing discrepancy, which depresses me immensely. You can beat about the bush, say that there are nations that are worse off, how much better it is now than it used to be, etc. I, too, could blame conditions for their adverse influence... But tell me, where can you find a pure world where all enterprises, all thoughts get the go-ahead? In his book about Petőfi, Illyés described how a nation gave birth to her son... If you look at Bábolna that way, you won't see it all that beautiful, either."

"Yet Bábolna is still in the international vanguard."

"According to western specialists independent poultry-breeding must be launched on a five hundred million selection basis. Right now we're at the hundred million level, following the course of the international minimum. And even in the course of six to eight years we have managed to rank fourth or fifth on the international market. No western enterprise can boast of the same in such a short period of time.

Poultry-farming is concentrated in the hands of ten to twelve companies worldwide. We're among the first four of these twelve companies. But rather than look back, we're meant to look forward."

Burgert jumped to his feet and walked up and down in the office in a burst of fury.

"Multilateral companies have invested in food production because of the world food shortage, buying up all the poultry-farms. The smaller farms could compete with even the great names two or three years ago, but today it is the Rockefeller group that dictates, even though the signboards remain the same. Who do I compete with now? How can we maintain the position we have achieved up to now and advance, say, a millimetre? We're up against the multilateral groups. They have the advantage with their money for research, knowledge of the market and know-how. This is no longer a rural agricultural game. The question arises: what ought to be, and what can be done? The investment mechanism in Hungary is one that suits the average Hungarian co-operative farm. How can I alone compete with the multilateral companies? When among wolves, you have to howl. There's no other way. Bábolna must be turned into a multilateral enterprise too. But what will *Der Spiegel* and *Neue Zürcher Zeitung* write about us then? We need dollars and technological development. So what do we do to achieve both? This country has the potential. We're no less talented than any American or West German farmer. Our peasants have much more wide-ranging interests than western farmers. Now think about it and tell me that after all this how we, with our profoundly rotten work ethic, can compete with multilateral enterprises. It's like a dumb shepherd and a lame sheep setting the pace. Help is always offered from somewhere, and we also want to help those wretches in need. But we don't need anybody's help, why won't they let us work in peace? All we need is air. Nothing but air to breathe, do you get me?"

"And the human factor?"

"Tension sets in at every step. For instance, we work on Saturdays as well. But I'm aware that good production hinges increasingly on people's wellbeing in the workplace. If I wish to create conditions that will assure their wellbeing without neglecting efficiency and order, I find myself faced with a daunting task. We have two hundred drivers who transport the chickens all over the country, subjected to outside influences which they bring home. The chickens have to be received at thirty-two degrees centigrade, but some places cannot fulfil these requirements, in which case the driver refuses to allow the unloading of the container. He tries to locate the manager, but usually finds neither the head of the co-operative, nor the agronomist, nobody. He finds a lack of work discipline and meets provincial thinking even in Budapest. The capital has become more provincial than the country. Tell me, have you read anything by Gergely Berzeviczy? What he says about the peasants holds good even today."

"Do people really understand what goes on in Bábolna?"

"Well, that's another thing that causes friction in Bábolna. Here we have a centuries-old farm and the average age of our employees is 32 years. We employ 1,500 women, their average age being 29 years. Our team is young and the leaders are old. This gives rise to constant friction. Another thing is this special mixture of the character of the puszta, the village and the small town. That's another problem. We know all about horses, poultry and pigs, but what do we know about people? How can we make people fulfil their potential? If I had to give an honest account of that, I'd be at a loss for words. I'm not quite sure when I do good and when not. Meaning well and intending to work well have no merit in themselves. A man may go unnoticed in one place but may flourish and excel in another. One of our poultry-keeper girls, for instance, was transferred to the computer centre. Although her work is excellent, I simply cannot pay her as much as somebody who has graduated from the technical university, merely because she has no papers testifying to her talent or her knowledge. Some amazingly talented people have sprung up here, but the opposite has also happened. When we changed over from horses to poultry, many people turned out to be completely useless. In other cases building workers have proved to be talented electricians. Talent is our national treasure. So how do I husband this treasure? I wonder. But we seem to be fertilizing this soil with lost brains. Many young people begin their career here, so talented men retire at fifty."

He went to the cupboard, opened it and turned around.

"I'll give you a book, *On Peasants* by Gergely Berzeviczy. Do you like Széchenyi? This was printed here in 1973. Do you know his book *On Horses?* I'll give you that too. As well as my quotations. I always carry quotations with me, so that I can meditate during meetings. Goethe, Széchenyi, Marx, Benjamin Franklin, Socrates, Aristotle, Gorky."

I accepted his gifts and took out two of the quotations right away to read them. One was by Gergely Berzeviczy and ran: "A stupid man is idle as well because by not knowing a better fate he makes no attempt to strive for it. A wise man will become idle when he reaches the sad conclusion that not even with utmost diligence can he manage to rise in society." The other quotation was from the March 12, 1977 issue of the German poultry-farmers' magazine: "The Ten Commandments consist of 279 words and the

American Declaration of Independence of 300. A Common Market decree concerning the importation of caramel candies, however, runs to 25,911 words." Although I picked these two quotations at random, they both epitomize Burgert's way of thinking. Now that I have put all this down on paper, I feel kind of emotional. That might be the reason why an answer given by György Aczél to Jacques De Bonis, editor-in-chief of *France Nouvelle*, comes to mind now: "We regard the leading role of the Hungarian Socialist Workers' Party as a service. A communist is a servant of the people, in the most honourable sense of the word. Any other interpretation of his role would be wrong and dangerous. Nothing and nobody is capable of replacing the people's participation in the affairs of the country."

I turned to Burgert:

"Then everything depends on people and the quality of human life."

Burgert looked at me as if longing for some kind of challenge. He had a belligerent air that morning.

"We often do the servicing of brains well," he told me. "I once sat down with the technicians and discussed to what extent their talent fitted their occupation. The final answer was simply to leave it at that. Somehow nothing matched. Dealing with people is really the most depressing part. It's just as well we don't have to give an account of that. How to deal with people is not taught at the universities either. Someone graduates from a college and right away he flops before our very eyes. Why? On this farm I feel the greatest responsibility for what I never have to give an account of. Can you imagine how they steal?"

"Yes, I can."

"I don't understand why they steal. In former times people went hungry, but today they have no real cause to steal. They steal a lot. I wonder why. I try to work out my part in this, since stealing, like everything else, is obviously the result of antecedents. But what are the antecedents? One man steals, the other seems to lose his talent overnight. I think what we're squandering most is our greatest national treasure: man. Do you know the scene from Anouilh's *Becket* where the cardinal turns to the Pope and says "We have great power, Holy Father, and our power lies in that we do not actually know what we are about. Out of a deep uncertainty concerning our designs follows an amazing freedom of manoeuvering."

"How does Bábolna influence its surroundings?"

"It's a very long process, but all in all Bábolna gives out a certain light; people around us seem willing to learn and to acquire industrial know-how. The new system of production is forging ahead. If you had a good look around, you will have seen how the poultry-rotation works. Our partner co-operatives must adapt to this routine. Bábolna used to be as punctual as Greenwich mean time. Yet recently co-operatives in Vas County criticized us because our transports hadn't arrived on time. They had compared us to our own standard and punctuality has apparently become a requirement with our partners as well. I see the essence of the whole production system in the existence of mutual critical pressure. We have a co-ordinate relationship. It's a good thing to have alternatives in intensive agriculture. And it's bad if Bábolna is left without competition. We have a presence in the Arab countries, which is undoubtedly a basis for comparison. You can't imagine how dark the Thousand and One Nights can be. We build there and do well. When the American Secretary of Agriculture paid us a visit, he quoted a Chinese proverb: 'If you give a starving man a fish, you save his life once. If you teach him how to fish, you save him for life.' We're still at the stage of giving away fish, but a small European country cannot give as much fish as is needed. The real thing is that people should not be given fish but should be taught to catch fish themselves. We're there in Iraq on a construction, and all's going well. I think people can be taught how to fish. I'm optimistic. But the fundamental thing is to think. We talk about the law of value, yet people here often do not appreciate good ideas. Yet thinking is the hardest of all physical work. What matters is the standard we set for ourselves. I often watch the gypsy-quarter nearby. For many people it provides moral absolution. Even if they don't work, and go drunk to bed every night, they are still happy because they feel superior to those gypsies."

Burgert is full of dynamism, strength, ideas and eagerness to act. If he had not had to rush back to Budapest, we'd still be sitting there, me listening to him. I'd be listening to him, because here you have a man who thinks and acts and when something is said to be impossible, he doesn't believe it. Burgert is not alone in Hungary. Just think of the co-operative farms of Barcs, Nádudvar or the Rába Railway Waggon and Machine Factory of Győr. I'm convinced I could cover pages enumerating the excellent co-operatives and outstanding factories with the same conditions as Nádudvar or Bábolna that will, no doubt, produce more and better in the years to come.

Shortly after the miraculous multiplication of bread, Jesus was crucified and John the Evangelist, son of Zebedee, fisherman of the Sea of Galilee, and Salome, his wife, he who wrote an account of Jesus's acts, was thrown into a barrel full of boiling oil on the order of Emperor Domitian. People were like that in the old days. It's just as well that we live in the second half of the twentieth century.

Translated by Judit Házi

The Great Adventure

BY ISTVÁN GÁLL

Two men lean close in the underground passage and whisper.

"Password?"

"The Great Adventure."

"Time?"

"This afternoon."

"Place?"

"Lujza Blaha, bottom-view."

The chubbier one with the beard can't keep a straight face. He guffaws goodhumouredly.

"Oh, you donkey!"

"Oh, you ass!" responds his friend with relief. "You haven't changed. As far as your gray matter's concerned, I mean. And what now, Fer ..."

"Don't say my name!"

"Why? What's wrong with it? It is Hungarianized?"

"This is a secret operation," the fat one warns him severely. "Didn't I tell you? Double oh-oh."

"Yes, siree, Chief!"

"You see, Beanstalk, you're not a bad conspirator after all, though you're in your infancy still. You haven't stopped growing, I see."

"Neither have you, Chief! Widthwise. And that beard! Looks like a flea market reject."

"It's the Hungarian blade."

"The air's running short down here in the underpass. It's afternoon high hubbub time again."

"Let's surface."

The two men join the stream of people.

"Fire away! What are your plans? Curiosity killed the cat," says the tall, lanky one.

"Wait and see. Trust the Big A."

"Your're as mysterious as a lead article in the Sunday papers."

"You think I asked you along on a wild goose chase? I never congregate if I can help it. You know our national history."

They roll along the Boulevard with the crowd in the direction of the Western Railroad Station. Two men in springtime, for it is spring now, moreover, they have not yet reached the summer of discontent of their lives. They are confident that on this afternoon, on which they have managed to find time to be together at long last, something will surely happen to them.

"I haven't seen you in a year and a half, Chief, if my memory cells serve me right."

"It's been over two. When the peach trees were in bloom," the man with the beard corrects him.

"How time doth fly! Like camel shit in the desert."

"If Alexander Graham hadn't invented the telephone, you'd still be sitting on your ass. I had a hell of a time getting you to come."

"The rat race, Chief. And the family. I think twice even before I breathe."

"And in the meantime, you've grown worn as a doormat."

"And you've got basting thread in your beard. Why don't you tear it out in the morning?"

"I do... You know, Beanstalk, sooner or later it's going to be Closing Time for us, too."

"Eh, you'll love it in your urn. You can stretch your ashes."

"Still, we're closer to thirty than to our Christmas bonuses."

"Thirty? That's positively antique! Will turn into our ancestors. Think it can happen to us too, Chief?"

"Sure thing. Life is like a drawbridge. Up one moment, down the next."

"Life is also like the common cold. You can't get round it."

"Yes, siree, ladies and gentlemen! That's what I call Truth. But no sentiment, Beanstalk, no panic. The afternoon is ours."

"We'll fool around like we used to. Like in the Ice Age."

"And the Great Adventure waits!"

"Funny you should mention it, it was just fermenting on the tip of my tongue. What have you cooked up?"

"I didn't want to say over the phone," whispers the rotund one with the beard mysteriously, "it might be bugged."

"You needn't spell it out. I'm prepared for anything! My trigger's cocked!"

"You won't need your trigger at the bank. We'll be using gas and dynamite. You didn't leave any telltale signs, I hope. Sure Interpol isn't on to you?"

"Definitely not! Not Interpol. My cleaning lady, perhaps. I owe her money."

Nonplussed, the one with the beard loses his train of thought as he glances anxiously up at his friend.

"What makes you say that? Don't you want me to ask you for a loan?"

"I didn't know you had intended to," answers Beanstalk, playing the innocent.

"What makes you think I had? You the National Savings Bank or something?"

"Chief, I honestly don't know who I am any more. Haven't known for some time. But I can assure you I am definitely not the Savings Bank."

After a long pause. Beanstalk sighs.

"The assumption hurt me to the quick, anyhow."

"Chief ...!"

"I just wanted to see an old pal. Have a chat. Bosom to bosom, soul to soul. To discuss the various ways of saving the world. And clean out the World Bank. Free the Zulu tribes. And then ..."

"Oh, Chief ...!"

"And then, my pal presses his purse to his heart's core because he thinks I want to ask for money! In other words, we spent a month planning, telephoning, synchronizing watches, listening to mutual reproaches about how we never meet any more, reminding each other of the sacred oath we took in the Sweatshop that our beloved teachers should live as long as we stay friends, we went through all this so now I should come and ask for money?"

"Stop playing on my emotions, Tiny Tim, or I'll cry ... All right, so you didn't want to talk about money."

Tiny Tim snaps back at him.

"Aha! So you did? A friendly little handout, eh? And you passed on the right so you'd come out ahead? Now was that a nice thing for a Comecon member to do?"

"Forget the mercantile trash, Chief. We went to the same sweatshop, resisted our teachers' efforts like true heroes, and though Time's winged chariot's hurrying near, friendship stands eternal! Let us take a solemn oath on it."

"A peck on the right cheek, a peck on the left," says the fat one mechanically.

"And arm in arm, let us face the Great Adventure!"

"Full speed in reverse!"

"But where?"

"We're together, that's what counts. United we stand. With a whole afternoon at our disposal ... Life is like an unopened telegram. Full of mysterious promises."

"Bologne! Life is like the cleaners. You take them a new shirt and get back a pair of torn trousers. But let's have a stroll anyway, Chief. You're bound to let me in on your plans sooner or later."

They walk along leisurely, like loose-limbed marionettes ignorant of who or what moves them, or why. With the wild self-confidence of youth they know only one thing—chance will surely throw something their way.

"It's hot," pants the heavy one with the beard. "Like an oven."

"And in your case," jests his friend, "the sun's got more to shine on."

"We could've gone out for a swim, like we used to."

"Great! Let's go."

"You ever go swimming these days?"

"Regularly. I even went the summer before last."

"I should've known. A busy father uses water only for brushing his teeth."

"So now you know why I want to have some fun today. How about that swim?"

"It's too late."

"It wasn't my idea."

"I didn't say we should go. I said we could have."

"Provided?"

"Provided we had agreed beforehand and brought our swimming trunks."

"We can rent them."

"I refuse to wear somebody else's."

"At one time, you went girl hunting in my nylon shirt, Chief."

"Think you still know how to swim, Beanstalk?"

"Better than you, at any rate. You swim only with the tide, don't you, Chief?"

"You don't trust me, Jack the Bean. I told you, the Great Adventure is just around the corner."

They come up to a crowd of people.

"Look! The old movie theatre. It's still here?"

"The Rat Hole. We spent a lot of time in there."

A boy sidles up to them.

"I got just two tickets left," he rattles. "My girl couldn't make it, you can have them for what it says. The box office is sold out. What about it, Boys?"

"We'll think it over, son. Take out your barnacles, Bean, and spell out for your old man what's on the menu."

" 'Stress'. Shall we go inside, Dad?"

"What on earth for?" asks the fat one with mock consternation.

"Because it's there."

"You never can tell, child."

"They say it's dynamite. We've got to trust public opinion, you know," argues Beanstalk naively.

"We're not that old yet," counters Tiny Tim.

"You want these or not?" the stranger asks impatiently.

"Business must be slow today, sonny boy."

"Buy my tickets first, pauper," says the thicker tout as he backs away, "we'll issue a joint communiqué later."

Beanstalk pretends disappointment.

"I thought you wanted to go to the movies, Dad."

"Not now. I'm hankering for a greater adventure."

They saunter along the noisy crowded street.

"Swimming's out, the movies ditto... What else did we

do in the good old days?" wonders Beanstalk. "I got it! The games. We used to go to the games."

"The games? What games?"

"Soccer games."

"Soccer? What on earth was soccer?"

Beanstalk catches on.

"It's rather hard to explain. They used to play it with the feet."

"I see. Like the organ. It must've been some kind of religious spiel."

"Something like that. It was the Hungarian national religion. Had millions of followers."

"If it's gone, why discuss it?"

"Have you a better idea?"

"A tiger hunt. Sleighing on the ice. Parachuting. Flying Dutchman."

Beanstalk interrupts him with a shout.

"Dancing! Dancing! It just dawned on me. Dad, we used to go dancing! Rock'n roll an' do da twist, and other such imperialist opiates."

"Today, there's just disco," shrugs Tiny Tim. "Pressing out cabbage leaves as you stomp your feet in place. Behinds clashing in the night. That's no dancing, that's dodge'em! Besides if I start throwing my weight around, they'll have to renovate the premises."

"You know, we're as boring as a running debate in the Sunday papers. Perhaps you will be good enough to reveal what your plans are, Chief. Come on, give! What about the Great Adventure?"

"Don't get ants in your pants, Comrades! Everything is progressing according to plan, Comrades. The Great Adventure? You'll get it, Comrades. Right away! Actually, it's happening bit by bit, Comrades. Permanently! We denounce pseudo-adventures, Comrades!"

"You mean you just wanted us to knock around?"

"Considering the difficulty we had agreeing on a time, that's nothing to scoff at. And once we're tête à tête, I figured something's bound to come up. And it will. Just wait and see, it will."

"I had great expectations ... Tickets to the flicks. You with a new wife... You inheriting half a million, and needing someone to help you carry the gold bullion home from the pawnshop."

"Money! You're talking money again!"

"I'd gladly talk all day for a mere hundred. Not that I'd mind a hundred-thousand."

"Sorry to disappoint, you, Beanstalk, I just wanted to be with you and gab, like in times of yore. That's all. We'll just have to be satisfied with that. We've grown richer by one more experience, and that's like money in the bank. Let's walk along like wise old gents and be grateful we've got the sun in the morning and the moon at night. Such is life."

"No. Life is like chewing gum. It's so utterly boring, you never get tired of it... Okay, let's walk and enjoy the quartz substitute, I dig the sun."

But they are not enjoying the sun now as they squint and blink and wrinkle their brows and turn their heads to avoid the glare. After months of overcast skies, the city is suddenly as suffused with light as a stove with embers, and it takes time to adjust to spring too.

They stop at the same time under the cool awning of a furniture store. Behind the plate glass several armchairs flaunt themselves in poses as vacuous as two politicians debating before the cameras.

"Take a seat. These have been waiting especially for us," says the fat one with false nonchalance. "Won't you be seated?"

"Only after you, Chief," answers the lanky one as he pushes his friend closer to the shop window.

"Take that tall chair so you can let those long legs dangle."

"And I suggest you take that armchair over there. It's ample enough for your behind."

"Did I ever tell you, you'd have to gain weight so I could call you a skeleton?"

"I could scrape some of the blubber off you. That way, we'd both come out ahead."

The short one, who looks fat because for the past fifteen years—ever since he got tired of growing—all the extra weight has settled around his hips, is looking hard at something further inside the store.

"See that set? It's forty-eight thou. A sofa, two armchairs, an ottoman and coffee table. Five pieces in all. What has that set got to offer for forty-eight thou?" He raises his voice. "Can it come running when you whistle? Can it conduct a conversation? It's so priggish, you'd have to send a letter of apology before you could touch it!"

"It's pure leather. It takes nerve to sit cheek, to cheek with pure leather." Balancing on his long legs, Beanstalk squints down at his friend treacherously, like a room painter from the top of his ladder. "You got exhibitionist excrescences like these in your office, Chief?"

"My office is a pigeonhole. A glass pigeonhole. It's so tiny, I have to step out the door every time I pull a drawer. It was supposed to be a telephone booth, but it turned out too small. One thing's for sure, even the ringing won't fit inside. The moment I hear it, I grab the receiver, it makes such a racket."

They continue walking. The tall one murmurs pensively.

"Still, you're the only one from the bunch with his own pigeonhole, telephone and key. You're as high up, Chief, as a sputnik! Reaching for the stars, eh?"

The short, fat one with the beard (with time, the too objective teasing of the aesthenic type always gets under the skin of the endomorphic type) stops dead in the middle of the pavement.

"You're nuts, Beanstalk, an ass and everything!" He waves an arm up in the air, where his friend presides. "For your information, I'm fed up with this shit! You called me Chief on the phone as well. Some funny joke! Can't you force something else out of your grey matter?... And don't interrupt! It's my turn. Tell me what's bugging you. Why're you needling me? You must think I'm off my rocker. We studied technology together, the whole bunch of us. But for the rest of you chaps, work stinks, that's the point. So get off my back with the you've-got-your-own-cubby-hole number. If you'd condescend to visit me in the shop, you'd hear how those machines clank and pound, and then maybe you'd get it through that peasize brain of yours why I need that glass cubicle. Otherwise I couldn't hear what anybody said whether I was on the phone, or facing him, mug to mug, if you know what I mean. Besides, there's such a draught in the shop, if they open the door at both ends, all the diagrams and requisitions, all that goddam paperwork goes flying off my desk all over the place." His summary is bitter now. "You're acting superior because I stayed with production, I stuck it out in the plant. 'Your own office,' and 'Chief'... Very amusing, Ha-ha-ha."

Beanstalk bends down to him, sympathy gleaming in his eyes.

"But aren't you chief of the Fart Distillery division?"

"No!" The fat one realizes his answer was too abrupt, and blushes behind his beard. So he repeats himself, just for spite. "No. What do you think of that?"

"Sorry, Tiny Tim, I must've been misinformed." Beanstalk apologizes with relish, it's his ballgame now. "You know, I reckoned you had become alienated from the Masses. Your own office. Armchairs with built-in ass-warmers. Oriental rugs. A bar. A redhead secretary who comes equipped with the Pill and everything else needed for the earnest retardation of progress. But if things stand as you have outlined above, respect goes right out the window as far as I'm concerned, anyhow. I won't call you Chief any more if you're still the same old Tiny Tim, the fattest fatso in the class, and if you're just stagnating, like the national income."

The fat one's eyes flash up at his friend.

"Stop beating around the bush. You sound convincing, I admit, but it's just the dregs, no meat. Since I threw a nice juicy problem your way, why don't you deal with that? Work stinks for you guys, isn't that right?"

Beanstalk flaps his two thin arms as if he wanted to fly away.

"Active rest, that's what you said over the phone, and that something's bound to come up once we're together again. That's what I'm programmed for. There was no previous mention of a political screening."

"The Champ works at a gas station, right?" asks Tiny Tim abruptly. "And Phil?"

"Married a share in a chow house."

"And Patchouli?"

"Drives a cab," admits Beanstalk.

"And you're a supplier at a producers' co-op. None of you sweat under the arms from a little hard labour."

"Punch and Judy fought for a pie, Punch gave Judy a bash in the eye." The skinny man drops his weasel head. "I've got to make ends meet, Chief, I picked up a loan at the bank against a promise of three kids. We had one when we got the flat, and pulled off the second soon after. Erika's just on maternity leave with him. And this year she'll have to litter the third. It's breeding time again."

"Are you bragging or complaining?"

"Take it as you will. But there's five of us, and that's a fact. Four club members, and the fifth in reserve in mummy's tummy. A mortgage on the flat, and the furniture bought on the never-never. My in-laws took out a loan for us, and we'll have to pay them back, too. We spend the first of the month filling out money orders and lugging the dough to the P. O. in numbered bags. Every moment of my day, including the time I spend fooling around with you, is being financed by the National Savings Bank. Continue your questions, and I'll just pop down for another loan so I can answer them. Go right ahead, ruin me. Friendship comes first!"

Tiny Tim stops and scratches his beard thoughtfully.

"You wouldn't happen to have a picture of the kids on you?"

Eagerly, his friend reaches for the inside pocket of his coat. His hand freezes in midair, "Shithead," he murmurs, and retrieves his empty hand with a begrudging smile. He's been trapped in his father role.

"I was just wondering whether the kids look like you or the National Savings Bank," grins Tiny Tim.

"Well, they don't look anything like you, thank the lord! They have intelligent faces."

"Good boy. Bravo! But for the sake of the record, let it be noted that Erika was some dish, it couldn't have been much of a sacrifice killing two birds with one stone."

"Why're you using the past tense?"

"Are you trying to tell me that girl-hunting is out?" asked his friend like the devil's advocate. "Where does that leave the Great Adventure? I was hoping we'd pick up some chicks."

"Well, count me out! I haven't got a vacancy."

"We wouldn't have any place to take the little charmers

anyhow. My landlady sits at home all day, dusting her pictures. I bet she spends the nights, too, up on the wall, sliding around, inspecting them."

Beanstalk sees his advantage, and his spirits soar.

"I hope you haven't turned into a saint! Anything, even marriage is better than that."

"That's what Mari says." Tiny Tim slows his pace. "And she says I should go back and start all over again. But I won't want to play hanky-panky with her family any more. The warmest greeting I ever got in that house was from their refrigerator. Maybe if we had our own apartment ... I could be one of the bank's customers now, like you."

"With a picture of the kids in your pocket."

"With a picture of the kids in my pocket," the fat one murmurs with resignation.

"Okay, we're quits," sighs Beanstalk. "Ooooh, you donkey!"

"Ooooh, you ass!" Then the fat one stops and expands his chest like a cock in the ring. "No! We will not surrender, Bean. Let us shake off our shackle of slack! All is not lost! Our troops may be beaten, our planes blown to smithereens before takeoff, our tanks shot to pieces by our own men in the fog, but our fighting spirit stands adamant. We'll throw in our reserves!"

"Reserves? What reserves?"

"Search your noddle, man! I'm thinking of spiritual reserves."

He continues with eloquence.

"Are we forced to the negotiating table? So be it. We'll have a business lunch! Today, there are no final defeats, no lost causes. At the negotiating table, everyone can force through a nice little dietetic compromise." He looks at his partner soberly. "We'll have lunch. A great big lunch. I wouldn't call that a Great Adventure, but it's something."

"But I ... She's expecting me, Erika has cooked lunch, and..."

"It was my idea, you're my guest, I'll foot the bill."

"That's not what I meant."

"Yes, it is. It's written all over you."

"Well, if you insist... I can't resist brute force."

"Besides, I've got to talk to you," confides Tiny Tim with embarrassment. "That's why I called you. There's something I want to talk to you about."

"That makes two of us." Beanstalk is uneasy too. "Actually, that's why I called *you* ... It's urgent ... You see, there's this chance of making some money ..."

"Hold your horses! Let's attend to spiritual matters first! It's late afternoon, and my spirituals are starving. Let's grab some lunch." And he goes through the menu, practically drooling at the mouth, "Chicken soup with quail's egg, bird's nest, shark fin, followed by à Chateaubriand with Cumberland sauce and goulash à la puszta, then trout with sponge cake and whipped cream, stuffed Csárdás with strawberry frappé, vintage wines with champagne, cognac and a double portion of bicarbonate of soda."

"I've graduated to Di-Gel ages ago!"

The spring sunshine seems too expensive for the narrow streets; it hardly has enough room even on the wide boulevard. A yellow tram glides ecstatically along its shiny rails, springing off the ground now and then as if in pursuit of the sky. But the two men don't care, they pass through the reluctant door of a restaurant.

"Not a soul."

"So much the better. Maybe we'll get treated like a capital investment," Tiny Tim sticks to his high spirits as he looks around. "Just look at that waitress, Beanstalk," he whispers with satisfaction. "All breast and thigh, and no unnecessary garnish. My mouth begins to water ... Something tells me she's going to be our Great Adventure."

"What'll it be?"

Fixing his glare on the tightly-wrapped hips of the waitress, Tiny Tim goes into action.

"We wish to have some lunch, Miss," he cooes ingratiatingly. "And don't bother your pretty head about the spoon. I'll eat my soup with a fork."

"Excuse me, sir?" The waitress's eyes, indifferent until that moment, open wide. "Why a fork?"

"So the soup'll last till closing time. I don't think you can get off before then."

The waitress gives Tiny Tim the kind of look she usually reserves for a stained tablecloth in bad need of prompt removal.

"The boss takes me home in his sports car. If you happen to be a long-distance runner, sir, you might try following." She turns away from them. "I'll call the wine steward."

"Hey! Hold your horses!" Tiny Tim shouts after her. "We drive around ourselves in a car at night. You can have your pick of brand names."

Beanstalk stretches his long legs under the table.

"You've fallen on your ass, like the rain in Spain."

"I had no intention of catching her, I just threw her a line."

"Sure. Because you didn't know she was the big man's broad ... What did you want to talk to me about?"

"Let's concentrate on lunch first. Besides, the girl's probably bluffing."

A bald waiter shuffles over. He is as red in the face as a turkey. The girl must have passed the word.

Something's gone wrong. Several waiters appear in the empty restaurant, along the back wall.

They move around ominously, rearranging chairs and keeping an eye on the two men.

"Cocktails? Beer?" the waiter asks heavily.

"The menu! I've already told your colleague. Couldn't you send her back?"

"The kitchen's closing soon. Beer?"

"Fine. And bring the menu with you. Me and that waitress were just coming to an understanding."

The waiter stands, staring into space.

"You'd better make up your mind. The boss, you see... Not that I care. Ask for something ready made. Like two consommés, two porkchops with vegetables." He grinds this out and leaves the table, shouting to someone in the back. "Two beers coming up!"

Beanstalk looks around with apprehension.

"There's a lot of movement back there. The waiters had a good look at us."

"The guy in mourning must be the boss." Tiny Tim grins. "What does he need all that breast and thigh for?"

"Even the washroom attendant's staring. Shouldn't we make a quick exit?"

"Ugh, she's already hooked, the little darling, just keeping it a secret," says Tiny Tim, leaning back in his chair. "Sooner or later her little hams will quiver like aspic, the heart-stew in her bosom will go pit-a-pat, and she'll throw herself at me. Just wait and see."

Beanstalk grins meaningfully.

"This girl reminds me of Mari. You know, your ex."

"Now that you mention it..." Tiny Tim is playing with the fringe of the tablecloth. "I guess this type must be coded in my genes."

They spoon their soups dejectedly.

"This reminds me of the school cafeteria. There's something in that soup, and it ain't meat!"

"Very thin stuff ... And how much longer, I wonder? When will we get something more substantial?"

"The finish line! Increase your speed, Tiny, here comes the meat!"

"How long does it take for rat poison to be absorbed? D'you think the boss could have ... If you know what I mean."

But the waiter just smiles. When he speaks, his voice is ingratiating.

"Two prime pork chops. Dessert-coffee-two-more-beers?"

"Two more beers."

Beanstalk glances at his retreating back.

"He's so obliging all of a sudden."

"He'd gladly cook ... He'd gladly serve up the boss's pussycat himself," murmurs Tiny Tim as he chews and swallows. "Money speaks. A tip ennobles and depraves ... Pour!"

Now that their stomachs are full, they feel relaxed once more. They gulp down their ice-cold Kinizsis and stare with glassy eyes as the foam slides down the insides of their mugs.

"What did you want to talk to me about?"

Tiny Tim is busy with his digestion.

"I just wanted to gab, that's all. It's the gab that counts, not the what ... We've lost touch. I don't see any of the boys any more. At one time we had nothing to discuss, but we were together all the time, and talked until we went dry in the mouth. But now ..."

"Things were different when we attended the Sweatshop. If we wanted to hear anything worth hearing, we had to do the talking ourselves."

"Remember Outer?"

"Outer the model teacher? How could I forget!" answers

Beanstalk in a throaty gurgle. "*Out,* boys! Parades are *out!* Rioting is *out,* understand?"

"But on March 15th, we marched anyway."

"And the cops gave us a run for it, even though the shindig was organized by the Young Communists' League. But Outer's paternal heart could feel the imminent danger, bless his soul."

"Ugh, he couldn't know the cops would be all over us. Of course, shouting 'Che Lives' wasn't part of the programme. The shopowners quaked and quivered for a full hour."

"And their shopwindows went slam-bang!"

"And they salvaged their display shoes and junky knits..."

"We created a stir, and then, nothing ..."

"Don't say that," snaps Tiny Tim. "Those were the days, my friend. In Paris, the students occupied an entire arrondissement. In West Germany the city guerillas kept the population popping. In the U. S. of A., there was shooting on the campuses. And in South America, the Tupamaros thinned out the ranks of the police. That was something! The world was afraid of the young. And we in the Inner City, in beautiful downtown Budapest, were in sync with these out in the big wide world ... Don't you see? That was our past, and it was something, after all! But Europe is silent, silent again, her revolutions gone, as the poet said. And behold, next came the Seventies, then the Eighties, all stuffy silence, not a spark of revolutionary fire."

"Not so loud. The Mortician's men are listening in over there."

"They can shove it ... Yes, old boy, we were witnesses to great times. The kids today don't even know that we fought for their long hair."

"And for the hitchhikers, so they wouldn't be picked up by the police."

"The beat concerts at the Metro Club, remember?"

"And the old Illés Band. Their song that went, 'It hurts, hurts, huuuuurts!'"

"Don't even mention it, or I'll start weeping through ears."

"To make a long story short, things were different in our day, old friend."

"For us, who were there at the Don, during apple blossom time."

"And at Doberdo, in a shower of arrow."

"At Világos, in the dead of night ..."

"And with Attila the Hun on the first IBUSZ trip to the West ..."

"Oooooh, you donkey!"

"Ooooh, you ass!"

"Comrade in arms, how about another round? Waiter, two more beers," shouts Tiny Tim. "It wouldn't do, him eavesdropping for nothing."

Beanstalk heaves a melancholy sigh.

"Life is like ulcers. It never passes without a trace."

"Life is like the elevator at home. Neither up nor down. We push the buttons in place."

The headwaiter brings their beers.

"We're changing shifts, gentlemen," he says, slapping his leather billfold open in his palm. He is as fat as an advertising pillar, and blocks the restaurant from their field of vision. Neither of the two men would be enough to fill a cavity in one of his teeth.

Tiny Tim makes a gesture of annoyance, but Beanstalk prepares his long legs under the table for a speedy departure.

"Six beers. Isn't that right, gentlemen? I hope you don't mind, gentlemen, but we're changing shifts." The headwaiter's manner is obsequious, yet threatening. "We're closing, but you just go right ahead, finish your beers ... Take your time."

"Don't blunt your pencil," says Tiny Tim as he flings some bills on the table. "And keep the change."

Although they are by themselves again, Beanstalk shifts his weight restlessly.

"Well, what is it? Come on, out with us, I've got something on my mind too, you know."

But Tiny Tim is in a state of beer euphoria, and responds with an unhurried, philosophical belch.

"What was it, what was it... Let's see now ... I've said it, Bean. Neither up, nor down. We're punching the buttons in place. I'm not kidding, Bean, I'm on the level. I've been worrying myself a lot lately, asking myself, what else is there? Is there anything else? I sit in my pigeonhole from morning till night while outside, the rest of the guys work the conveyor belts. In the afternoon I vegetate in my room, while next door my landlady slides up and down the wall among her paintings. At night I stare at the boob tube, and then, off to sleep. And the following day, the same merry-go-round goes round and round again. Sometimes, I feel like asking somebody: isn't there a terrible waste here? Because if someone were to tell me to whitewash the sky, polish the sun, sieve through the sand of the Sahara, sprinkle the North Pole with salt, I wouldn't ask why, I'd ask, will tomorrow do? Instead ... Put the kids' pictures on the table, Bean. Right here, in front of me. Show me some hope for the future. If Mari and I could have another go at home-making, maybe I could talk her into delivering triplets, and we wouldn't have to fall behind ..."

"So that's what's bugging you. Mari! And you need somebody to encourage you ... Tiny, go back to her! Please, I beg you! I'll go down on my knees if I have to."

"Hold your horses! It's not as simple as that. I won't go

to live with them again. Dadsy-mumsy are detrimental to my health. Believe me. I've tried it."

"But any other solution would mean money."

"Ay, there's the rub. Money!" recites Tiny Tim, leaning his bulk over the table. "I know of a flat. The owner's going abroad for two years. I'd have to pay one year down. But where should I get the dough? Ask mumsy-dadsy for a handout so I can abduct their little baby? And the car needs repairs. It'll be six years old this fall, and the testing takes money, as you know ... I didn't want to ask you, though, that's not why I called."

Beanstalk sees his chance, and takes it on the run.

"You couldn't have called at a better time! I need money, too, to pay off my debts ... So I have a business proposition. That's what I wanted to talk to you about. You drive a sedan, don't you?"

"A Moskwich sedan. But it's old."

"All it's got to do is roll. Listen! I know a greengrocer who needs some shipping done. And that means good money."

Tiny Tim shivers.

"You want me to fill Ivan Ivanovich with lettuce leaves?"

"Lettuce is big business. And fruit. At dawn, we'll go out to Bosnyák Square and load up."

"What do you mean by dawn?"

"Two o'clock. Maybe three. We'll take the stuff into the store, unload, and go to work. The widow will pay through the nose. Saturday and Sunday we'll go down to the countryside. From the farmer to the store, that's double pay! The widow needs us bad, she kicked out her previous shipper. She'll dish out anything we ask. Might even give us an advance. Ten a head. Probably even more. We'll be millionaires by autumn ... Well, what do you say? We could start tomorrow. Let's go to the widow right now and strike a deal."

Tiny Tim shakes his head morosely.

"I need my beauty sleep."

"So you'll hit the sack early, and watch less TV."

"No. Beside, there's such a thing as self-respect in this world."

"But you can't turn it into capital."

"And pride! Remember Outer lecturing us on pride?"

"Yes. In his threadbare pants."

"And how about socialist mentality? Would you have me sweat for a capitalist?"

"The public interest demands that the stores be well stocked."

"For all I know, this thing could even be against the law."

"Think of your oncoming triplets. How will you support them?"

Tiny Tim continues to resist, but with less conviction.

"I just can't see myself pressed inside a car stuffed with wilted cabbage."

"Then try seeing yourself inside a brand new car, you fat, indolent swine!" snaps Beanstalk. "If you continue this shilly-shallying, someone'll take the business away right in front of our noses. I told the widow we'd go see her today. If you're pigheaded, she'll find somebody else. It's goldmine for anyone with a car."

"Before we were just talking about lettuce and cabbage, now it's gold."

"Listen. The widow promised ten grand a head in advance. But we could get thirty. And you can have it all. We could settle our accounts later. You'll rent the flat and move in with Mari. And from then on, when you go home, Mari will be waiting with dinner. You'll stuff those calories down, and off to bed. You'll work on the triplets, then sleep. At dawn's early light, you'll leave for Bosnyák Square fresh as a daisy. And by six, you'll be at the factory. Well, what do you say?"

"When do I breathe?"

"I'll tell Mari," says Beanstalk with a sinking heart, "that you refuse to make sacrifices for her sake."

"Don't bother. She knows. Ever since I stepped out of the family frigidaire."

"In that case, do it for my sake. Do it for and old pal!" pleads Beanstalk. "I need that money... Do you know how healthy it is to rise early? And how gorgeous a sunrise is? Dawn in purple mantle clad?... Come to your senses. Let's go to the widow, all right?"

"It's too late," says Tiny Tim, leaning over the table meaningfully. " 'Don't move! We've got the house surrounded!' I should've settled for your lettuce instead of the boss's moll."

Beanstalk looks up questioningly.

"A cop at the door?... What's going on?"

"The Mortician looked us in and called the fuzz."

Meanwhile, the boss is eagerly explaining the situation to the policemen:

"They're sitting right over there, Comrade Sergeant... They acted and talked pretty suspiciously... Said that they go around with a car by night, that's what they said, word for word, Comrade Sergeant... And since you mentioned how there's this gang of car thieves in the neighbourhood... Well, we believe in vigilance, Comrade Sergeant...!"

The waitress, too, puts in her shrill two-cents' worth.

"Yes, they told me, too. We said, we have a car, too, at night... Or go after cars at night... They're the ones, all right!"

Tiny Tim nods with satisfaction.

"You were right, Bean. She looks a lot like Mari. And you want me to sit in a carful of wilting lettuce for this? Ooooh, you donkey!"

"Oooooh, you ass," whispers Beanstalk nervously. "If explain quickly, we can still make it to the widow."

Saluting stiffly, the policemen towers over them.

"Good afternoon. Your IDs, please."

Tiny Tim winks sarcastically at Beanstalk.

"It's gonna take time, that's the problem. We might as well make a full breast of it, they'll write that to our credit in court, and we won't get the Chair." He turns to the policeman. "Comrade Sergeant, life is like every big adventure. All our dreams end at the police station... We give up. What do you want to know? We're international drug smugglers, and white slavers, not to mention wanted terrorists. And patricides! But we never deliver lettuce and cabbage, we'd never stoop that low. That's an extenuating circumstance, I hope!"

The policeman ignores him as he leafs through the two IDs, subjecting them to a thorough scrutiny. Then he takes a good look at the two suspects. After a long pause, he gives back their IDs and turns away from their table.

Tiny Tim and Beanstalk have hardly a chance to get to their feet before the disappointed headwaiter shoves them towards the door like a bulldozer.

Outside, the afternoon crowd sweeps the two men along; in no time they merge with the people and cannot be differentiated from the others, to whom, just like to them, nothing extraordinary happened that day, except that the spring sun shone on them perhaps more brightly than usual.

Translated by J. E. Sollosy

A Story that K. Did not Like at All

BY FERENC TEMESI

I.

We had been trying to destroy each other for a year. Since I still hadn't realized what I was getting into, ignoring my love's ominous forebodings, I joined an amateur dramatic society. Actors were in short supply, I speak Hungarian fluently—I was invited to join.

It immediately became obvious that I was among the most original of characters. First of all, there was F., who—the only real actor among us—was, reluctantly, studying to be a literary historian, but enjoyed writing short humorous pieces on bits of paper in the library. Then N. whose back was straightened out in the mines. He avoided people ever since discovering that his manuscripts had for six months been used as toilet paper by his high-school classmates. There was D., who at about this time—a bit late—was developing a personality for himself, and Z., the respected alcoholic. Then there was B. who played the middle-class roles, and even carried the weighty volumes of Georg Lukács's *The Characteristics of Aesthetics* to the toilet. He associated only with Peter, who was debating whether to follow Marxism, Existentialism or his natural *joie de vivre*. The girls were less interesting because in secret they all wanted to be actresses, except perhaps for H., the exemplary student, who joined us to lose her virginity, and G.—she was widely passed round in our group too.

That's about what the company looked like when we started rehearsing the unknown work of a celebrated Hungarian writer. I recognized his name because it was the first thing I had ever read of his. In other words, "contemporary Hungarian literature" was completely unknown to me. A long story should now follow, but I'll try to squeeze it into one sentence: IF ONE IS THE LAST REMAINING WRITER ON EARTH, THERE ISN'T MUCH ELSE TO READ THAN ONE'S OWN WORK.

That's where I was when I became a member of the troupe, and got to know a blonde, daisy-faced girl and "contemporary Hungarian literature".

2.

She had blue eyes. These two attributes (remember: blonde hair) constantly kindled my imagination during this sad period when I seemed to outgrow my trousers in a matter of days. That is, I tried to hang all the Christmas decorations of my artifical love on girls of such appearance. Quite unsuccessfully, thank God. To anyone else this girl would at times seem to possess black eyes. In addition, she had the kind of timid gestures that would invite any young man to offer her his arm. The only thing unusual in all this was that at the same time I should have been head over heels in love with a somewhat horse-headed, tall, thin girl named Andrea. As indeed I was.

And newborn too. To be exact: "Second Newborn.' I must admit it was not a big role, but I liked it. The play ended with me. I did hate that inconvenient jock-strap sort of a thing, in which I had to jump, creep, bend according to a predesigned choreography. Our director, who in private life was an assistant director of a theatre, was a fan of Jancsó films. That damned thing kept wanting to fall off me but didn't. It drove me positively wild. Also, I couldn't get my part right with Blue Eyes (let's call her that for simplicity sake) who appeared as a sad star on the not too bright sky of our company; she played the role of my mother and I was unable to pretend that I was afraid and attracted all at the same time. For that's exactly how I felt off stage. My particular stubbornness made me an actor able to portray anything on stage, except what he really wanted.

We rehearsed the play diligently, but it didn't work. That's how we found ourselves no longer in the period of rehearsals, but in the period of "there's no more time left".

3.

One would certainly not expect it of a decent Latin-Greek student, I said to Blue Eyes in the ante-room to the toilets that served as dressing room in the small town community centre, when she blurted out that she wanted to be an actress.

Why not? It's every girl's dream, except they won't admit it, she said, fixing her eyes on me by way of an irrefutable argument.

Well, look here, I said. If you mean me, I can only tell you it's just another role as far as I'm concerned. Just one of many. And because I cannot take any one seriously, I am everything to everyone. So now they assume that I am a harmless, irresponsible actor, you see? I assure you, I am neither harmless nor irresponsible. Even less, an amateur actor.

Then what are you?—she became serious. The wrinkles on her forehead appeared to me as much out of place as a function graph in the hands of a doll. I did not know her yet.

I took a deep breath and looked into her eyes, as if I could give a serious answer. I was lucky, the stage manager rushed in: Let's go, the homecoming is next. He meant the homecoming of my father, that is, of Blue Eyes' husband. He was returning from shopping, quite done in, because in the meantime somehow they also executed him. So I was left alone with a book given to me by a mother studying Latin and Greek. I had lots of time as I hadn't even been born yet.

That happened during our umpteenth performance. We visited many towns and that gave us an opportunity of getting to know several local taverns. By about the fifth performance I knew that we were the first to perform the best Hungarian avant-garde work, although I had no idea about Hungarian avant-garde drama. In fact I still don't know such a thing exists. Even the Master (I named him that in private) said that although it was his first work it was his best. However, I bravely read all the rest, then all his short stories and novels lent me by Blue Eyes for strictly defined periods of time. I liked her more and more. I liked both of them more and more, Blue Eyes a bit better, perhaps, than him. But the night was still far off when, throwing all caution to the wind, I decided to fall in love with her.

4.

The Master liked the show, he saw it at least six times. I must admit, I liked it too. I became more and more comfortable in the play. Less and less in the group. Perhaps because I got to know them better. Or they got to know me better. It was hard to tell. During the long hours of travel, I mostly talked with F. and N. using very few words, because we understood each other.

The Master's invitation did not come as a surprise. It was a kind of charity performance at the Master's summer residence on lake Balaton. I went down there immediately after my exams. My love suspected that the rest were not going alone, and she wanted to come too. I don't remember how but I talked her out of it. I knew that because of the company's easy ways and my cosmic jealousy, the week would rush by several quick changes of blows. We both deserved a bit of rest, I thought, because if she were not with me, not for a moment would I be tormented by jealousy.

I regretted my decision on the rainy day of my arrival. For a day I roamed about the building of the school of viticulture where, in Classroom II/A, they put us up. In a rush, they left off the "V" before ACATION, an oversight I hastened to correct. I climbed up to the teachers' room where I found an old radio suffering from cancer of the larynx, a flag and a small book titled, *Methods of Wine Judging*. From the latter I learned that "Those wines that are rated O in all measurable categories must be rejected." I imagined being a decent little table wine preparing for the judging, but then... I fell asleep.

On the afternoon before the performance, the Master invited us to his house. Z., who was responsible for discipline and money (he wanted to be everything from journalist to radio reporter, but only made it as far as executive in charge of cultural affairs, asked us specifically to leave the dog alone, as he was quite old and the Master was very attached to him. At the house we were welcomed with enough sandwiches to fill a wagon and wine the like of which I had never tasted before. I tried to recall what I had read in the *Methods of Wine Judging*, but even today all I can tell you is that it was good. We settled down on the grass and did't wait to be served. The Master, sitting at a round table fashioned out of a mill stone, approved our greed with benign dog eyes. In return, we entertained our host with spontaneous nonsense.

When we had more wine in us than in the gallon jug, the company began to disintegrate. The Master returned to the house. The dog followed him. D., who at one time played in a rock band, sat down beside me and we began to entertain ourselves. Can't you be a little more quiet?—B. looked up from the second volume of *The Characteristics of Aesthetics*. We didn't bother to answer him.

I noticed that those next to us did not hum the refrain with us. I looked up: the Master sat among them on a small garden chair. I poked D. We stopped. Play on, the Master said, that's why I came. Contemporary Hungarian literature, I thought. We played another four or five numbers, but it wasn't the same. The Master noticed it too. What do you think this music means? he asked after one of the numbers. I don't know, I said. This is our religion. I giggled because it sounded so absurd. In their embarrassment, the others laughed too. And you believe in it? In the music, yes, I answered. But not in anything else? he asked with slight irony in his voice. Well, I said, but Blue Eyes, who had been silent during our playing, suddenly interrupted: That it could be a solution. It's a third class lie, that's all. What sort of third class?—I asked. Blue Eyes looked at me with disdain: Well, that all we have to do is to wait for the older generation to die out and everything will be fine in this world. Because we stick together.

The heat of emotion made her beautiful—if that's at all possible with someone whose otherworldly beauty had already disturbed the whole company. You don't believe in action? asked the Master. He was very polite. The sexual revolution is the only one we'll see, if that's what you mean, answered Blue Eyes. Interesting, said the Master thoughtfully. His pronunciation gave the words style. It's too bad, said Blue Eyes. The Master fell silent, offended. We began to play slow numbers, *Helpless, Fourth Time Round* and *Cry Baby, Cry*. N., who was quieter because of the wine, suddenly said: I would like to ask a question about the character I'm playing. I don't understand him very well. N.

played the role of a monster (one of the major roles), who symbolized government and the financial oligarchy. Yes, it's a complicated figure, answered the Master thoughtfully, he constantly borrows... I was the first to speak in the silence that followed the explanation. The day after tomorrow one of the best rock bands is giving a concert here. Come with us if you feel like it. Thank you, said the Master. I'll see. I'll let you know after the performance.

We stood up, it began to get dark. The dog was reluctant to give up one of the legs of my jeans, that is, its smell. Tell me, please, is this dog a pure breed? It is, said the Master. I only wondered because mine is black and white as well and it's a mongrel. The true fox terriers have a brown spot too, I said. You're wrong, said the Master with irritation. I don't know much about it, I said, I only heard, and that was the truth. L., a teacher at a university, looked at me meaningfully. For the moment he abandoned his role, for in general he desperately wanted to appear cool, and he often called people's attention to the fact that he was a writer. During our farewell, F. conveyed to the Master greetings from one of his relatives. I never liked him, answered the Master simply. We stumbled down the mountain.

5.

Forming a chain we pulled them through the crowd. I have never been to a rock concert, said the Master, enthusiastically, considering his seventy plus years. And Hamburg? interruped his wife. That was different, answered the Master. That's how it was left. The audience was quite mixed, the best seats were occupied by those over thirty. It's not going to be real, I said to the Master, pointing to them. I noticed, agreed the Master. His young eyes darted restlessly around. He took out a notebook and wrote in it. You left your pen with the flashlight in the car, said his wife.

Yes, the Master said, not even looking up. For reasons incomprehensible to me, his wife repeated the sentence two more times. Finally, the Master looked up and said, the pen with the flashlight. I think I left it in the car.

Then he said, I'm working on a novella. You'll be in it. he smiled, and asked about the band. He was as impatient as a teenager. I don't think those things should be written about, I said, trying to speak with the self-assured tone of intimates. Our kind is not interested in literature. Then, what? he asked. I pointed to the stage where only yesterday we had played our roles, where the band was now tuning up. I don't know much about it, he said, but I don't like those things that appeal to the instincts alone. But that's the only thing we can trust, I answered. That's what they take advantage of, he noted quietly.

During the intermission we went down front, as far as the orchestra pit, where there was standing room only. The Master, taking notes, asked me the titles of one or two numbers. A few people noticed it. Look at the old fool, one of them said. Shut up, I said, agreeably. Z., who was a wrestler before he began drinking, stood beside me and did not need to speak. The Master noticed nothing.

Let's go up to the boys, said the Master's wife, when we got back to our seats. Why should we, said the Master. But of course, we went.

I don't think this generation wants to grow up, said the Master, as we hurried to the band's dressing room. It still wouldn't be able to change anything, I said. But unfortunately, everyone must grow up some time, the Master said. Just look at me.

I looked at him.

6.

We'll say that guests were already sleeping in our beds, said E., as we staggered home from the farewell party. He was a third-year law student, a mayor's son from a small, dusty town. Although he lacked any conviction, he became a stage hand in order to run around with us. I'll sleep with the blonde one, he said in front of the door. By "blonde" he meant Blue Eyes, who, together with our prompter, was sleeping in a separate section, because they came hitchhiking and arrived later than the rest. Why you? I asked, surprised and drunk. Because you're already going with someone, E. raised his index finger in explanation. That's true, I said, not realizing that I could have said the same thing to him. We went in. The girls were not very surprised. The only question now is who should sleep where, announced E., after we told our transparent lie. Let's toss a coin, I said, because ever since I could remember, I found the role that chance played exciting. Except that I always confused it with something else. As now. If tails, the bed on the left is yours, I said to E., who was not very enthusiastic about this solution. I won Blue Eyes. Go on, there, your lie there, I said, and I climbed in with the little tangled-haired prompter, who must have been waiting for such an opportunity, as she immediately started caressing me. In my confusion, I began kissing her, while watching the other bed with all of my back. The girl whispered something, but I didn't understand. I mumbled something with closed lips. The sound of rubbing grew louder over there. I lay on my back and tried to hum *Bridge Over Troubled Waters* to myself. I couldn't. I didn't know what to do. Come, I said to the little tangled-haired prompter, who, in her surprise, obeyed me. I gathered up the sheets and pulled her upstairs. I made up a bed on top of the teacher's desk in classroom I/B.

Well, how was it, my boy?—E. woke me up in the

morning. Tangled-haired was long gone. I showed him. Shit, old boy. E. grinned. The other was a virgin too. And how she had talked about the sexual revolution the other day. If I hadn't been so sapped and tired, I would have kicked him all the way to the bus. But all I said was: We did it for our country. By then I knew I loved Blue Eyes.

7.

I only told the news to Andrea, of course. And as always, when I didn't know what was going to happen, I began working. I drank for a week, in three shifts, then I ran into Andrea on the river bank. I went to bed with someone, she lied. I'm not good enough for you, was all I could manage to say as if I had pieces of broken glass in my throat. With Blue Eyes I got as far as taking her to dinner with money I got by selling three of my books. We ate tenderloin à la Kassa, something I had been dreaming about. Andrea could never forgive me for that. Shortly after, N. fell in love with Blue Eyes, and I would have stepped aside even if I had not been head over heels in love with Andrea. I usually step aside.

I soon gave up acting. It took me a year and a half to find out that I had no business with them, and three days to write this story.

Translated by Georgia Greist

Snapshot

BY ÁKOS KERTÉSZ

Shortly after midnight, three women sit alone on a bed. They are very young (the oldest just over twenty-three, the youngest just twenty), young and pretty; attention accidentally shifts from them, just as the group accidentally ended up together a few hours ago, four men and five women, of these, three had never met before; across the room, in front of the bookcase, stand three men, glasses in hand, exchanging ideas (fixed ideas as the host says with mild self-criticism), serious and important ideas; on the left, near the right corner across the room in darkness, where a couple sit kissing on the sofa (no one knows them well); the dog walks nervously around, there are too many strange legs, strange smells, strange voices; a stereo plays quietly in the corner, the host, who is divorced, likes young women and music; the fifth woman (a divorcée, about thirty-five, thirty-eight years old, without a partner) is busy in the kitchen, she is the soul of the party, takes care of everyone, cooking sausages and making coffee, slicing bread, looking for mustard in the cupboard; then the oldest woman on the bed, just barely twenty-three, speaks, she begins the conversation in that unobserved moment when the three women are left alone for a while on the bed, shortly after midnight. Of those present, only a few know each other (one never quite catches names during an introduction), they came separately in small groups, why not give Z's a call, they are at home, but have guests, doesn't matter, bring them along, let's drop in to X, who is a bachelor, divorced, lives alone, has an incredible stereo system with lots of tape and records, let's take wine and liquor, perhaps some cognac, some people prefer that, Mártika remembers that one must eat too, she suggests the sausages and bread, so now they are together and are having a good time, a pleasant exchange of ideas; the three men are holding their glasses (the host, a young man— some assistant professor—and a very good-looking boy who works in the hotel industry, speaks several languages, and knows famous artists personally), the purpose of existence is being considered and everyone has an opinion, they forget to drink, and forget about the three girls on the bed, where the oldest, a blonde girl, asks (in that moment when they are left alone) what the others are taking, because she left her Ovulen (she does not say where, and the two others do not ask), she can only get it tomorrow, but is afraid to skip a day, could someone lend her one; only as a loan, says the youngest, a thin girl with brown hair, a philosophy student, she is taking the same thing, but does not have any extra, only as a loan, of course we'll fix a date when we can meet; the dog nervously walks between the legs, suddenly licks one of the girls' hand, she is twenty-one years old, recently married (her husband is talking in front of the bookcase, the one who works in the hotel industry), she is a small woman with brown hair and a childlike face, one would think her seventeen, she has a pleasing smell, it seems, for the dog licks her hand and for a moment lays head on her knee, then moves on, stops behind the men, his master is there, his leg familiar, the dog relaxes, lies down behind his master and listens to the sounds, the recordplayer plays jazz, it's an excellent Dutch group, playing cool jazz, the assistant professor is speaking, physics does not know progress, the universe is rushing head on toward destruction with explosive speed because the universe is made up of materials splitting and fusing, a permanent atomic fusion, the elements lighter than iron are fusing, the heavier splitting, "eventually everything cools down and the neutral cinder is left," as the poet also suspected, iron is left, cold and still; on the sofa, the youngest woman, the thin philosophy student with brown hair said her doctor prescribed the Ovulen after her D. and C.

She reaches for her purse, looks for the pills, while the other two shield her so the men would not see, not that they are ashamed, but it's their business only, nobody else's, the men are not curious anyway because they are involved with the future of being, and this theme creates a pleasant thrill in the pleasant apartment, in the pleasant semi-darkness, beside the pleasant drinks, while pleasant music plays and the girls sit at an arm's length, and it seems that they are getting along well together, and they do not disturb the pleasant conversation of the men in this pleasant hour, shortly after midnight. The three girls watch the small, white pill travel from one purse to another; I fell asleep before it happened, says the thin philosophy student suddenly, as she passes the pill and quietly laughs, they did not put me to sleep, said the other, the blonde girl, the philosophy student interrupts her, that's not what I mean, I fell asleep because I was so nervous, in the doctor's office; the young wife, who was sitting between them, doesn't say anything, quietly calls the dog, coaxing him back; it happened six months ago, said the philosophy student, she did not want a child, it was impossible in her circumstances, there was never any question but that she would have an abortion, even then, when it was certain, she became hysterical, couldn't stop crying, and was afraid that her man would misunderstand, and she would lose him, she was afraid of that, not of the operation, she didn't know what it all meant, it was the first time she had a vaginal examination, she didn't know what to expect, that's why she fell asleep, because she was tired and nervous, because the doctor (a woman) who was a friend, let her lie down in her office, so she would be comfortable while waiting for the operation, because in the common waiting rooms the women make each other nervous, and when the doctor came to get her, and saw her asleep on the examining table, just like a snotty-nosed kid, she made fun of her, and she was embarrassed, although it was natural, the numbness of the cortex, nature's way of protecting itself, but during the operation, apparently, she cried out in pain and swore, that's what the doctor told her after, but she didn't remember anything. The blonde girl, on the other hand, was not put to sleep; it happened in the country, and they didn't put you to sleep in that hospital, that's how it was done, only the piercing hurt, because they pierced up in the uterus, of course she could feel the rest too, it didn't hurt, but she felt it, it's impossible not to feel it when they are prying in your insides with a sharp-edged spoon, she could, it seems, hear in her belly the tearing of tissues, she broke off with the guy then, because he was dirt, he said it was her business, it was in her belly, all right, she said and went ahead with the whole thing on her own; in her case, interrupted the philosophy student, she and the boy agreed, it never occurred to her that she should bear the child, yet when she thought that at thirty-five she might have a sixteen-year-old boy or girl, she cried, and constantly cried up to the operation, and the boy thought that she wanted to keep the child, he didn't understand that she was crying because she wouldn't keep it, she was afraid the boy would think she was blackmailing him; she called a cab, says the blonde girl, she says it lightly now that it's over, she called a cab, went home, went to bed, and her mother called her a lazy dog because she didn't believe she had a headache (that was her lie, she didn't get out of bed to help with supper, didn't lay the table and didn't wash the dishes), her mother almost slapped her, her parents scolded her, that's when she came to hate her mother, not because of the scene, but because she could not confide in her, that's the way she was brought up, the atmosphere of home forced her to lie, that's what she could not forgive her mother (if she ever has a daughter, she says now with determination, she would bring her up to trust her, so she could turn to her, if she were in trouble, she would take her to the doctor, she would not let her work the next day, because she went to work the next day, her insides hurt so, she could hardly walk), that's when she decided to go to Budapest, she came and will never return, she adds, she stands up and stretches, she has a beautiful athletic figure, and the other, the philosophy student is silent, she still had something to say, but did not want to brag, because her man sat by her bed for three days, because he was a decent sort, they are still together, and the blonde would probably not understand what she had to say, she is a tough woman, takes life in her stride, although it was not easy for her either, that's obvious; the dog was again in front of them, because the third, the brown-haired young wife called him to her, the dog came and once again lays his head on her knee, and closes his eyes, letting her pet him and pull his ears. The brown-haired young wife, whose husband is standing across the room from them, in front of the bookcase, talking with the other two men, scratches the dog's head, says quietly that they filled her with water or some other liquid, she could not tell, her belly swelled up like a barrel, because the child had to be drowned in it, because she was past the fifth month and it had moved, that's when they did it, not where they lived, but in another town in the doctor's home, no one was at home, the doctor sent his family away, only her own parents were there, but she was not allowed to cry out, because what happened was that they got her drunk at a party, she was sixteen then, she didn't even know who did it, she was so dumb that it was her class-teacher who noticed something, called in her mother, but by then she was in her fifth month, her parents pulled her out of school, and took turns beating her for a week, trying to find out who did it, tried to have her confess who the person was, but she didn't know, honest to God, she didn't, the young, wife with the brown hair smiles with her child-like face, and with her almond-shaped eyes, the shape of which she accentuates with eye-make-up, looks trustingly at the philosophy student and at the tall blonde girl, as she repeats, honest to God, as if it were terribly important that she did indeed not know then who it was, then they got on the train, they paid an enormous amount to the doctor who induced her labour, and so that she would not yell, said the doctor, he stuffed a rag into her mouth, because if someone found out, they'd hang him, otherwise all went smoothly, it was a simple case of premature labour, she knew that the child was not alive, still it was strange, said the child-faced young wife, and she looks at her husband, since then she had finished high school, now they are saving money to buy a flat, she looks at her husband, who is now listening to the professor; according to the professor, the sun will blow up in six million years, like the other supernovas, and all life will cease, what was strange, says the young wife, and pets the dog's head, that she waited for the crying, but the little one didn't cry, of course it could not cry, it wasn't alive any more, that's what the doctor said, he said, unexpectedly, in the dark, it was a well-developed child, she knew it could not cry, that it was impossible, but she was still expecting it, it's strange that she was so dumb, she could not return home, she had to stay in that town, with her godmother, later she ran away to Budapest, met her husband, now they are renting a place, and she works in an office; the dog tires of the petting, moves once more to the centre of the room, and not far, near his master's familiar shoes, he sniffs nervously, the young wife's hand stops in mid-air, now that the dog left, she does not know what to do with it, she hitches up her legs and wraps her arms around her knees, then repeats that it was so strange that she waited for it to cry, what was terrible was that she did not hear it cry, yet she knew that she could not hear it cry, for it was no longer alive.

Three women are sitting on the bed, they met just a few hours ago, the men look at them now and then, and note, satisfied, that they are talking quietly, have become friends, nothing is wrong; Mártika is busy in the kitchen, on the sofa, which the standard lamp leaves in semi-darkness, the lovers are kissing, no one knows exactly who they are, three men are standing in front of the bookcase, holding glasses and they are so preoccupied with great thoughts that they forget to drink, the dog is nervously moving around in the middle of the room and wriggles under the sofa where the pair is kissing, he is looking suspiciously at the strange legs, quietly growls because the woman put her right leg on the man's left knee, the dog doesn't understand which leg belongs to whom; and the three women are silent on the bed, for a moment they are thinking of the same thing, just what that is, cannot be fixed exactly, probably not one of them could say for sure, they don't feel sorry for themselves, or for each other, they don't love each other more, nor do they hate each other, yet there is some sort of trust in this silence, a peace, perhaps the security of knowledge, perhaps they were partners in a sin, sharing a secret, while the men exchange lofty ideas, not quite three metres from them, Mártika has already poured out the coffee and is putting the sausages on plates in the kitchen, and the dog is quietly bar-ing its teeth under the sofa; the picture, in this moment's silence, becomes rigid and fixed for the three women: the three men in front of the bookcase, the couple on the sofa, the dog, the room with its corners in semi-darkness, and they themselves, three together on the bed, but then the moment passes, those present move out of frame, the host empties his glass, the assistant professor crosses over to the blonde girl, the dog wriggles out from under the sofa, the small, child-faced young wife stands up, walks over to her husband, and the blonde girl once again concludes that the young wife is stupid and has an unattractive figure, and it's irritating that the professor stares at her, his eyes practically bulging, the tape ends, the couple stops kissing, and Mártika brings in the sausages.

The exact time is 12:51 a.m.

Translated by Georgia Greist

Showdown

BY GYULA KURUCZ

A crash from outside. His mother cast a furtive glance around her: no one saw the cup break. She picked up the pieces and threw them into the plastic bucket, stirred the garbage up a bit so that the pieces didn't show. She sucked her lips in angrily, pursing them up into a thin straight line, body heaving with the indignity of hands now unsteady, the broken cup, and everything else. She stared bitterly ahead of her. It was her nose, the smell of bubbling soup that brought her back to the present, into her kitchen; she came to life again, her movements flurried.

His father heard the cup break. The sound startled him; he sat silent, uncertain eyes roving from object to object, searching for a foothold, a place to rest. He found it in the tangled fringe of the carpet. He rose laboriously, groaning, took the worn plastic hairbrush from the chest of drawers and bent double, knees trembling, brushing it straight, first on the further side, by the two beds, then by his door. He dared not crouch for fear of being unable to get up again. And he knew that when his son came out of his room the heels of his tattered, over-large slippers would scuff the fringe of the shabby old carpet out of place again. No one saw him working. He lowered himself back into the armchair, and hurriedly lit another cigarette. He smoked it quickly, avidly, until a third of it had gone. Then he could pretend that it was a stub had gone out and had to be lit again.

His son heard the scraping of the brush, first from a distance, from the other side of the room, then from close by, from the side nearest his door. No use hiding the brush; his father had appropriated, monopolized that backbreaking task. The scraping of the brush grated on his nerves and the click of the lighter aroused a nagging fear that his mother would come in and find his wheezing father puffing away at yet another cigarette.

He rubbed the tabletop with clammy palms. He could have read ten pages by now; instead, he lit another cigarette. The flat in fact was quite large: fifty-two square metres, two medium-sized rooms, large enough for three people "by our standards". And as it was on the first floor it lessened the danger of his father toppling down the stairs, clumsy-legged—he walked stiffly, jerkily, bouncing from step to step—tripping at each—maybe the last—turn of the staircase. Each day was fraught with danger, the danger of becoming the last; each homecoming a sigh of relief and anguish until the next departure. Fifty-two square metres, and in his name, as if it were his own.

He heard a door squeak from the direction of the kitchen. He hastily counted the butts in the ashtray—one-two-four-seven-eight-eleven—pictured his mother's face at the sight of them—snatched a paper handkerchief from the desk drawer and blew his dry nose into it: blew to muster a little damp, enough that the butts would adhere to it. He shook seven butts and a proportionate amount of ash into the handkerchief, rolled it up into a ball, stuffed it into an empty packet of cigarettes, crushed it negligently so that the contents would not show and threw it into the wastepaper basket.

The smoke was thick enough to cut with a knife. True, the room was small; the bookshelves, the wardrobe, the desk and the narrow divan bed along the wall took up a lot of airspace. And the butt-hiding game was in fact purposeless, unnecessary—in the fever of Sunday dinner-making his mother would not bother to come and fetch him, would be content to call. He couldn't open the window; his father would surely protest against the 40 fillérs per kilowatt warmth seeping, squandered out into the raw spring air. He could not open it noiselessly enough for his father to fail to hear in the larger room, could not prevent him from appearing, face aghast, to say: "Why do you switch the heating on if you're hot?" His father sat in his armchair, bored, waiting for dinner to be ready, one way of whiling away the hours; his father sat, hiding the second butt in the pocket of his jacket, and trembled expectantly: would his wife be able to tell that the smoke in the room was produced by two cigarettes, not one, or not?

A rapid inspection of the room followed the squeak of the kitchen door. Number of butts—acceptable, smoke thick, tell-tale amount of ash reduced, cubic airspace demonstrably small—they both knew that he smoked a great many cigarettes, the difference being only that he knew for certain that the total was eleven while his mother suspected fifteen, until the moment she could lay her hands on the hidden packet to reproach him with each and every one.

Her voice reached him from a distance:

"Lacika, dinner's ready! Come and eat!"

And the prompt echo resounded from the armchair:

"Son, your mother says dinner's ready! Come and get it!"

He jumped up before either of them could come to fetch him.

"Come on," he said to his approaching father, "let's go and eat".

"Yes, let's", his father replied.

Dinner was over quickly and without fuss. Holding back his father's avid spoon his mother urged him to eat. Portions were meted out inexorably, their size determined by indisputable laws—he had to eat more than he desired, his father less than he craved. His mother watched his father like a hawk to make sure he did not "gorge himself", over-eat, make himself ill. His father had never managed to accustom himself to moderate eating; he watched his son eat with envious eyes.

With a cup of coffee and a bloated stomach he retreated to the sanctuary of his room. And waited for his mother to appear.

There was not the slightest sound—not even the rustle of a newspaper—from the other room. Ears strained to catch familiar sounds, they both lay in wait on either side of the door. The smoke irritated his throat, made him want to cough; he choked it back—couldn't—and from holding it back had to gasp for breath and began to cough in earnest. Immediately the door opened and his mother's face popped in:

"Have you caught a cold? Where did you catch cold? I'll give you something for it, shall I? Take an antibiotic and some cough mixture."

"No!"

"Why not? It'll make you better!"

"No!"

"Then stop taking tranquillizers and sedatives! And stop eating aspirin! And if you must take sedatives, then you can take an antibiotic and some cough mixture too! I'll fetch it for you, shall I?"

"No!"

"It's those damned fags that make you cough! How many did you smoke today?"

"Forty-one."

Doubt washed off the expression of horror that was beginning to settle on his mother's face.

"Not really?"

"Really. Tell me what you want."

"Why should I want anything?"

"Mother, tell me what you want."

Thoughts racing behind those thickening features, thickening nose.

His mother retreated. The sound of her feet from the other room.

"What's up?" asked his father in a subdued whisper, so as not to disturb his son. He probably received a shrug for an answer—the hunch of his shoulders became more pronounced. His mother tugged open a drawer, went out into the kitchen, came back with a glass of water and some pills.

"You know I'm not going to take them."

"Stubborn, that's what you are."

She put down the glass and the pills on the side table and went out.

Malevolent joy: he had managed to send her out a second time. His father fretted about the unexplained pills, rummaged for cigarettes in his pockets, but did not dare light one, did not dare ask questions. He squirmed restlessly in his seat, stood up, scuttled timidly for the toilet, locked the door behind him, unbuttoned his trousers, sat down on the cover and lit up with trembling hands. As soon as the cigarette was alight he switched off the light in the toilet. Unless something happened out there to distract his wife's attention she'd be down on him as soon as he stepped out: "What were you doing in there? You didn't take a laxative today! Smoking again, weren't you?" and she'd sniff into the smoke-filled closet. Nonetheless he puffed avidly at his cigarette until the ash grew inch-long and the filter became hot to the touch, just like a teenager in the school loo. He reached blindly for a bit of paper, kneading his stomach with his left hand until—with an effort—he managed to belch. He didn't need to pee, he went not more than an hour and a half ago.

The son waited, face turned towards the door. His mother opened it and began to speak rapidly to ward off all interruption.

"Oh, Laci, I almost forgot to tell you. There's been a letter from your Aunt Edit. She's coming up for a visit around Easter."

He sat silent, waiting.

"She's planning to stay with us."

He looked at her. His father had come out of the toilet; under the cover of the water flushing loudly in the bowl he swung the door to and fro to dispel the smoke. That was all right: what he'd lost on heating he'd saved by switching off the light. He strained his ears for the sound of their voices, opened the kitchen door—no one there, stepped into the bigger room—no one there either. Through the opaque glass of the door to the smaller room he could see his wife standing inside. Was his son lying on the bed? What could be the matter with him?

His mother did not notice the eavesdropper's shadow on the pane of glass.

He suddenly decided to answer her after all.

"Well if she's coming, let her come. She can sleep in one of the armchairs."

"Are you joking?"

He forced himself to smile. 'Look, son,' that's what would come next.

"Look, son, like it or not, she is your father's sister. After all, she's got a right to celebrate Easter too, hasn't she? And you can do something for your family this once, can't you?"

Since when was his Dad "your Father"? And what did

she mean by this "after all" business? After all? Before all? Above all?

"So?"

"So I thought you could go and stay at that woman's place again."

"What woman did you have in mind?"

"That person you took yourself off to the last time you started carrying on about it being impossible to live under the same roof with us. You could go and stay at her place for a couple of days and we could put Editke up in your room where she'll be comfortable, like a guest should be."

"Was it Dad who asked her to come?"

"Him? He wouldn't ask anybody, old skinflint that he is."

"So it was you who asked her."

"Well! Well of all the...!"

She left the sentence unfinished; she needed him. She needed an ally against his Dad; he couldn't stand his sister.

"Don't be flippant now, son. You'll go and stay at that person's place, then?"

"No. She hasn't got a place of her own."

"Well!... I always said you should have gone in for engineering or medicine but you wouldn't listen to me."

"I'm listening now."

"What?"

"I said I'm listening now. Envy is an insufficient incentive to make one act against one's best convictions."

"What are you blathering about?"

"Let's go next door, shall we? Dad's dying of curiosity."

He opened the door; his father just managed to plump down in the armchair in time. His mother followed him in hesitantly, leaned on the armrest of the third armchair.

"How are you feeling, my boy?"

"Your sister Edit is paying us a visit at Easter."

"Edit? Coming here?"

"Blood counts, after all, and all that. Like it or not. Love, peace, bunk beds."

"What have bunk beds to do with it?"

"A nice brother you are."

"And where is she going to sleep, if I may ask?"

"Come on, Dad, where would she sleep? In my room, of course. And for those two or three days I can always sleep in the servant's room."

They looked at him, shocked.

"All right, if you think it beneath my dignity to sleep in the servant's room I can always sleep in the hall."

"But we haven't got a servant's room, my boy, or a hall either."

His mother began to see the light.

"You know what he's doing? He's making a fool of us as usual, that's what he's doing."

"But what's all this about Edit coming here?"

"She's your sister, isn't she?"

"Yes, but what's all this about..."

"Oh, shut up will you?"

Blue seawater surrounded him, waves of infantilism washed over his body, bland to the touch. A pleasant sensation. The number of times his students used it to get the better of him, the number of times he had to put up with their gay, unfettered cynicism—and always came up helpless, powerless against their mischief. And now the time had come to make use of what he had learned from his slick-mannered students with their oily grins. For he was a quick learner, and he ought to make use of their cynicism, polished by constant use on targets provided by their environment.

The unaccustomed, open attack, the spark of hatred flashing from narrowed eyes, took him completely by surprise:

"You never listened to us, you ungrateful wretch!

Wasted our breaths telling him to go in for engineering or medicine but that was too good for him, school-teaching snotty kids was what he wanted, nothing else would do…"

"They're not snotty kids, they're teenagers," he snapped back.

"What's the difference?' And what have you made of yourself, may I ask? Three thousand seven hundred you earn. I ask you, how much is that?"

"As much as both your pensions," he stammered.

"Have you got a place of your own?"

"But Lujzi, how can you ask that?"

"Shut up!" She turned on him again. "Where would you be today if it wasn't for your old parents? There wouldn't even be a roof over your head, I can tell you. Couldn't even stick out your marriage decently, could you, even your wife would have none of you, and no wonder! We put him up, look after him, take care of him and what do we get in return? Insolence, that's what we get. When he should be going down on his knees to kiss our hands for putting the house in his name! It's because of you that we have to live packed together like sardines in a tin and even then it's your poor father who has to do the shopping!"

"For two thousand a month, let me say, it's…"

"Two thousand nothing. We gave up our lives for you and all the thanks we get is he makes our old age miserable! We should have beaten you with a whip to put an end to your impudence! We should have beaten you with a whip until you did as you were told!"

"Lujzika! That's our boy you're speaking to!"

"Shut up! He's full of hatred against his parents! You'll get your share of it, don't you worry!"

"That's right, Mum, let it all come out, all the filth you've been saving up for me. So you gave up your lives for me, did you? Fine. Instead of a tumbledown shack in

360

a small town suburb with an outdoor shithouse and a coal-stove for heating you got a self-contained flat and me into the bargain—yes, you got me back so that you could ruin my life for free, for fun! No one else could have thought up such a sneaky way of laying their hands upon the better part of my lousy salary, not spending it, mind you, just making sure I'd have nothing to put by, because then I could have saved up for a one-room flat or something by now, a place of my own at least. Because then you couldn't have borrowed my name, couldn't have made sure I'd never again be entitled to any manner of housing in our sweet land—I can never again apply for any kind of flat to our gracious and almighty council, I can never again lock my own door behind me. You have made me into an unpropertied proprietor, a beneficiary cheated out of his lawful rights, who, out of the twenty years that are left to him can spend the next ten tending you, and the last ten tending himself."

"So it's our death you're lusting after, is it?"

"You're so stupid!"

"Boy!"

"Leave it, Dad, you can't mend things now."

"A viper, that's what you are! A viper we've been nurturing in our bosom!"

Slowly he stood up, quite calm now. Two people sat facing him.

He went out into the vestibule, put on his shoes, his coat.

He could not put the twenty years divided in half out of his mind. Ten here, ten there. The first ten were a bit exaggerated perhaps: give his father another couple of years, if that; he'd be happy to enjoy a couple of days given the chance. Should he go to his sister's? There were four of them there in a two-roomed flat, each prepared to fight to the death for their self-allotted corners. And what would he say? Why would he explain? It wasn't justification he sought. No? They set upon each other because the Hungarian housing laws left them no choice: his parents, coming up from the country, had no legitimate "right" to buy a flat of their own with their money and so bought the flat in his "legitimate" name. They fought because the law said: let us set the small fry against each other so that all that we want to escape their notice will remain hidden in the shadow of their antagonisms. An old Roman practice, that, very prudent, a trifle hackneyed perhaps, but time-honoured. Why did I have to take part in the humiliating game of the humiliated? The wish to command, to rule is so deeply ingrained in Mother that I have no choice but to resort to trickery. With nothing but my magical—magical?—personality and professional skill on my side, how can I become a respected authority in the eyes of the youngsters I teach, pupils of an elite grammar school and all more affluent, more widely travelled, and in many respects more experienced than I? In one respect they certainly eclipsed him: in their repeated, in indirect experience of the futility of rational struggle, in their exact knowledge—and scorn—of the game. Were they children at all, these adolescents wearily attempting to come to terms with their age, running the risk of contamination every single day of their lives? If one had to face the truth, he did not really know them, he simply perceived and registered the incomprehensible symptoms of this our modern age through them. His mother had still been the absolute ruler of her class when she stopped working; she could still believe in her power, to shape the destinies of the gawky country kids held firmly under her thumb. His lot had been a couple of dozen attentive eyes, interested, despite the law, ready to be captivated by the subject—that had been his lot in life, and the hope that some of what he taught would take root, that they would multiply his aims as it were. That and the dream of not having lived in vain.

A broad-shouldered man in a tweed coat passed by him. The white, grey and brown threads mingled in the coat. The stifling silence of the larger room weighed heavily upon the threads. Timidly his father walked up and down between the two beds and the kitchen, his mother pouncing upon him every now and then, checking his hard-earned courage. His mother, too, was unable to sit still; she padded up and down, bearing the burden of her anger everywhere with her. With the first great outburst spent and over she was now content to nurse her wounded pride, her anger, and eagerly awaited him so that she could cast all the insults she forgot to think of in his teeth. His father watched her heavy-eyed, trying to think up ways of smothering the glowing embers of her animosity. He did not know his wife; he did not know that a single sentence would suffice: "I just hope he doesn't get himself run over," for her vibrant love for her son, quenched by stubborn pride and hurt, to surface and be transformed into self-reproach.

The man in the tweed coat turned off into another street. If he followed him now he would be tempted by the easy way out: to go home with brows wrinkled in agony, face tortured with pain, wordless, and to falter out, in answer to her expression of concern: "Headache". A handful of pills, a cool cloth for his forehead, tender care would follow.

The soles of his feet warned him he had been walking for a long time. He glanced at his watch—two hours had passed since he left home. He began to walk homeward. Wouldn't it have been better to choose marriage and the solace of children, regardless of deepening divisions and the growing autocracy of the stronger-willed? Ten years of solace his children could have given him, then disappointment would have come, and they would have been two people left to fight each other again. Belated thoughts, there was no going back, no changing things now.

He turned the key carefully in the door and slipped in only to be immediately confronted with his mother's questioning face, eyes expectant for a split second, quickly turning to ice. For a minute they stood hesitant—to fall on her neck then would bring him instant forgiveness—then each retreated to base, pulses racing madly.

In the larger room his father made as if to rise from his chair—a gentle pat on the shoulder would win him over to his side. He made no such gesture, passed by. He pitied the old man, turned away from his beseeching eyes, deserted him, shut the door behind him. There was nothing he could do for him. He sat down and waited for the first attack.

Stray thoughts helped pass the time. Sounds of activity from the kitchen, but no sight of her yet. Thin panel walls transmitting the message of panel society, and the only one unaware of the message was she who was preparing to attack.

A heavy shadow passed by the old man as he sat huddled in his armchair, the door emitted a protesting squeak —bodies tensed themselves in readiness—he awaited the depression of the unwieldy aluminium handle of the door. The door-handle was pressed down, a dish of stewed apples appeared, flourished with a lavish gesture and placed on the side table, the face hovering above it guarded, watchful, then her back was turned ostentatiously and the door closed behind her.

"I don't want it!" he groaned helplessly, belatedly, "I dont't want it!" he roared to the silent room, and because he encountered no resistance, because he was in such need of it he jumped up, stamped out into the other room and banged the see-what-good-care-I-take-of-you-ungrateful-wretch gift down on the table. His mother turned back from the door, his father covered in his armchair, licking his parched lips.

"Ask him why he won't eat his stewed apples on a Sunday of all days, when he's always stuffed it down before!"

His father forwarded the message with silently moving lips.

"Not this way, I don't want it!" he snapped back.

"He wanted it all right when we washed his dirty knickers for him, and his smelly socks, he wanted it while we educated him, and clothed and fed him, and cared for him, and even took him back, helped him become what he is today, he wanted it all right then! Didn't he? Go on, ask him!"

Sunk between huddled shoulders the face was rigid, lips unmoving as they passed on their message.

"You took me back?" he shouted. "Took me back!"

They turned upon each other.

"Think it yours, do you, because we put it in your name?"

"Gobble it up then, the walls, the furniture, the carpets, the bed, the air! Gobble it up and swallow it, and I hope it satisfies you! I hope, I really do hope you'll be satisfied for once in your frustrated life!"

"Lujzi! Lacika!" the armchair cried out.

"So you're on his side! All right then. You can have each other to gnash your teeth on until there's nothing but the bones left!"

The door banged loudly behind her. The armchair gave a plaintive squeak under its meagre load.

He pushed the tranquillizer down his dry throat. Waited for it to take effect in the growing darkness with his ears strained. His mother fiddled with glasses in the kitchen, preparing to clinch the game with the aid of the paper-thin walls dividing them. His father lit a cigarette—come what may, nothing would make any difference now. Face growing ever paler he waited for his wife.

The kitchen door opened, then the door to the larger room: breathless silence for a second, then with heaving, impassioned breath the volcano erupted.

"What an ungrateful wretch! Call that a child!"

"Lujzika!"

"What do you want me to do? Ask for his forgiveness? Me, his mother? For putting up with his insolence?"

"Still, wouldn't it be better to..."

"What would be better! Who's the boss around here! Should I kiss lordship's hand, or what? No respect for his parents, nor for his elders, that he hasn't! Let him go back to his depraved students, those degenerates who won't be content with looking down upon their parents, but will soon be beating them up. Let him go back to them where he belongs!"

"Lujzika, you know he's not like that!"

"Why, what have you got from him to be proud of? Rudeness, unkindness, contempt, that's all you've got. A worthless, doddering old fool, that's what he thinks of you. Didn't he say we are in the way, didn't he say he'd take care of us for another ten years and if we don't kick the bucket by then he'll have done with us—from then on he'll only be looking out for himself! That's right, back him up, maybe you'll live to see him do us out of our house!"

And after a short silence a carefully calculated cry of surprise:

"So you're on his side! You both want to see the back of me! All right then! All right!"

In his lair he sat expectant, trembling, until the voice came again:

"I'm sending a telegram to Edit right away. I'm going

to tell her that her brother and nephew refuse to allow her into our home."

"You can't bring such shame on us..."

"And that's not all by half! I'm going to tell her that it's me who'll be taking a train tomorrow! I'm leaving! For good!"

"Lujzi dear!"

"Don't you Lujzi dear me! You can stay here with your degenerate son, let him take care of you, let him wash, cook and clean for you, and when he's had enough of you just see if he won't send you packing! In the poorhouse, that's where you'll end up, in a home for the aged!"

He tore the door open and glowered in the doorway like a caricature of an avenging deity.

"You can stop the dramatics, mother. I'm leaving tomorrow."

"I'm the one who's leaving!"

"I am!"

"No, I am!"

"Oh, God, oh God, why did I have to live to see this!"

"Because, you were born, Dad."

"See how he talks to you already! You'll soon learn what a wretch, what a rotten beast you've raised!"

"Lujzi dear, please don't leave me!"

"You're the one who's left me! And you can just face the consequences. I'm going to Edit's, to the sister you've turned away! And don't either of you come pleading to me!"

"Pleading to you! Never!" the son raved.

His father was deathly pale; he looked at his son reproachfully, but dared not say a word.

He turned away silently. He knew her irrefutable logics. She had defeated him.

He sat down at his desk and stared out at the four-storied

houses bathed in the evening light. His whole body seethed, frothed with anger. Of course his mother would not leave. She would send the telegram by phone and it would run something like this: first the address, then: "Dear Edit, something has come up, your trip must be postponed," then she would cover the mouthpiece with her palm and continue: "Shall be arriving tomorrow afternoon, expect me at the station." Removing her palm from the mouthpiece she would add: "Lujzi". And the telegraph clerk would read the text back to her, but of course they would be led to think the whole text had been sent. And in his fear and shame his father would shrivel up still further in his chair.

In the vestibule a wardrobe door squeaked, followed by a thud, one-, two-, three loud groans she had lugged the suitcase out into the hall and had begun to pack. His father mustered up his strength, the door opened. Only his mother's repeated no's could be heard clearly. His father would renounce him gladly if only his wife would stay, he would do anything to keep this, last, domineering distributor of favours and tender care beside him. The suitcase was filling up. Right this moment she was doubtlessly saying: "I'll arrange to have the rest of my clothes, my crockery, furniture and carpets sent after me." The word "arrange" stabbed his father to the core, brought to mind lawyers, emptied flats, lawsuits, divorce courts, irreconcilable warth. He regretted his futile attempts at reconciliation, remembering his son's gruff rebuffs: chastized or repudiated by his wife he had often tried to seek refuge by his son's side, only to have him look up sullenly from his book, remove the wax plugs from his ears and say: "Go on, fight each other, all you want to if you aren't old enough to know better". If there would be just the two of them left, he wouldn't have anyone to talk to throughout the day and might not even be allowed to watch telly in the evenings. Under the shadow of his wife he could watch every programme with impunity. He stared beseechingly, terrified at his victorious, icy-eyed wife.

The lid of the suitcase banged shut: her decision was final. The door closed: she had probably gone into the kitchen. He was to suffer another stab, then, he was to be shown a last, a final proof of her illimitable goodness.

His stomach rumbled hungrily: his gastric juices, stimulated by the pills he took and the tense, idiotic Sunday clamour for supper. Feverishly he searched for the last of his antacid pills prescribed for his marriage ulcer, because whatever the cost, he would not eat, even if it killed him. He found the pill, crumbled it into pieces, and as he did not want to go out, swallowed the fragments dry, almost choking on them.

The flat was in darkness. His father sat huddled in his armchair, smoking dejectedly. No one noticed, but if they should he could always say: "What harm can anything do to me when you're ruining my nerves in any case?" Only the kitchen light was on: that was where supper is being prepared. The last supper.

His father did not echo her call and he forced himself to ignore it. He waited for her frozen face to appear. It loomed up before him in the darkened frame of the doorway:

"Supper's ready. Come and get it."

"I don't want it!"

"What did I make it for then?"

"That's your headache."

Familiar features dissolving into familiar contortions before his eyes, then the door banged shut.

Down in the streets of the housing estate the street lamps went on, casting their light into his room.

"Come and have a decent meal for the last time," she

called to his father, and out he went obediently into the kitchen, obediently sat and ate, staring pleadingly at that distant, frozen face, getting the last dietary morsel down silently, without an appetite.

He was tired. Listlessly he stared out of the window until—he did not know himself how much time had passed—the sound of her voice startled him.

"Let's spend our last evening together pleasantly."

What was that? What new trick had she thought up now? One thing was for sure: her tactics were superb. She had devised a new method of shutting him out, humiliating him. "The Week" came on the telly; he could almost see the jumbled snippets of newspaper converge and assemble to form the outsize letters of "The Week" before his eyes, and was reminded of a crafty counting game they used to play as children: reeling numbers off rapidly, fingers of a closed fist unfurling before the astonished eyes of a playmate, the tenth finger would appear as nine, nine would be ten and he would never guess where the trick was, in those fast unfurling fingers.

He rested his head on his folded arms and dropped off in the cosy, familiar tranquillity of the television programme.

The opening theme music of the Sunday special startled him awake. I must have dropped off, he thought to himself. Over on the other side of the door dreamy heroes rode horses or drove cars across the screen, robbed banks or stole pretty sums of money, while the viewers identified themselves vicariously with the heroes of the autoroute or the breezy hired prairies. Young people prepared themselves for life, comparing what they saw to their everyday experience.

Nine o'clock—he had gone without food for almost nine hours. The urge to pee encouraged him to use the loud flush of the toilet as cover to steal into the kitchen and snatch something to eat. In darkness he slipped across the room, passing in front of the eerily flickering screen—his father dared not call out to him: "Aren't you going to watch it, son? It's an American film!"

Meticulous order reigned in the kitchen. His supper was laid out for him on a plate—he would not touch it for the world. Neatly spaced items on the shelves of the fridge, easily checked—she'd notice at once if something was missing. His stomach bellowed for food, he could not resist its call. He cut wafer-thin slices of fat bacon and swallowed them raw, without bread; swallowed them disgustedly, gulping down innumerable glasses of water to force them down, then left the kitchen, confidently flushed the toilet, and finally marched past the finale on the screen. His father sat hopefully in his armchair: maybe things would revert to normal after this communal watching of the film. His mother paid no attention to the flickering screen, allowed the grandiloquent music to flood through her while she hatched new plots.

The light changed in the other room—they had switched off the beast. Familiar sounds of doors closing, water flushing in the loo, tinkling in the basin in the bathroom. For a moment he wavered: was there to be no more retaliation for his sins?

The light went out on the other side of the door. Conditioned reflexes made him jump up, hurry out to pee and wash his teeth, face averted from them lying in bed. On his way back he mumbled goodnight under his breath. He'd not give her anything to hold against him; hostility did not exclude politeness, but the absence of politeness would add fresh fuel to her hatred.

Everyone was in their proper place, tiny night-lights winking to inform others that the day—a Sunday, a holiday of State and Church—was not yet done. The participants were well-versed in the game: schooled by the reflexes of pupils and colleagues, well-trained offspring, apprentices, anointed knights and self-appointed popes for society and class.

He undressed and put on his pyjamas. He took the book he had been longing to read all morning, opened it, and began to listen. A programmed attack of illness, that would be next on the agenda, lights snapping on and off, searing his eyes through the glass every half hour until he had no choice but to go out there and ask what was the matter. He could not ignore the distress signals, he could not go out, not he, ungrateful, unloving, unfeeling traitor. Two people determinedly getting on each other's nerves, each secure in the belief of being the injured party, the cheated, the humbled, the misunderstood, deserving of and destined for better, for higher things, unaware of sharing the same rocking boat—they had broken him, reluctant witness to their games. Would marriage have been better after all? He had always lived among she-wolves, hungry jaws opened wide, as wide as they would go; he had never needed to worry about which of them should finally swallow him up, the problem was always how could his wife and mother both have their fill of his flesh?

In his hands the book remained unread; the strong light from the other room remained unlit.

The last half-hour was spent getting ready for bed. And still there was nothing but the creaking of bedsprings, the squeak of a drawer being opened and shut, and the faint glow of the night-light from the other room. What could she be plotting in there? She'd break him in the end—of that he was sure—she had only to think up and force upon him conditions in the face of which he would stand helpless. In a degenerate battle such as theirs the enemy would usually come to his opponent's aid to facilitate the making of amends; the slightest gesture could prove sufficiently humiliating. The assailant had to plot carefully in order to elude the necessity of carrying out his own threats.

He did not understand the silence. His mother got up only once to fetch a glass of water or a wet cloth, and even then she had gone out stealthily, silent-footed. His father was no doubt asleep: the spark of life glimmered ever more faintly in his frail body; he was grateful for the refuge of sleep, dozed away the afternoons if there was no shouting to disturb him. Perhaps it was a good idea to have that night-light remind him of the suffering which he had caused by—borne patiently, without a word of complaint.

Leaning on an elbow he sat up and lit a cigarette, listened with a drumming heart.

Listened for an hour.

His father's cry broke the silence.

"Whaaa... Whassemader?"

Then, barely awake yet, but petrified out of his wits:

"What?... Good God!"

The hoarse, frightened voice jolted him upright. He heard his father come stumbling towards him, bearing the tidings of the dreadful calamity that had befallen them: colic, palpitations, fainting fit, blood pressure.

A sleepy, bloodshot, panic-stricken face:

"An ambulance! Right away! Son! Your mother! Lujzika has committed suicide!"

He leapt to the door—suicide? but if she was able to tell him that, it would have to be another trick?! Even his tyranically inclined, eternally warring mother, forever thirsting for dramatics, would not dare tell a lie this size! Committed suicide? How? Not with a razor-blade, no, she was much too squeamish for that, no, it would have to be pills, of course, that was what the silence was all about, that was why she let his father fall asleep, that was why she let him watch the telly, of course, the plan had been ready and set since supper-time. No, she couldn't have left out a magnificent bit of drama like this, and of course she took care with the dosage, but maybe...

Only the current of air that brushed his skin as he rushed to the door made him aware of the beads of cold sweat breaking out and coursing down his body.

On the bed his mother lay terrified, fear for her life barely piercing the blanket of drowsiness weighing, pressing down upon her, limbs visibly heavy from the sleeping pills, an artistically scattered heap of an apparently large number of silver foil leaves by her bed; caught hold of her limp wrist, felt the slackening pulse, jumped to the phone, had no time for his terrified father kneeling by the bed; dialled for the ambulance. At last a weary voice replied, hallo, and they haggled for a while. Deadlock—nothing could be done without the panel doctor's transfer order—until he demanded the name the weary voice answered to, threatened to hold him responsible, threatened lawsuits, threatened to knock his brains out until at last the weary voice replied that they would be there in twenty minutes.

He dressed hurriedly, resisted his father's imploring voice: no, he was not to accompany them to the hospital, he'd phone; urging him to take a tranquillizer he poured lukewarm, bitter strong nescafé into his mother's slack mouth and forced her to swallow. No, a taxi would not be quicker, his mother was far too heavy, far too dazed, he would not dare to attempt to drag her down the stairs single-handed, they might both fall and break a leg or something, to crown it all. He wrapped a housecoat around the flaccid body, pulled socks on her feet, rummaged for identification papers, crammed his pockets full of money, blood-group certificates, medical certificates, final reports; hung out of the window, ears strained for the siren, poured another cup of nescafé down the throat of the drooping head (the drooping head was contentedly drowsy: the boy had broken, he loved her, tended her, begged her forgiveness by deeds, not by words), kicked the silver foil aside into one heap, had no time to notice that half the wrappings were old, lustreless, worn, smoothed out for tonight's performance. He opened the door, switched on the light, ran out into the corridor to check whether the downstairs door was open, did a quick reckoning in his head: if it was half past ten now and the film finished at half past nine, if his father fell asleep at a quarter to ten then she couldn't have taken the pills more than forty minutes ago, which meant there was every hope that...

The ambulance man did not allow his father into the ambulance:

"Only one escort allowed!" he shouted when he discovered that it wasn't the old man he'd come to fetch, though he looked sicker than his wife.

"I'll call you, Dad," he said in passing, and already they were lifting, lugging his mother down the stairs and into the van with the flashing, revolving blue light.

He slipped two hundred forints into the pocket of the attendant's coat:

"Make sure she's taken good care of," and took it ill when he replied, upon examining the pulse and pupils:

"She'll make it all right."

He slipped another two hundred into the pocket of the nurse who rose tiredly as they entered, said "Thanks," smiled, made a phone call, and disappeared.

"Money down the drain," rumbled the ambulance attendant, "she isn't the night nurse, she doesn't even work on this ward. She just came over to look out for her girl friend who's off philandering some place."

He never saw nurse "Thanks" again. In her stead another

arrived accompanied by a bald-headed, heavy-eyed doctor. The minutes spent in the making of arrangements and the giving of particulars seemed like hours. At last they awoke to the consciousness of his mother, the ambulance man departed with his papers signed, the sleepy-eyed nurse found a stretcher upon which his mother was placed; to speed things up he placed a five-hundred note in the doctor's pocket. The doctor looked away, then, after feeling her pulse, looked into his eyes:

"She'll be all right."

The doctor asked when, how much, what type while he urged him to hurry and, as an afterthought, rapidly slipped a hundred note into the nurse's pocket.

"Wait here."

The smoke stung his eyes, making them water as though he were crying. He sat, tired, knees cramped. No escape: the image of his mother blocked out all else from his sight. He could half-hear but ignored the sound of her vomit bubbling up beside the tube stuck down her throat. His mother trotting about the flat, her tread too rapid, unsteady because of her short sight; his mother preparing breakfast, serving tea, cooking lunch and supper, her hand always ready to fly out for support; his mother, seemingly concealing, in fact proclaiming her passing—illusionary, but earnestly, sincerely imagined—indispositions, flaunting the wrinkles that demanded to be noticed at the start of a job of work, at the end of a period allotted to day-dreaming; his mother, never a second late with the dietetic lunch, with the dosage of pills, with the overdosage of pills, with the activities with which she kept this family bound tightly up together. Short-sighted, stumpy, heavy-handed, clumsy, she fumbled, making people helpless by necessity, feel the weight of her importance, salvaged from her teaching days, from the great mission that swayed destinies.

In the flat she kept scrupulously clean and had forcefully monopolized she was in continual search for caches in which to secrete her treasures: pills, toothpicks, salt, paper napkins, toilet paper, batteries, and anything else that might come in handy, for who knows what might happen: another world war, another Rákosi era, a shortage, whatever. Once a hiding-place was discovered it was immediately put out of use, so that they could not find anything without her, so that she could forever direct the two destinies at her mercy, destinies that could not be fulfilled save through herself. She would have preferred to take her married daughter back under her wing, though hating her for her meagre allowance of grandchildren, hating her for having had the impudence to live her own life, but saddling the stranger, her husband, with her sins. And when, on an evening, she was entrusted with the children, she spoiled them shamelessly, mollycoddled them, showered them with presents so that they would feel neglected, uncared-for at home. Shortsightedly she fumbled, hiding money so that they would all depend upon her financially as well, so that she would always be prepared and capable of giving whenever they asked, whenever they were in need. She harassed and pestered her two remaining charges to death: you've got a cough, you've caught a cold, you've got a temperature, constipation, circulation trouble, sniffing out, devising, contriving, forcing their illnesses upon them. And she tended them when they were ill, for she was the doctor of the family, locked them up into over-heated rooms, bundled them up in sheets, aired them and steamed them, now its a cross-current they needed, now a simple opened window, now a blanket, now an eiderdown; she distributed and confiscated, forcing T-shirts, woollen undies, woollen and cotton socks upon her protesting loved ones, always too quick, always to full of her own importance. She was a raw force that commanded destinies, her tyranny ostensibly philanthropic, her life an infernal road paved with good intentions. On this road his mother trotted along, rapidly, myopically, and if the ground was to be cut from under her feet she would strain every sinew to get back upon it, at no matter what cost. At whatever cost. Her own life at the cost of others.

He jumped up, looked at his watch. Half past twelve. He broke out in cold sweat, rushed to the surgery door, knocked, opened it at the answering silence. The surgery was dark and empty.

He ran along the corridor, the ward sister's room was empty, back up the stairs from where the doctor and nurses had taken their time arriving earlier that night. He put his ear to the door of every ward, at last found a "doctor on duty" sig nand music from Radio Luxembourg filtering through the door. Quaking, he knocked. A grumpish, bristly, familiar face appeared:

"Yes?"

"How is my mother?"

"Don't shout."

Behind him the light went on, the nurse's sleepy face looked up.

"How is she?! Is she all right?"

"Yes. She's asleep. You can go home now."

"No! I want to know!"

"You're creating a disturbance!"

"I gave you enough for you to answer me!"

He points to the doctor's left pocket, the doctor slipped his hand inside—bare, hairy legs under his coat—and forced a smile:

"Your mother took fewer pills than you supposed. We have given her a gastric lavage and she is now peacefully asleep in ward 21. Do you wish us to wake her?"

"No, not if... If you say she's all right."

"She is out of danger. Come and see her tomorrow, formalities must be attended to in any case."

"So she only took a couple?"

"Even if she had remained at home she would only have slept for a day or so."

The doctor tended his hand, smiling.

He trudged down the stairs. He was almost out of the door when he remembered his father. He went to the reception desk, rummaged in his pockets until he found his last ten forint piece to make a phone call.

He let the phone ring seven times then replaced the receiver. His father must have fallen asleep in his armchair, he'd surely find him with his head lolling. He'd brighten up when he heard the news and after a couple of minutes would lay his tired body down on the bed for a hard-earned rest.

The trams weren't running and he hadn't enough money for a taxi. He had paid a thousand and ten forint fine for this Sunday. He pulled his coat tightly around him and set out into the metropolis. It was a hell of a long way home.

A quarter past three. He might as well have waited for the first tram. He opened the downstairs door, fumbled for the staircase light switch. It had been a long while since he came home this late at night.

He took care to be quiet opening the front door, though he knew he would wake his father up for one reassuring minute. In the large room the nightlight was still on — his father must have been sitting in his armchair waiting for the phone to ring when sleep overcame him.

He took off his coat and shoes, and went into the room. In the dim light he saw his father lying peacefully on his bed, clothing and bits of paper scattered in their rush to be gone strewn around him, and there was something else which he sensed rather than perceived. He went up to his father and touched his arm: the lukewarm arm of an old man enfeebled by sleep. The arm felt limp to the touch. He took hold of his father's shoulders and gave it a gentle squeeze to wake him. Above the shoulders, in the half-light, the skin of the face was yellowish, wrinkled, the head lolled forward. He shook him: the shoulders were slack, the body was limp, much too limp! Terrified, he slapped his father's face—he had hit his gentle, quiet little dad. He collapsed by the bed and knew now what he did not notice before: the foil wrappings of sleeping tablets screwed up, crushed into tiny balls in the ashtray, all in a heap. Not a very large heap, for his father's hand retained its strength despite the bad back that would not bend, despite the operations that had left him with one kidney and a patched-up stomach. Had retained its strength until the very last moment of his life when, horrified by the act of she who had made him her captive for the duration of his life, and had then decided to end her own, he had found himself lacking the courage and resolution to go on living and had followed the course she set out for him even in death, crushing a great many leaves of silver foil holding a dozen tablets each into a pile of tiny balls that corresponded as near as possible to her spectacularly scattered heap. Being unversed in the dosage of pills he had gone the round of the flat, gathering the familiar packets from their various hiding-places and then, with the telephone—a tool he had never grown accustomed to and from which he now awaited his acquittal, his absolution—within easy reach, he had stripped the packets of their contents with his careful, trustworthy, dependable old hands. Unversed in the dosage of pills, then, he had compared the scattered heap of foil with his own growing pile until he was sure that the amount he had crushed with an iron hand finally matched the amount strewn about the floor—the amount that had silenced the phone. Sitting there beside the telephone, its silence permitting no leeway for doubt, his father had swallowed the tasteless, indifferent pills with an unchecked amount of soda water.

He held the limp, mottled, lukewarm hand in his. He knew he should ring for the ambulance and he knew that this time it would be in vain. Slowly he walked to the telephone, explained where, why and when, then went back to sit in the chair beside the bed—he did not make coffee, he knew he would not have the strength to pour it into a slack mouth, a lifeless face and neck. He held the lukewarm hand in his and watched the yellowish, wrinkled skin cleaving to the cheekbones; as he had done at the time of his father's kidney operation, he had then relayed resurrection through the skin, in transfusing his own energies he had forced his father to get well quickly, and the doctors had let him do it without a word, for they saw how rapidly he was able to heal his tiny, frail, incredibly disciplined father.

The feel of his father's skin, the touch of his tired, familiar fingers, lifelessly cooling fingers on his palm. He gave up counting the beats of the sluggish pulse and waited, holding the parting hand. Between their hands time slowed down, was almost stilled. His father lying down, himself sitting— the difference was slight, almost negligible.

His eyes lit dispassionately upon a white blotch in the darkness: an unsealed envelope. He reached out for it without relinquishing his father's hand, opened the sheet of paper folded into four with his free hand and began to read:

"Ungrateful son!

All your life you have reproached us with being nothing but a burden to you. I always gave you everything you asked for and never got the slightest bit of tenderness in return. So I have decided not to stand in your way any longer. Trample on my dead body if you wish: you are now free to possess yourself of our home, of my jewellery, may you be happy with them. I am taking my life of my own accord. It is because of you that I have decided to go. And I hope you will learn in my death what I was to you in my life. I do not disown you, I do not disinherit you

Your loving Mother"

He folded the paper back into four. He looked long at the parchment skin, passionately fondled, stroked the cooling hand, running the dry, brittle, thin old fingers through his own, tasting, storing up the feel of them. Shrill and loud the door-bell rang and before opening the door to the ambulance people he bent low over his father's brow.

Translated by Eszter Molnár

A Very Private Affair
BY MIKLÓS VÁMOS

Peter sat at the large oval dining-room table. He turned back a corner of the sheet-size tablecloth and laid a newspaper on the polished wood to protect it. His mother would not let him use the elegant table for his homework otherwise. "You'll give me a fit on the spot if you spill ink on it!"

Peter was dawdling over his history homework. The objects lying on the newspaper in demure disarray—books, notebooks, writing tools, notes—were all the appurtenances of concentrated effort. There was just one exception, a shiny sheet of paper propped up against the inkwell, which contained six typed lines. Some kind of poem, as its title suggested.

POEM
Oh, how I love thee,
In rain and in hail,
Whether grieved or gay
In fine weather or gale
And love thee shall I
Till the day I die!

And at the bottom of the sheet, in ink, stood: "Julika!" Just like that. With an exclamation mark.

"What's this?" His father stood leaning over his shoulder, reading the poem.

"It's private!" Peter grumbled. He grabbed the sheet and shoved it inside his pocket.

"Too late," said his father with an apologetic smile. "I've already seen it. You shouldn't leave your secrets out on the table."

"It's not a secret," stammered Peter. "It's just that…" At a loss for anything more to say, he bit his lips.

The man looked at his son. 'He's grown up,' he thought. 'I should pay more attention to him. A lot more, while he'll listen to his old man.'

"Say. You write poetry?"

"No!" That was too quick. "Just this… Just this one."

"Well, it's nothing to be ashamed of," said his father. "But this poem is bad, you know. It's mannered, if you get what I mean. It's so…" He was searching for the apt word. "So… sentimental! Sounds like other poems, and not like you."

Peter crumpled the cover of his senior history book. The cardboard cracked.

"If you don't mind me saying, son," his father began. 'He doesn't answer,' he thought. He expected his son to defend his poem. Or to argue with him, at least. 'He's always so silent.' When he himself was young, he fought desperate, noisy battles with his own father. He remembered distinctly the furious struggle it took to win his independence. But this boy, he just keeps silent and stares with those sad, balck eyes he inherited from his mother. His son, it seemed, was made of different stuff.

"Is it a girl, son?"

Peter hesitated, then, with cheeks red as tomatoes, he nodded diffidently.

"It'll pass," said his father. "Just as well. You'll have more time to devote to your schoolwork. Seven months, and you'll be taking your exams."

'I shouldn't have said that,' he thought. 'What he needs is sympathy and understanding.'

"I work hard enough!" Peter's voice quivered almost imperceptibly with indignation. His lip curled. Just like his mother before a fight.

His father's mood darkened at the frown. He waved a hand and walked away.

Peter met Emilia one Vietnam Sunday, at the chocolate factory. Three high schools had volunteered for social work in order to donate the proceeds to the Vietnamese people.

The students sat around a long table, wrapping chocolate bars in aluminium foil, struggling with the crackling foil under the guidance of a woman with a worn expression on her face. They watched in sheer exasperation. The woman's hand moved like lightning.

"You'll catch on," said the woman with a smile. But her fingers never stopped. "It's nothing, really."

The chocolate had to be tapped with the edge of the palm, while the other hand folded under the corners of silver foil. If this hand fell behind even a fraction of a second, the whole thing tore to shreds.

Peter's job was to collect the débris from under the table. He was glad, because he proved hopelessly clumsy at folding. Besides, from down there, he could peep under the girls' skirts and get to know them, so to speak, from a new perspective.

Time passed quickly. They walked most of the way home together. The noisy group took up most of the sidewalk. Those coming towards them moved to the side and watched them pass with something like awe. The youngsters enjoyed it. They sang folksongs and working class songs, which echoed through the street.

"Why don't you sing as well?" a thin, black-haired girl

asked Peter. Two dimples appeared on her cheeks as she spoke.

"I'm tone-deaf," Peter observed.

"So what? So the others are Carusos?" And with that she put her arm through the boy's. Peter tired to look away. He knew that his head had turned into an enormous, blood-red ball. He sang as loud as he could to make the danger pass. The song rang out: We're off to battle with sturdy, firm resolve, our single weapon an unshakeable drive. Join us! Join us! Join us!"

Later, they introduced themselves.

"Peter Bucsai."

"Emilia Rácz."

The girl's tiny, warm hand was lost in the cradle of Peter's own stubby fingers.

The group broke up at Marx Square.

"Which way?" asked the girl.

"Same as you." He'd been mustering his courage and practising the sentence for the last ten minutes so that he could walk her home.

"Okay. Let's head down to the Danube."

They wove their way among the crowds on the Boulevard. "So far so good," Peter thought. He was wondering what he should talk about with the girl. His former girl friend always stopped him when he burdened her with expositions of literature or history. "You're boring, pal!" Julika only cared about dancing, music and clothes. She didn't take school seriously, and barely made it from one year to the next. Peter had decided that with time, he would shape Julika into his own image. He began by taking her books. "Read them, then we'll discuss them, okay?" Julika returned the borrowed books—Tomas Mann, Hemingway, Camus—unread. "They're so boring, they put me to sleep!" Then after a while, she found Peter boring too. When she told him so, Peter cried.

It had been almost three weeks ago. Julika was a charming blonde with a turned-up nose. With the constancy of the young, Peter pined for her for days. One of his schoolmates suggested that he think of the girl, constipated, sitting on the toilet. That would cure him of her once and for all. Peter could imagine Julika under a lot of circumstances, but not that.

"Why so quiet?" inquired Emilia. The two had reached the quay by the Danube. They sat down on the steps, among couples and anglers.

To the right, a lanky, long-haired boy embraced his pockmarked girl friend. Peter jerked his head away, but his eyes retained the image of the squat girl's scarred forehead. He'd have liked to touch Emilia's smooth, clear skin and her neck with its fine hairs. But he didn't dare. Not yet.

"The Danube's nice," he murmured.

"But filthy."

" 'And I watched a melon rind float by...' " he quoted.

The floodgates of conversation were open at last—Attila József, Thomas Mann, Camus—but the boy was sailing on different waters now. On the sea, where the Old Man fished alone along the Gulf Stream, but hadn't caught anything in eighty-four days.

"Hemingway is the greatest writer in the world!" he said with enthusiasm.

"Don't exaggerate," answered Emilia. "The world's big, there's room for lots of great writers. I don't like superlatives."

Peter shrugged.

"Okay, but for me he's still the tops. The way he begins a story, from the first sentence to the last, it moves along like a torpedo. And the names he uses!" This was his pet theory. "Like gunshots! Nick, Al, Max, Jack. All one syllable."

"Most words in English are one syllable," Emilia added.

Peter made no answer. He didn't know a word of English.

"He wouldn't have known what to do with my name E-mi-li-a. Four syllables. Nice and long."

"Emilia," Peter repeated pensively. Then his countenance brightened. He made a face like the farmers in American films, and said in a deep play-acting voice, "Hi, there, Em. Where's the whisky, Em? I lost ten grand at cards again, Em."

Emilia came back with "Hello, Pete. You gambled away the money we planned to send to the Vietnamese? Now was that a nice thing to do, Pete?"

"You're right, Em. It'll never happen again, Em."

Then Peter said that Emilia is actually a peaceful little country somewhere at the end of the world. Emilia is the country of the Emils. And he proposed that on this day, its capital be renamed Peter in his honour.

"That's impossible," said the girl. "In Emilia they don't like personality cults."

"I dont't wish to interfere in your affairs, son, but let's be honest, you've been neglecting your schoolwork," said Peter's father one afternoon. He twisted the corner of the chintz sofa upholstery between his fingers. Old, yellowed issues of the "Hungarian Gazette" lay on a table before him.

"You should cut back on your meetings with that girl."

"But dad, we barely see each other once a week!" He didn't sound convinced.

"And political work? And the steeplechase?"

"That's different. I don't go because of Emilia. I'm the Youth Party secretary, dad! Don't confuse private and public affairs." And he wrinkled his brow like a teacher.

"Fine," said his father after a pause. "I'm glad you take an interest in politics, but don't forget. Your job is to study. You know what Lenin said…"

"I know," countered Peter. The motto hung in his classroom, painted on a glass sheet in Russian and Hungarian.

"I'm not young any more," his father began. "I'd like to see you get a university degree. Yes, I'd like to see the day," he repeated.

"Oh, dad!" broke out Peter. It was unsettling to hear his father talk about death.

"You know, every father wants to see his son do more than he did. But I suppose you can't understand that…" And he stared at the ceiling. "I would like you to get into the university, and after graduation…" His voice had trailed off. "Here. I've brought home some 'Hungarian Gazettes' from the factory. It's the country's official paper, you know. It contains the latest law provisions. I figured it wouldn't hurt you to read them. After all, you want to be a lawyer. Read them, then we'll discuss them." And he pushed the lot towards his son.

"Yes, we'll discuss them." Peter remembered Julika. He rose and snatched up the Gazettes.

"And don't forget what I aid," his father called after him.

Peter went to see Emilia with slight pangs of conscience. It happened that some time later Peter's parents went to Bratislava for the weekend to visit relatives. The flat was free, and Emilia moved in for the night. "The class is going on an outing," she told her father.

They had a very agreeable and pleasant dinner. Emilia made baked potatoes. Peter swore that he'd never eaten anything so delicious in all his life. In the evening, they made up the parents' double bed.

The next morning, Emilia was the first to wake. She slid cautiously from under the bedclothes and looked at the boy.

'Sleeps just like a child.' She walked out into the hall to the bookshelves, to look for something to read. And found the POEM. By then, in a moment of inspiration, Peter had crossed out the old name at the bottom of the sheet and had written 'Emilia!' instead. Just like that, with an exclamation mark.

The girl read it, then went back to the bed.

Peter opened his eyes and stretched like a great big cat. "Oh... Hi, there."

"What's this?"

"Nothing," said Peter and tried to take it from her. "It's private."

"Poetry is never private," said Emilia. "Did you write it?"

"Yes."

"For me?"

Pause.

"For you," he answered softly. "Are you pleased?"

"Of course I'm pleased."

"And the poem. You like it?"

"Well..." Emilia threw her head back. Her hair flew like a dark flag. "It's short."

"Short?"

"Six lines. Men who are really in love write epics at least. Or plays. Or Divine Comedies, in triplets."

"You're insatiable," said Peter dejectedly. He thought the poem would impress Emilia now that she'd found it. "Thank God I crossed out Julika," he thought.

"So it's Julika," said Emilia. "Julika was your girl before me."

"What?" stammered Peter. 'Jesus!'

"If you don't want me to read something, don't just cross it out, blot it out," said Emilia. "You should've re-typed the whole thing on a clean sheet of paper. New girl, new paper. Since it's recycled, why not at least type it out afresh?"

Peter hunched his neck deeper into his pyjama collar. He took the unhappy poem and crumbled it up. 'It's over,' he thought. 'Now she'll go.'

"Em," he began timidly. "I... I... I'm sorry."

"That'll do for beginners."

"Em... don't be cross."

"All right. I'm not. Not any more."

Meanwhile, Emilia had crept back into bed. They embraced.

And Peter decided he'd never write a poem again as long as he lived. Or if he did, it would be about some serious issue of social concern. But a private poem, never. Never again.

Translated by J. E. Sollosy

On the Authors

ANÓKA, ESZTER (b. 1942) graduated from university with a degree in Hungarian and library science. Her first volume of short stories, *Hála* (Gratitude), appeared in 1975, the second, *Búcsú a nőktől* (Farewell to Women), in 1980. She is also a book reviewer and critic.

BEREMÉNYI, GÉZA (b. 1946) is considered one of the most talented prose writers of the middle generation. With a diploma in the humanities, he now works as a scriptwriter, and has just directed a film of his own (The Disciples). His novel entitled *Legendárium* (Book of Legends), a *Bildungsroman*, has been reprinted several times. His plays, regularly produced in Budapest, were collected in *Trilógia* in 1982. His short stories have been translated into several foreign languages.

BERTHA, BULCSÚ (b. 1935) is a prose writer and journalist. His first volume of short stories, *Lányok napfényben* (Girls in the Sun), was published in 1962. His journalistic works, dealing with controversial social issues, have appeared in a separate volume. His novel *Tűzgömbök* (Fireballs; 1970), which was made into a film, portrays the horrors of the World War II as seen through the eyes of a child, while *Kenguru* (Kangaroo; 1974), which was also made into a popular film, reflects the life of working-class youths. In *Balatoni évtizedek* (Decades on the Balaton; 1973), he deals with Hungary's biggest lake in the form of literary reportage.

BOLDIZSÁR, IVÁN (b. 1912) is a writer and journalist, editor of the English-language *The New Hungarian Quarterly* and the journal *Színház* (Theatre), and president of the Hungarian P.E.N. Club. After attending medical school, his first work, entitled *A gazdag parasztok országa* (Land of Rich Peasants), a literary reportage or sociography which reflected his impressions of his trip to Denmark, appeared in 1939. His selected short stories were published in 1979 under the title *Örökké élni* (To Live Forever), while his recollections of life between 1942 and 1947 were published as *Don-Budapest-Párizs*. He plays a significant role in cultural diplomacy, and his works have been translated into several foreign languages.

CSALOG, ZSOLT (b. 1935) studied ethnography, history and archaeology and presently works as a sociologist. His first volume of short stories, *Tavaszra minden rendben lesz* (Everything Will Be Fine Come Spring), appeared in 1971. His works, *Kilenc cigány* (Nine Gypsies; 1976) and *A tengert akartam látni* (I Wanted to See the Sea; 1981) comprise a series of sociographical portraits.

CSURKA, ISTVÁN (b. 1934) is a prose writer and playwright. He studied dramaturgy at the Academy of Dramatic and Film Arts in Budapest. His first volume of short stories, *Tűzugratás* (Leaping Fire), appeared in 1956. Both his short stories and his novels stand out for their grotesque and satirical style. He is also a master of the *feuilleton,* some of which appeared in 1980 in the volume, *Kettes kolbász* (Cheap Sausage). He wrote the script of several films. He is also one of the most popular playwrights in Hungary, whose comedies are popular abroad as well.

FEJES, ENDRE (b. 1923). His first book, *A hazudós* (The Liar, 1958), a collection of short stories, appeared in 1958. His novel *Rozsdatemető* (Scrapyard; 1962) brought him international acclaim. His many short stories, novellas, plays, radio and television plays portray workers and the average man struggling through a life of hardship. His novel *Jó estét nyár, jó estét szerelem* (Good Evening, Summer! Good Evening, Love! 1969) was made into a highly successful play and television series. His collected plays were published in 1969 *(Színművek)*.

GALGÓCZI, ERZSÉBET (b. 1930) published her first volume of short stories entitled *Egy kosár hazai* (A Basket from Home) in 1953. Her literary reports (*Nádtetős szocializmus*—Socialism under Thatched Roofs; 1970) depict the results of agricultural reform, while her novellas, short stories and novels reflect the problems of life in the Hungarian village. Several of her works have been adapted for film and television. Her plays and television scripts have been collected in two volumes, *A főügyész felesége* (The Attorney General's Wife; 1974) and *Úszó jégtáblák* (Ice Drifts; 1978).

GÁLL, ISTVÁN (1931–1982) grew up in the mining town of Tatabánya, and his themes therefore revolve around the lives of miners, as well as military service. His career was launched in 1954 by a volume of poetry, *Garabonciás diák* (The Wandering Scholar), but he is best known for his prose works. His volume of novellas (*Patkánylyuk*—Rathole; 1961) and his collection of short stories (*Kétpárevezős szerelem*—Love and Double Sculls; 1962) deal with the political and social conditions of the Fifties. His two novels *Az öreg* (The Old Man; 1975) and *A ménesgazda* (The Studfarm; 1976) were popular successes. The latter was made into a film.

GYURKÓ, LÁSZLÓ (b. 1930) is a prose writer, playwright and journalist. His first book, a novella entitled *Bűnösök* (The Guilty), was published in 1961. His books, *Lenin, október* (1967) and *Négyszemközt a forradalommal* (Face to Face with the Revolution; 1970), draw a picture of the Great October Socialist Revolution on the basis of largely till then unpublished documents, while *Arcképvázlat történelmi háttérrel* (Portrait with a Historical Background) offers a biography of János Kádár, the First Secretary of the Hungarian Socialist Workers' Party. His novel, *Faustus doktor boldogságos pokoljárása* (Doctor Faustus's Blessed Descent to Hell) of 1979 draws on the history of Hungary since World War II. (It was subsequently made into a successful television series by Miklós Jancsó.) His plays are collected in two volumes, *Az egész élet* (A Whole Life; 1970) and *Utak* (Roads; 1977).

ILLÉS, ENDRE (1902–1986) was a writer, playwright, essayist and director of Szépirodalmi publishing house in Budapest. *Zsuzsa,* his first volume of short stories, appeared in 1942. A master of psychological portraiture, he has published novellas and novels as well. His collected essays (*Mestereim, barátaim, szerelmeim* – My Teachers, Friends and Lovers) were published in 1979. His plays have been successfully produced, and his works are also known abroad.

KARDOS, GYÖRGY G. (b. 1925) wrote his first sensational novel (*Avraham Bogatir hét napja*—Seven Days in the Life of Avraham Bogatir; 1969) about Palestine during

World War II and the complexities of establishing a new nation. The theme is further developed in his novels *Hová tűntek a katonák?* (Where Have All the Soldiers Gone?; 1971) and *A történet vége* (The End of the Story; 1977). He also wrote a rock musical entitled *Villon és a többiek* (Villon and the Others; 1976).

KARINTHY, FERENC (1921 b.) is a popular prose writer and playwright. His first novel, *Don Juan éjszakája* (The Night of Don Juan), appeared in 1943. His most popular novel *Budapesti tavasz* (Spring Comes to Budapest; 1964) was made into a film. His plays are frequently produced in Budapest, and his works are well known in most European countries.

KERTÉSZ, ÁKOS (b. 1932) is a novelist and playwright. His first volume of short stories, *Hétköznapok szerelme* (Weekday Love), was published in 1962. He has published several novels since the early 1970s, the best-known being *Makra* (1971). His plays are also popular.

KURUCZ, GYULA (b. 1944) graduated from the University of Debrecen in the humanities. He is editor of the journal *Hungarian Book Review*. His first literary success came with the publication of his novel, *Nohát meséljünk* (Let's Tell Stories), in 1970. Since then, he has written several other novels as well as novellas and short stories.

MOLDOVA, GYÖRGY (b. 1934) studied dramaturgy at the Academy of Dramatic and Film Arts. *Az idegen bajnok* (The Foreign Champion), his first volume of short stories, appeared in 1963. Several of his novels deal with the Stalinist era of the 1950s, while *Negyven prédikátor* (Forty

Preachers) goes back to the time of the Counter-Reformation. His many satirical writings, such as *Magyar atom* (Hungarian Atom; 1979) and literary reportage (*Az Őrség panasza*—Complaint of the Őrség; 1974) became especially popular thanks to their sociographic detail. Moldova, who has also scripted several screen plays, has been translated into many foreign languages.

ÖRDÖGH, SZILVESZTER (b. 1948) graduated in the humanities from the University of Budapest. *A csikó* (The Foal), his first volume of short stories, was published in 1973. His novel, *Koponyák hegye* (Golgotha), which was inspired by the Bible, appeared in 1976. His play *Kapuk Thébában* (Gates of Thebes) was produced in 1978.

ÖRKÉNY, ISTVÁN (1912–1979) came to literature from the sciences. His first volume of short stories, entitled *Tengertánc* (Dance of the Sea), appeared in 1941. After returning from a POW camp, he wrote the play *Voronyezs* and a sociographical work entitled *Lágerek népe* (People of the Camps). *Emlékezők—Amíg idejutottunk* (Remembrances—Till We Got Here), a personal confession, was published in 1946. In the early Sixties he wrote two novels, *Macskajáték* (Catsplay; 1963) and *Tóték* (The Family Tót; 1964) of which highly successful dramatic versions were later produced and performed in many countries. His volume of short grotesques, *Egyperces novellák* (One-Minute Stories), was published in 1968. His writings have been translated into several languages.

SÁNTA, FERENC (b. 1927) published his first volume of short stories, *Téli virágzás* (Winter Flowering) in 1956. In his novels, he is primarily concerned with questions of integrity and morality. *Az ötödik pecsét* (1963; *The Fifth*

Seal; 1986) and the literary reportage *Húsz óra* (Twenty Hours; 1964), were both made into successful films. A selection of his short stories appeared in English, entitled *God in the Wagon* (1985).

SÜKÖSD, MIHÁLY (b. 1933) graduated in the humanities from the University of Budapest. A writer, critic and essayist, he began his career with the non-fiction volume *Tudós Weszprémi István* (The Scholar István Weszprémi), published in 1958. His collection of short stories, *Ólomketrec* (The Lead Cage), appeared in 1960. He has also written several novels, literary and sociographical studies.

SZÁRAZ, GYÖRGY (b. 1930) is a dramatist and prose writer, who favours essays and literary reportage. He is editor-in-chief of the literary monthly *Kortárs*. His first book, *A vezérkari főnök* (The Chief of Staff; 1969) is about Aurél Stromfeld, commander during the Hungarian Republic of Councils of 1919. His documentary novel, *A tábornok* (The General; 1981) portrays György Pálffy, victim of the purges during the personality cult of the Fifties. *Történelem jelenidőben* (History in the Present Tense) appeared in 1984.

TAR, SÁNDOR (b. 1941) works in a factory. His first poems appeared in the monthly *Alföld*. Since 1975, he has also written short stories and sociography. His first volume of short stories, *A 6714-es személy* (Passenger Train 6714) was published in 1981.

TEMESI, FERENC (b. 1949), who graduated in the humanities from Budapest University, is a writer and translator. His volume of short stories, *Látom nekem kell lemennem* (I See I Must Go Down Myself), was published in 1977.

VÁMOS, MIKLÓS (b. 1950) was already an accomplished writer when he graduated from law school in 1975. His first volume, *Előszó az ábécéhez* (A Foreword to the Alphabet), appeared in 1972. It was followed by nine others, including *Zenga zének* (Singa Loud; 1984), which describes his generation's search for self-identity. He has also written plays for the stage and the radio.

VÉSZI, ENDRE (b. 1916) is a writer, playwright and poet, whose first book, *Végy oltalmadba* (Take Me Under Your Protection), appeared in 1935. *Felszabadultál* (You Were Liberated), a novel published in 1937, brought him critical acclaim. His collected poems were published in 1974 (*A teljesség igézetében* — Under the Spell of Totality). His novel, *Angi Vera*, which deals with the psychology of the 1950s, was made into an internationally celebrated film. His plays have appeared in the collection *A piros oroszlán* (The Red Lion) in 1971.